ROAD TRIPS, HEAD TRIPS, AND OTHER CAR-CRAZED WRITINGS

Road Trips, Head Trips, and Other Car-Crazed Writings

Edited by Jean Lindamood

Introduction by P. J. O'Rourke

The Atlantic Monthly Press
New York

Published simultaneously in Canada
Printed in the United States of America

FIRST EDITION

Library of Congress Cataloging-in-Publication Data

Road trips, head trips, and other car-crazed writings / edited by Jean
   Lindamood: introduction by P. J. O'Rourke. — 1st ed.
      p.   cm.
   ISBN 0-87113-654-6
    1. Automobile driving—United States—Literary collections.
    2. Automobile travel—United States—Literary collections.
    3. Automobiles—United States— Literary collections.   4. American
   literature—20th century.   I. Lindamood, Jean.
   PS509.A89R63   1996
   810.8'0355—dc20   96-23030

Design by Laura Hammond Hough

The Atlantic Monthly Press
841 Broadway
New York, NY 10003

10 9 8 7 6 5 4 3 2 1

CONTENTS

CONTENTS

THE MACHINES

IN MOTION

MAN VERSUS MACHINE

THE OPEN ROAD

PREFACE

You may think it unusual to find yourself perusing a book of automotive writings compiled by a woman. Car stuff is usually guy stuff, right? Well, I've been doing car stuff for a living for the past twenty-four years, so I'm your guy on this one. But let me attempt to explain myself a bit further.

The question I've been asked most in my fifteen years as an automotive journalist is what it's like to be a woman in a business that is primarily the domain of the male child. I have spent a good deal of my forty-two years on the planet trying to ignore that fact—to pretend it isn't so, at least to get over it. So I don't want to talk about being a woman. I have *never* wanted to talk about being a woman. Because it occurs to me that, for lo these many years, I've been trying to be a guy.

This has come naturally to me—I grew up in the country, in the middle of five brothers. I had no sisters. I found out early on that guys seemed to have all the fun—they at least never had to do the dishes—and that's where I headed. If I could only be a guy, I thought, everything would be all right. The best guy in the world, of course, but a guy nonetheless.

My dad noticed that I was a girl and tried to steer me in the right direction with this little bit of advice. "Learn to be a good waitress," he said, "and you'll never starve."

So in addition to all the other things I have tried to learn well, I am also a very good waitress. This may explain why I have approached my life so fearlessly—because I know that if the shit hits the fan, I can always go back to being a waitress. I will never starve.

Unfortunately for my dad, I had already discovered cars. My father worked for *Automotive News*, and he was the editor when he died in 1988. That meant he brought cars home. Different cars every night, some of them quite exotic, like the first Avanti. Or the Mercury with no steering wheel. Or the experimental turbine Chrysler. I was the star of the playground at recess. My interest in cars blossomed from there.

As a teenager, I didn't approach cars the same way boys did. I didn't tinker with them. I never read car magazines. I didn't stand around and stare under the hood at the engine the way guys do. Cars were bigger than that; they were freedom and motion and beauty to me. Cars seemed to be the key to everything I wanted. I was driving by the time I was fourteen. A guy's date potential hinged on if he owned a car, and if he'd let me drive it. I drove fast. I drove everywhere in my teenage years at 100 miles an hour—it seemed like a good round number. Cars were my escape from the country. I left home when I was sixteen, tried college for a year and failed miserably.

Turning again to the car, I got a job driving a cab when I was eighteen. A year later, I owned my own taxi. I bought a used car with 56,000 miles on it, installed a top light and a meter, painted it yellow, and joined Ann Arbor Yellow Cab. Within six months, I had to teach myself how to work on it because the repair bills were staggering. I taught myself tune-ups in my friends' gas station. I did a brake job in the street in front of my house by drawing a picture of every part I took out, so I would put it all back together right.

I was *so* tough. I was so *cool*. I was a cabbie. My cabdriving outfit was bib overalls and a ski hat, or skirts down to the ground with army boots. You could see the salt stains along the bottom edges of the skirts in the winter. I didn't shave my legs, I smoked cigars. I, of course, had to be the best cabbie ever. I wrote a training manual for new drivers, rewrote the company bylaws, revised the structure of the city cabstands, and became the president of the cab board.

About once a year I'd have someone like Jason Robards in the back. But most of the time it was junkies and drunks. I carried one guy into his house over my shoulder after he'd been slashed in a bottle fight, cleaned him up, and put him to bed. It got worse. Another time, I had a guy who'd just escaped from the state mental hospital and kicked his wife to death. A driver began stalking me. Another woman driver was murdered. I was robbed at gunpoint. After five years, the party seemed to be over. So I moved out to the country and got a job as a test driver with Chrysler.

Chrysler hired me because the government made them. There weren't enough women working there and it was the mid-seventies—so I lucked out. The Chrysler Proving Ground is where I learned that the government can get you a job, but you have to earn your own respect. It was clear from the start that Chrysler had created this job for women to appease the government. It was worthless. A sham. All the women who weren't secretaries were part of a group that took new production Omnis out on the track every day, drove them 400 miles or so, then wrote up a little report about how the seat belt chafed their necks. Then they went home. There was no opportunity for advancement and no merit raises.

I immediately began angling for a transfer to be one of the guys; specifically, a mechanic in the Impact Lab, where they crashed cars into the wall. No one wanted to work in the Impact Lab (which mystifies me. There was something *so wonderful* about running an Imperial into the wall at 30 miles an hour). But they needed a warm body, so they were forced to hire me. I lied to get the job, I told them I could weld. Luckily, welding came naturally to me. And, luckily, I didn't have to buy a new wardrobe. The overalls, work boots, and ski hat worked very well.

I loved being a mechanic because of the big, scary tools I got to use every day, like the belt sander and the band saw and the arc welder. They actually shouldn't *let* people like me around tools like that. Luckily, my only mishap (other than ripping out an overhead garage door with the fork truck) was the time I was trying to drill a hole in a bumper with a dull drill bit. One of the other mechanics asked if he could help, and I told him I could DO IT MYSELF. It was evening break, about ten o'clock—I was alone in the shop pushing and pushing on this drill motor. I had long hair, and as I leaned forward the drill suddenly caught my hair and in a flash had sucked it into the motor. I was saved from being scalped because I was wearing a hair comb, which stopped the drill. I was stunned. You can imagine how relieved I was that none of the guys was in the garage. I tugged. I pulled. I tugged some more and nothing budged. My hair was cross-threaded and stuffed up into the motor. I had to walk into the break room, drill motor attached to my skull, cord dangling, and say, "Uh, guys. I have a little problem." They were thrilled.

Chrysler laid me off before I could *really* hurt myself. And that is when my life took off. I had been bored and putting out a little mimeographed newsletter for the local UAW. It won some awards, and, based on that, David E. Davis, Jr., invited me in to interview for a writing position he had open at *Car and Driver* magazine.

I bought a dress, washed my truck, and headed for Ann Arbor. But I felt so uncomfortable in that dress, I went home and put my blue jeans on. And so it was I interviewed with the man who would change my life, while wearing the dress *and* my blue jeans underneath. He was so amused, he hired me.

How fortuitous that I would start my life as an automotive journalist under the tutelage of David E., one of the most wildly imaginative, iconoclastic, bigger than life people I have ever met. He was astounded by my inability to put two sentences together without saying "Them boys" and "We was." Luckily, he decided to make me his lifelong ward and Pygmalion project. I was thrown to the technical staff for basic automotive training, and Mr. Davis himself took on the delicate task of throwing out the bathwater without losing the baby.

The first two years were a nightmare. I knew nothing about cars that weren't Chryslers. I'll never forget my first trip to Europe—where I was expected to file a report on the new cars at the Geneva Auto Show. Within fifteen minutes, I was in tears. I couldn't figure out which cars were new because I had never seen *any* of the cars on display in my life.

And I couldn't drive, which was a terrible piece of news to someone who had been driving for a living. I couldn't drive like *these* guys drove, anyway. I was dispatched to racing school. My first car race, I was up against a guy from *Road & Track* who owned his own race car. And I was under strict orders from *Car and Driver*'s technical editor to bunt the guy off the track if I couldn't beat him. I was distraught. I was sure I would be going home to Michigan in disgrace. Luckily, he wasn't very good. We were driving side by side down the back straight at Mid-Ohio, and another driver smashed into my bumper, knocking me right past Mr. *Road & Track*. I beat him.

Trying to prove myself at the magazine, I made it my mission to propose the wildest assignments. Like test flying an ultralight airplane, and racing in an off-road truck race with Walker Evans. I wouldn't have been racing with Evans had he known from the start that I was a *girl*. He just assumed the magazine would be sending a guy. He was not a happy camper. "If you pee your pants or throw up, I *ain't* stopping!" he sputtered. It was like an all-day plane crash. My body was covered with bruises, and my organs were all messed up. I wore a kidney belt about six inches high—and that was the only place that didn't hurt.

And then there was the demolition derby. I drove up to the gate of the fairgrounds in my heavily modified Plymouth Satellite, and the official said, "The powder puff heat is tomorrow night, honey." You can imagine how well *that* went over. "Well, you can *take* that powder puff . . . ," I said as sweetly as I could. He was astonished. "Why don't you want to race with the girls?" he asked. "Would you like to get beat by a girl?" I asked him. "Well *neither would I.*" He let me in and I won. I got fifty dollars and had to wear a neck brace for two weeks. I wore a T-shirt that said, "I've got tough nuts," from a lug nut company. I will admit that even *I* cringed when I saw that picture in the magazine.

My testosterone poisoning was so pervasive that I was amazed when *anyone* treated me like I was a girl or something. I have learned over the years how to handle these moments gracefully. Like the time the wild chairman of Saab here in the United States pinched my behind at a formal cocktail party in Europe. "Get your hand *off* my ass," I boomed. He almost fainted. He's still telling that story. "My *boss* was there!" he says with mock horror.

The readers, right from the start, have taken my female intrusion into their domain very well. For instance, I still get plenty of letters from guys on death row asking me to slip a tit shot in the mail to them. How flattering. Of course, there has been some negative feedback, too, like the letter from the guy who wrote, "You didn't hit a cow in Baja with the Dodge 600, it was Lindamood's butt." Lovely.

All joking aside, other than the occasional marriage proposal from the guy who thinks I would be the only woman in the universe who could understand his devotion to his massive collection of Saab Sonnets (and he would be *wrong* by the way), the people who write don't seem to notice or care if I'm a man or a woman.

I could have saved myself a lot of agony over the years if I'd known then what I know now. As it turns out, my life has not really *been* about being a guy or being a woman. All along I have simply been trying to do the things I love to do. To meet wonderfully interesting people. To have thrilling adventures. To be included in the gossip—when the story behind the story is being revealed. To have a really good time and then pass it along. Cars have been the central theme of all this goodness. Somehow I don't think that a love of cameras or, say, fingernail polish would have brought me such a full, passionate life.

Ten years ago, Mr. Davis and I started *Automobile Magazine*, and somewhere along the way, being a guy eventually lost its importance to me. I still have an occasional guylike moment: I sailed off a cliff in a racing car a few years ago with the

Japanese rallycross champion, and I raced the Baja 1000 with this Russian who couldn't speak English. And, yes, I bought a Harley, and I still talk kind of tough. But I just don't need to be one of the guys anymore. Life is full, life is sweet. My personal motto is "If you have a shitty time, nobody cares and you're still having a shitty time. So you might as well have a good time."

I'd like to think that this is exactly what will happen when you read the wonderful car stories I've collected for you in this volume.

INTRODUCTION

Why an anthology of automotive writing? Why not collect old articles from *Stereo Review*? Or publish a selection of microwave oven assessments from bygone issues of *Consumer Reports*? Why not gather together various scribblings that mention the washing machine? A car is just an appliance, after all.

Except it's not. The automobile bears a symbolic weight that fridge and toaster never can. The automobile is an icon of modern existence—more so than the electric dynamo, the skyscraper, the atomic bomb, or the awful sweaters of Bill Gates. The automobile *means* something.

The automobile means mastery over technology. It means power, speed, control. It means freedom, autonomy. It means we don't have to walk home.

Oh, sure, we could rely on other means of transportation—horses, sled dogs, our own two feet. But a walk-up movie wouldn't be much fun, standing outside in the evening damp with those big metal speaker boxes hooked to our belts. If we had a wrecked horse on cement blocks in our front yard, it would smell. And a wintertime shopping mall parking lot full of yelping, snarling, biting Alaskan malamutes would be an inconvenience, especially when we emerged from the supermarket with a bag of steaks. Then there's the train, but it won't fit in the garage. And can you picture the president of the United States scooting along a parade route with one knee in an armored Radio Flyer?

So can I. Therefore we should all be grateful to the automobile. But I in particular. I'd be a shoeless pumpkin-knocker rolling down his overalls to count to eleven if it weren't for cars. My grandfather Jake O'Rourke was born in an unpainted shack on a tenant farm in Lime City, Ohio. There were nine other children and Dad was a drunk. How much formal education my grandfather had I don't know. He may have finished sixth grade. His spelling was approximate. And his acquaintance with higher mathematics and the classical languages was slight. But then the car was invented. Jake went to work for the Atwood Motor Company of Toledo, Ohio. He started as a mechanic, became a salesman, sold the first Willys-Overland in Toledo, and went on to be the nation's top Willys salesman, averaging 110 cars per year.

By the 1940s Grandpa O'Rourke had converted to Buicks. He and his eldest son, my uncle Arch, owned a dealership on Main Street in East Toledo. My father was the sales manager. Uncle Jack was the ace glad-hander. Uncle Joe ran the used car lot. Cousin Ide was in charge of the parts department. Various sisters and wives kept the books. And my great-aunt Helen cooked midday dinner for them all in Granddad's house across the alley.

Everybody in the family worked for O'Rourke Buick, if work was what you'd call it. We spoiled, soft citizens of the 1990s define everything as work. Making pie graphs on the laptop is "work." Recreational sport is a "workout." Lollygagging on a couch in a psychotherapist's office is "working on personal issues." But the O'Rourkes came from a time and a social class where work meant lifting things. Loafing beneath the stuffed sailfish and mounted deer heads in the Buick showroom, smoking cigarettes and shooting the breeze with prospective car buyers was what my relatives would have been doing whether they had jobs doing it or not. And this left them with plenty of energy at the end of the day for smoking cigarettes and shooting the breeze with prospective car buyers beneath the stuffed sailfish and mounted deer heads of various bars, pool halls, and bowling alleys.

Cars made the O'Rourkes happy and prosperous. And it was as a happy, prosperous little O'Rourke that I was born in 1947. My first memory is of a car, a 1948 Roadmaster convertible in electric blue with rolled and pleated red leather upholstery. It was a thing of astonishing beauty. Automotive engineering and design have not been bettered since, in my opinion. All right, aerodynamics. I'll give you that. But there never was a quieter transmission than the Dynaflow, especially during the thirty to forty minutes required to reach 60 mph under full acceleration. And, talk about safety features, the '48 Roadmaster weighed 4300 pounds, rode on sixteen-inch wheels, and—observe the size of that bumper, the heft of those teeth in the grille—it could mash a Volvo flat.

My moral and emotional life was immersed in cars. I got my first feel of responsibility dangling from my father's knees steering his 1952 Special Coupe in erratic wiggles down the highway while he worked the pedals. I recall the moment I realized how truly beautiful and good was my mother. We were driving on Monroe Street in her 1950 Super four-door sedan, and I was so overcome with filial devotion that—Buicks still retaining the clamshell bonnet, which opened from either side—I reached down and pulled the right-hand hood release. My idea of loyalty was measured by the Buick trademark. I fought the kid across the street whose parents had gone so far as to buy a DeSoto. And when my father died suddenly in the fall of 1956, my grandfather could think of no way to console me except to bring over a 1957 Century hardtop a week before the introduction date and drive me around for hours.

Not to sound callous, but I think those 1950s new car introductions affected my outlook more than my father's death. The annual all-American excitement over the latest models shaped my philosophy and politics. I have faith in democracy and free markets. I believe in human progress. I know in my heart that given the vision, the commitment, and the will, all mankind can achieve attractively updated chrome trim. Indeed automobiles have taught me most of life's lessons. The existence of evil, for instance, was revealed in the person of a lumpen, bullying stepfather who also sold cars. And I found that evil did not go unpunished. The stepfather arrived at the beginning of the 1958 model year, and soon after marrying my mother he landed a job as a manager of an Edsel dealership.

My own first employment was, of course, at O'Rourke Buick. I worked on the used car lot cleaning and waxing clunkers with Shorty and Rubin, who had a number of teachings. "Always leave some lint in the corner of the windshield," said Shorty. "That way they know you washed it."

From my first car I learned how, if you remove the hubcaps, reverse the tires so the whitewalls don't show, ventilate the muffler with an ice pick, replace the giant oil-bath air cleaner with something cool in chrome, and pound aluminum spacers into the coil springs to jack up the front end . . . you'll still look like a dick in a 1956 four-door Ford Customline sedan that your grandmother gave you. The more so if it's salmon pink.

And there was my first wreck. I was driving my stepfather's appalling 1959 flathead six Plymouth. (He'd quit the Edsel dealership and bought a Dairy Queen on the road to Detroit, but the expressway opened in 1960 and it had been four years since anybody'd stopped for an ice cream cone.) I made an unsignaled left turn from the far right lane on a four-lane street and ran door to door into a passing Impala. This taught me that Satchel Paige was exactly wrong when he said, "Don't look back. Something may be gaining on you." My stepfather decided to teach me a lesson, too. He sold my Ford, emptied my save-up-for-an-MGA bank account, and declared I'd never drive another of the household vehicles as long as he lived. Which wasn't long. He got cancer in 1965, and I remember the words I used to comfort my mother the night he passed away. "Mom," I said, "can I borrow the car?"

Naturally there came a time when I rebelled against the automobile. For a while I was infatuated with motorcycles. But I kept falling off them. I had a nasty little X6 Suzuki that I put over the high side on a windy road through my college campus. I went sailing on my back across the dew-lubricated lawn, looking up and thinking what a beautiful night it was with the sky full of stars. And I saw all the more of them when my head hit the tree.

The bike was unhurt except the front brake cable was snapped and the rear brake pedal was jammed against the frame and useless. I rode home gingerly, parked the Suzuki behind my apartment building, and that night some idiot stole it. The police called a week later and said they had my motorcycle. I went to get it. It was a pile of rubble. Apparently the idiot cranked the Suzuki through all six gears, then came to a curve. "We found it *way* at the bottom of a ravine," said the police.

I owned some other motorcycles, too, but I fell off them and (possibly due to head injuries) became a hippie. Cars no longer meant anything to me. Except as a means to an end. That is, it's very rare to be given a lift by a pedestrian while hitch-hiking to Big Sur. I was above thinking about cars. I was concerned with political liberation, world peace, spiritual enlightenment, and convincing Moonbeam Feinholt that the ecosphere was in imminent danger from man's rampant waste of fossil fuels and that she and I had better double up in the shower to save earth's precious re-sources. I could care less about cars. Although I do remember sticking an enormous doobie out a vent window and attempting to use a Volkswagen microbus as a room-sized bong. I was so fully recovered from my boyish enthusiasm for automobiles that I made appreciative noises about an old bread truck somebody had painted with a five-inch brush in ten colors of Dutch Boy semigloss interior vinyl. Cars were for squares. Or so I said. But while leading life of outward conformity with drug binges, orgies, and rioting in the streets, I also maintained a fantasy existence. I'd get a haircut and a job and a Ferrari California Spider, an Aston Martin shooting brake, a Lotus Elan, a Morgan Plus 8, a Pegaso Z-102, an E-type Jag, a 289 AC Cobra, and, for practicality's sake, in case I daydreamed up a wife and kids, a Facel Vega.

There was another hippie with kindred secrets, Alan R. (now a respectable commercial artist). How we found each other out I don't know. Perhaps we were so stoned that right in the middle of a discussion of astral projection one or the other of us blurted something about Weber carburetors or de Dion axles. Anyway, we would closet ourselves in the farthest reaches of the crash pad and jabber for hours about the relative merits of Bertone, Zagato, and Pininfarina.

Alan R. and I did eventually get jobs and haircuts, if not Ferraris. And in 1975 I noticed I hadn't renewed my driver's license since the late '60s. After all, the world had been going to end in atomic holocaust and a revolution had been about to happen and I'd meant to move to Kathmandu. But I found these arguments unpersuasive with the Hertz rental car people.

To get a new driver's license I had to take driver's education as if I were a sixteen-year-old instead of just someone who'd been acting as if he had a sixteen-year-old's brain. Thus I wound up in night courses at a Manhattan high school. My class consisted of half a dozen Asians who spoke no English, half a dozen Eastern European women in babushkas who wouldn't speak at all, ten jiving teens clustered at the back of the room, and me. The instructor wore liberal clothes, a medley of corduroy in dirt colors. His pedagogical method was simple. "The function of the steering wheel is to control the direction of the car," he'd say. And then he'd ask, "Can anyone tell me what function the steering wheel performs?" The Asians stared politely into space. The babushkas looked at the floor. The teens continued to exchange high fives, dis each other, and rhyme things. "Can anyone tell me what function the steering wheel performs?" the instructor repeated. I lifted a mitt. "Yes, third row," said the instructor.

"The steering wheel controls the direction of the car," I said.

"Good," he said, and continued his lecture. "The function of the accelerator is to control the speed of the car. Can anyone tell me what function the accelerator performs?" No response. He repeated the question. Again, nothing. The instructor had the look of resigned insignificance that comes from years of inner-city teaching. I could see he was prepared to keep asking this question for the next fifty minutes or until I went nuts and strangled him. I raised my hand. "Yes, third row."

"The accelerator controls the speed of the car," I said. And so it went every Monday, Wednesday, and Friday for six weeks with the liberal in corduroy saying, "Yes, third row," each time as if he'd never seen me before. And to this day, if you want to know what function the steering wheel performs, I'm the guy to ask.

The written part of the driver's license exam was given in the horrible Department of Motor Vehicles building downtown and given in a number of languages fortunately including English. "The function of the accelerator is to control the speed of the car. T or F" was one question. We were given forty minutes to complete the test. It took five. I handed mine in to a large, irritable woman at the front of the room who laid a template over the pencil-checked answers and said, "Ditchyoo cheat?"

"Did I what?"

"Nobody got all them right before," she said. Which tells us everything we need to know about New York drivers. And apparently I'd become one because I flunked the driving test. I'd borrowed my boss's Oldsmobile. After an Age of Aquarius spent illegally driving paisley bread trucks and Volkswagen microbuses full of marijuana smoke, I was unused to automatic transmissions, much less power brakes. Attempting to back into my parallel parking space, I belatedly realized I'd put the Olds in drive instead of reverse. I gave a good, hearty Volkswagen microbus stab to the brake pedal and spring-launched the driving examiner (who was not, by the way, wearing his seat belt). His clipboard hit the dash, he hit the clipboard, and the clipboard clip left a big red ankh mark in the middle of his forehead. He drew an X through my paperwork.

I think it was that precise moment—seeing the ancient Egyptian symbol for eternal life impressed on my driving examiner's face—when my love of automobiles returned in full force. About this time I also quit smoking pot and began to drink again. And the next thing I knew I was waking up with a terrible hangover realizing I'd bought a 1965 Alfa Romeo GTC convertible from Alan R.'s brother.

This is how I happen to write for car magazines. A few days later I was in Brew's on Thirty-sixth Street, which was my neighborhood tavern and also a hangout for the employees of the old Ziff-Davis magazine companies. I was standing at the bar next to Jim Williams, then sports editor of *Car and Driver*. He said, "I heard you bought an old Alfa. It so happens I've got an old Alfa repair kit."

"You do?" I said.

"Yeah. A truck full of money to follow you everywhere you go."

When the editor in chief of *Car and Driver*, David E. Davis, Jr., learned that there was someone stupid enough to own an old Alfa and silly enough to be obsessed with Buicks, he gave me an assignment to take a silly old Buick on a stupid trip across the country. The '56 two-door Special broke down every day. I remember being somewhere in New Mexico, reduced to tears, beating on the fuel pump with the fat end of a screwdriver and howling words of Anglo-Saxon etymology.

That was almost twenty years ago. I remain absorbed in the culture of the automobile. Mr. Davis, who later founded *Automobile Magazine*, has sent me on numerous stupid trips since. And, although the GTC was sold and the Buick fixation eased somewhat, a succession of silly vehicles have accrued to me anyway, including, whoops, another Alfa, a pickup truck made from the front half of a Jimmy that had been in a head-on and the back half of a Chevy Fleetside that had been rear-ended, a Rabbit convertible for which I took cruel "chick car" ribbing from Jean Lindamood, a Subaru wagon so well built and reliable that I traded it in out of boredom, a BMW 325 convertible with more miles on it than the Jupiter probe, a 911 used mostly for urban commuting, and a Jeep I've just, unaccountably, had restored even though it's a 1984 and as rare as eating disorders in the fashion industry.

To this day I can be found out in the garage reduced to tears, beating on a fuel pump with the fat end of a screwdriver, howling words of Anglo-Saxon etymology, and causing my wife to say, "I thought you knew something about cars."

Perhaps this is the moment to confess that I do not. I mean, "The steering wheel controls the . . ." But I don't know much else. And I suspect none of the O'Rourkes ever has—at least since Grandpa quit being a mechanic about the time the acetylene headlamp was invented. As a kid I would be given a couple of simple tools and sent to amuse myself on the wrecked cars behind the O'Rourke dealership. This is how I learned to hammer on things with the fat end of a screwdriver. The rest of my knowledge of automotive construction and repair I gleaned from building AMT scale model kits. Whenever my car makes a funny noise I first see if the engine is still glued in and then check whether my sister has knocked the continental kit loose by sitting Barbie on the trunk lid during a doll homecoming.

I'm not much of driver either. That is, I'm OK on theory. I went to race car driving school and did very well in the classroom work. I remember the instructor telling me so, just as the large, irritable woman at the Department of Motor Vehicles had done. Though the race car instructor didn't accuse me of cheating, since, on the track, I was the absolute slowest of the ten people in my course. In fact, I believe the instructor's exact words to me were "You've got a fifty-dollar mouth and a ten-cent gas pedal foot."

Never mind. To me automobiles are not mere physical objects. My love of motor vehicles transcends the material plane. The flivver, the jalopy, the crate—

these are things of the spirit. The place taken by religion, philosophy, or art in other men's lives is occupied by cars in mine. Spend an hour in a church and where are you? Spend an hour in a car and you're at the beach. Three thousand years of Western philosophy has not been able to answer the question "What is the meaning of life?" But when you're driving a car the meaning of life is to find a place to park it. And, as for art, take the most beautiful and sublime sculpture by a Renaissance master— it brakes, corners, and accelerates like a large chunk of marble.

Cars have allowed ninety-odd years of O'Rourkes to earn a living without heavy lifting. Can God, Plato, or Michelangelo make such a boast? And this O'Rourke doesn't even have to sell the things. I can just ride around and tell lies about them.

The Source

DAVID E. DAVIS, JR.

The Freedom of Wild Ducks

My first car was a 1935 Mercedes-Benz roadster, purchased for one thousand dollars in 1951. An American colonel had brought it home from Germany, only to be defeated by its service requirement. That car was my friend and constant companion for more than a year, until I decided to become a racing driver and sold it to raise money for a competitive entry-level sports car. I was living in a very small town, a hundred miles from my parents and my childhood. I worked at a variety of jobs during the days, and drove to see friends and farmland and forests (and life) in the nights. The car ran like a train. It had a six-cylinder engine and an overdrive transmission. We were a team, that car and I. I accelerated through its gears, pushed the lever to the overdrive fourth gear, waited a moment for it to engage, then droned across high-crowned two-lane country roads in the gathering dark. The top was stowed out of sight behind the seats. The warm wind wrapped the back of my neck like a scarf and the moon lit the backs of my hands on the steering wheel. The instruments glowed softly, barely legible in their faint yellow light. Sometimes I drove for miles without lights, just following the road by its contour and by the march of the utility poles stretching away toward the ends of the earth in the moonlight.

Going where? Going to see women who were sleepy and tousled and warm when I parked beneath their windows and walked quietly across the grass to their doors. Going to see old friends, who wanted to drink and talk about women whom they used to visit in the night. Going to a gypsy restaurant where the owner played the violin and his wife accompanied him on the accordion and the hatcheck girl loved me. Going to the right, because that road led to a secluded lake. Going to the left, because that road seemed to promise more curves. Going to the end of the road, because I'd never been there before. Going to . . . I don't know where. Perhaps going to the future, to the rest of my life.

Then there was the MG. White, with black-edged yellow stripes over the louvered hood and front fenders. The grille painted checkerboard. The engine was tuned to its limit. The exhaust pipe was a copper tube, one and three-quarter inches in diameter. The sound was much greater than the performance, but to drive it fast was pure unbridled joy. The headlights were the best Marchals available at the time. On the badge bar stood a pair of Lucas flamethrowers that made the scenery of the night all flat white foreground, two-dimensional, pierced by the reflected light of deers' eyes in the forest that lined the road. My windscreen was folded down, and bugs stung my cheeks and forehead as I tore across the agricultural heartland.

We drive cars because they make us free. With cars, we need not wait in airline terminals, or travel only where the railway tracks go. Governments detest our cars: They give us too much freedom. How do you control people who can climb into a car at any hour of the day or night and drive to who knows where? An open car gives us another dimension of freedom. In an open car we enjoy the heightened freedom of the coursing hound, racing across the land with only the wind for clothing. It is the freedom of wild ducks, shining in their colorful plumage, flying at impossible speeds through the treetops to impress the duck-women they love. In a closed car, the world is a horizontal place, seen through windows that are too much like television screens. In an open car, the world becomes properly round above us, a vast dome of pure possibility, limited only by what we know of the universe. In an open car on an open road, we can feel what that man felt eons ago, when he first managed to grab a horse's mane, throw himself on its back, and feel himself transported at unthinkable speed into mankind's next stage of development.

In the beginning, all cars were sports cars. Only the most venturesome travelers chose the automobile over the more reliable trains and horses of that era. When the internal combustion engine at last became useful, it was simply bolted into the front ends of wagons and carriages, where the horses used to be. Those wagons and carriages suddenly found themselves being propelled at greater rates of speed than those for which they were designed, and it was all pretty exciting for their drivers and passengers. Over the years, as speeds increased, the vehicles became more comfortable and secure, offering better weather protection to their occupants, but the real sports, the true believers, still wanted to feel the wind and sun on their faces, and the cars that made it possible for them to do this were called roadsters, spyders, cabriolets, phaetons, touring cars, and—sometimes—sports cars.

A sports car is one which offers more sport than utility. One in which fun is a more important design goal than practicality. In the early days, sports cars were simply racing cars that had been modified sufficiently to make them legal, or appropriate, for use on the public roads. Today's sports car is more apt to be a fully tamed production model offering all the amenities, but still spiced with the zesty flavor of those great bellowing crudenesses that smoked across the country roads of our grandfathers. To quote a dear friend and mentor of mine, Barney Clark: The modern sports car is a "child of the magnificent ghosts." One puts down the top, sets off down a country road, and relives years and miles of automotive legends.

Once, years ago, I was involved in an imported car dealership in a university town. Our service manager was something of a loner, a man who kept to himself and told us little of his life beyond the hydraulic lifts and Craftsman tools. From what I knew of this guy, he loved four things: Three were tattered BMW 328 sports cars and the fourth was any woman who would go home with him. "Home" was a tiny rented house full of BMW 328 parts. One speculates as to why any woman would have gone home with him in the first place, but the mind boggles at what she must have felt when he unlocked the door and she saw that they would be sharing the single bed with a cylinder head and a bouquet of pushrods. Nonetheless, his enthusiasm for the 328 communicated itself to me, and I grew particularly fond of its lovely two-liter engine. I drove Arnolt-Bristols powered by that engine, and to this day I long to own a 328-powered LeMans Replica Frazer Nash, surely one of the most delicious sports cars of the automotive century.

I still drive open cars with great enthusiasm. I recently fulfilled two of my automotive dreams: one, by actually owning a beautiful Kougar-Jaguar, a modern replicar that looks a bit like my beloved Frazer Nash; and, two, by finally getting rid of it. I had begun to believe that I was the last man in North America to want a Kougar-Jaguar. It was a car without a top, without doors, without windshield wipers, and it taught me a great deal about the proper clothing for open car motoring. Sheepskin coats and trousers like those worn by air crews in World War II are very nice, and very popular, but they're bulky and restrictive, and they are not waterproof. I prefer the Barbour line of outdoor clothing, made in Great Britain. It is absolutely waterproof—being constructed of oiled cotton—and when worn in combination with wool, silk, cashmere, polyfleece, or quilted down, it will protect one from anything the weather gods have to offer. For headgear, nothing beats the old leather or cloth flying helmet that buckles under the chin. This is absolutely secure, will not blow off, and keeps the ears warm. It is hard on the coiffure, but it works. A full-coverage racing helmet is also warm and relatively comfortable, but it does make you look ridiculous backing out of your suburban driveway. English flat caps look wonderful, especially on women, but they tend to blow off at high speeds. Never, ever, wear the sort of baseball caps with advertising messages so favored by the more feckless Americans.

Is an open car the answer to all of your transportation needs? Probably not, at least not entirely. But, will a fast drive on an open road in an open car lift your heart and light your dreams? Of course it will, unless you have no heart and no dreams. Open cars transport us, not just in the sense of getting from home to work, but by showing us a side to life we might otherwise have missed. They put the fun back into driving, and they remind us of a time when automobiles represented the sum of human progress, and the people who designed, built, and drove them were heroes.

DAVID HALBERSTAM

How the Car Changed America

Nashville—

I remember the day I left Nashville after working there for four years as a young reporter. It was the day after John Kennedy's election in November 1960, and I was on my way to take a job with *The New York Times*. I had packed up my Triumph TR3 with all my belongings, such as they were, strapped on the outside rack. Off I headed for New York and what I hoped was my brave new future. The roads around Nashville in that day were hardly fancy. There were no superhighways leading into or out of Nashville. Highway 70 going east to Knoxville and west to Memphis was the region's best, and it was two-lane. The roads going north and south were markedly shakier and more irregular. The main highway north, 41, toward Clarksville and Fort Campbell, Kentucky, was a particular nightmare, and there were constant fatal accidents on it, when soldiers, having spent their weekends in Nashville, would race back to the base in time for reveille and miss the route's curves.

The TR3, my proudest possession—indeed, in terms of toys, virtually my only possession—was firehouse red. I had owned it for about a year and absolutely loved it. I thought in some way the car defined me: I was not part of the crowd that waited for Detroit to tell us what that year's look was going to be; I was not going to plow

15

a disproportionate amount of my small salary into horsepower I could not use. Rather, I was a man apart, with my own sense of style. A member of the new class, a man who allegedly made his own decisions and could not be hustled by the ads on television. I wanted everyone I met, particularly the young single women of Nashville, to know that. The Triumph's predecessor had been an MG TD, 1952, which I had also loved but which I had ridden hard—I was rough on cars in those days, and the MG had suffered accordingly. In the last six months I owned it, I had needed to park it if at all possible on an incline so I could be sure I could get a roll to start it in the morning.

But I had loved both cars. Tennessee, because it lacked superhighways, because of its natural beauty and its wonderful climate, and because of its contours (particularly to the east, where the roads rose and fell and bent and cut), was an unusually pleasant venue in which to drive a sports car. That summer I had covered the last senatorial campaign of Estes Kefauver. It had been a wonderful assignment—I would drive some 200 to 250 miles a day through the small towns and county seats of rural Tennessee following the senator, who would make about a dozen speeches a day, and I had managed to feel like something of a playboy in my sporty car. Even better, *The Tennessean*, my paper, had paid me, as I recall, eight cents per mile for the use of the car, which meant, given the wondrous gas mileage that I was getting, that I was making the equivalent of my salary off my gas expense payments.

The most distinct pleasure for me in those days was that of actually driving. It was nothing less than sensual: I loved the feel of the car as it hit sharp corners and the sense of strength and power that it seemed to convey. I as a driver seemed to be an extension of the car. I remember getting very few tickets and, on the occasions when I was stopped and handed one, receiving a certain grudging respect from the highway patrolmen.

More, the car seemed to fit the venue. Because Tennessee did not have superhighways, because its roads were old and bent, and because much of the terrain seemed hilly, driving a sports car there seemed the most natural thing of all. A lot of my friends had cars with far more muscle, but they could never beat me on those roads. The day I left to go to work for the *Times* was both a happy and a sad one: I was thrilled by the chance of going to work not just for the *Times* but soon to go to Washington to work for the most honored journalist of the era, Scotty Reston. But the truth was that I had never been happier in my life, nor had I felt more useful, than in those years in Nashville. Not surprisingly, I have always looked back on that time with great nostalgia.

I go back to Nashville a lot these days. I am doing a book on the young black students who were the first sit-in leaders, whom I covered in 1960, and my leg-work brings me back regularly to this city, which I knew so well and loved so much as a young man. And I am stunned by the difference between the Nashville that existed then and the Nashville that exists today. Much of that change, both physical and psychological, seems to have been wrought by the change in automobile usage.

In those days, in the middle and late Fifties, I thought we already lived in what would soon be known as the auto culture. But I was wrong—the true culture of the auto was still to come. Middle Tennessee in the fifties was still a relatively poor and underdeveloped region, just escaping from an almost feudal agrarian past. If, in America, the North and the East and California were enjoying the immense surge of middle-class affluence brought on by America's favored status as the one developed nation undamaged by World War II—a country astonishingly rich in a world that was desperately poor—the South and the Southwest were about a decade behind in gaining their fair share of that affluence. The region was just beginning to receive some measure of industrialization. Rural electrification, brought on by the Tennessee Valley Authority, was still relatively new. The revolution Henry Ford had wrought elsewhere in the country—the worker as consumer—was just beginning to take place there.

Today Nashville is an infinitely more prosperous city, and middle Tennessee a more prosperous region. The change is not only a reflection of the far greater affluence of the nation but of the changes caused by the coming of the automobile. The automotive revolution, I realize in retrospect, was just beginning then. Now it is, for better or worse, complete. In those days, we reporters occasionally wrote about something which was supposed to happen in the near future but which to us seemed quite distant. That was the coming of a great new national highway program that President Eisenhower had just pushed through, aided by the most powerful and all-inclusive lobby in the country's history. As with most things that seem to herald the future, I wrote some of the stories about the highway program, but I never paid very much attention to the highway program because I never thought of it as affecting me. Among other things, my heart was set on being a Washington correspondent and a foreign correspondent. I intended to be gone before the roads were built. And I was.

In those days, Nashville's rush-hour crunch was never that great. Anyone bothered by the idea of the worst of it—the worst of it on the Richter scale of contemporary traffic was very mild indeed—needed only wait another fifteen minutes to go home, and the worst would be over.

Today when I fly into Nashville, it is to a city with a dependence on cars at which we could only have guessed in the Fifties. I arrive, walk from the gate of my plane to the front of the airport, descend to the ground level, and choose among a vast variety of rental companies the one that gives me the best deal or at least pretends to give me the best deal. The lines are short, and I am usually processed through in about ten minutes. Then I walk all of about fifty yards to the waiting car, get in, and drive off to my destination—my first interview. I have set my schedule according to the normal waiting period of eastern airports and rental offices, and because the Nashville process is so quick, I often have an hour or two to kill. As someone who has rented cars all over the country, I am stunned by the ease and simplicity with which you can rent cars in America, but the Nashville process—the ready accessibility of the cars—seems particularly miraculous. It reflects something uniquely American, something conceived and developed in the land of the car and now copied elsewhere, although rarely so efficiently. I remain stunned by the idea of the American car rental: that each day so many thousands of Americans can start the day in one part of the country, travel to a distant part, and walk up to a counter and soon drive off with a nice, clean, virtually new car, often (except, it seems, in the city in which I live) at a remarkably low price. If it is normally an easy transaction, then in Nashville it is again and again the easiest and most pleasant I have ever been partner to.

I get into my car, and I head for town. Today six giant arteries lead out of Nashville in six different directions. Another massive multilane highway rings the city, allowing drivers the ability to skirt the city if need be, or to go from one section to another in a minimal amount of time. Nothing seems very far away. Distance within the city has somehow shrunk from the time in which I worked here; whereas when I lived here only a relatively small section of the lovely land surrounding the city was considered viable for real estate purposes, the coming of these new highways has made the surrounding region infinitely more valuable. Very simply said, more people of this city live significantly better than they did when I was here.

I am aware of the other changes that have taken place in a city I knew well. In 1960, my last year here, I covered the ongoing struggle of young black students to eat at downtown stores that were eager to have them as customers as long as they did not want to eat lunch at the stores' lunch counters. The irony of that struggle was that the downtown area was already virtually gone as a commercial shopping area. Whites, at least prosperous whites, were shopping there less and less. Using their cars as their legs, they were already shopping in the increasingly affluent new malls in suburban Green Hill and other places. The people who shopped downtown were black; they shopped there because the bus service was good, since many of them did not have cars. Even then the downtown, as far as the white middle class was concerned, existed more and more as a financial and government center. Now it is little else.

Today, changes that were just beginning to be visible in the late Fifties are more obvious than ever. There are more and bigger and newer malls. The city's best restaurants, once located downtown, now adjoin the malls. The area around Vanderbilt University is deluged by fast-food places. The rush-hour traffic is heavier now. There are more people with cars and more cars per family. In the Nashville that I knew well in 1960, the black middle class was very small. Most ordinary black people did not have cars then—they demanded too large a part of too small a budget (the cars blacks were able to buy were also clunky and likely to be expensive to keep up, and the ability of black people to get help in financing a car, as whites did, was dramatically more limited). The principal means of transportation for blacks was the bus. Often, if they could, black men walked to work to save money. Black women rode the bus from the black sections of town to West Nashville, where they worked as maids in the morning, and rode the buses back home in the afternoon. In the broader wealth that the city has attained in the thirty-five years since I have been away, there has been a dramatic increase in the black middle class. The automotive manifestation of that broad black middle class is obvious.

But the greatest change of all may be the invisible one. It may be that Nashville, like so many American cities, is for better or worse a less rooted city in a less rooted country, and that the coming of the great highway system and the coming of cheap transportation—for that is what we are talking about; elemental transportation in America has for those thirty-five years been relatively cheap—has dramatically changed not only how we live but where we live.

When I worked here in the Fifties, almost everyone I knew was from Nashville or from somewhere in the general region. Most of the people I knew seemed to have family members who had been in the city for two or three or four generations. (My own family, I might add, was in those days scattered throughout northwestern Connecticut, a member of our family, it seemed, in each town, with no town more than about twenty-five miles away from another. Now its members are scattered all over the country.) In Nashville, people who were ambitious tended to be from the smaller towns in the surrounding 150-mile range who had been drawn to the city because of its better job market and educational possibilities. Even on our paper, which was a particularly good one and which was, in the changing nature of journalism, beginning to hire college graduates, there was something of a split-level culture. The reporters who had been hired before the editor decided a college degree was an important credential for a reporter were all from within the region; those more recently hired who had college degrees were increasingly from outside the region.

In those days, if you went to a party and there was someone there from the North or the East (as far as I can remember, there was no one from California in Tennessee in the Fifties, although there was some talk of a local architect who did not like dealing with local building inspectors and was said to have driven off to San Francisco in a fit of pique), they were more often than not women, and they were there because they had married a young man from Nashville and had come back to live in his home. It was much more unusual for a man from the North to have come to Nashville to live in his wife's hometown than the reverse; the assumption in those days was that, when a man moved to his wife's hometown, it happened because she was from a privileged family.

The people who ran Nashville, of course, were from Nashville. In fact, they had always been from Nashville, or from the area, and they had, it seemed, always run Nashville. They were from what were known as old families; therefore, it was their right to run the city. It was not a city that ventilated itself economically or, of course, socially. If you were from a leading family, your family had always been a leading one. To say that some of the economic leadership was ingrown was an understatement. (There had been a memorable chamber of commerce meeting in which a local industrialist, hearing that Ford might locate a glass plant in the area, had argued vigorously against giving Ford any commercial benefits because he feared what the arrival of Ford would do to the city's then-suppressed pay scales.)

In Nashville, there was a traditional kind of mutation of wealth that had taken place over a century. A family would start off by being wealthy in land, and then in the next generation some of that wealth would be mutated slightly, perhaps into a share of a bank, which meant that the bank would favor the family's commercial interests (and look with disfavor on the interests of rival families). Then, in succeeding generations, the family wealth would be mutated into some kind of family business or into an influential law firm. But power, particularly financial power, and particularly the control of the jewel in old Nashville's crown, Vanderbilt University, tended to reside with people with whom it had always resided. In any business decision in Nashville, the past spoke as powerfully as the present, and usually far more powerfully than the future.

But this is a new Nashville. It reflects a new, far more mobile America driven by cars and by the movement of jobs and lives. It is an America that is less rooted, more open. In the late Fifties, jobs began to move, and the economy began to change more and more from a blue-collar to a white-collar economy. Companies that had once been located in the Great Lakes region or the East moved to the South. The new white-collar businesses found cities like Nashville, with its impressive hospital system and its powerful religious publishing industry, hospitable and business-friendly. As new job possibilities opened up, and as the roads became better and better, people were not tied to the locale of their parents and grandparents. Families scattered from the small geographic regions that had once bound them together. New money came to town, and it was less and less respectful of the past. Today, important people who make critical decisions about Nashville's economy are no longer products of Nashville's past.

I am impressed now when I am at small dinner parties in Nashville: First, that very few people seem to be originally from Nashville anymore and, second, that no one cares where they are from. The mayor, Phil Bredesen (who seems to be determined to bring this once small city a professional football team, something unheard of in my day), is typical of the new city. He is from the East, went to Harvard, arrived in Nashville in his early thirties some twenty years ago, and made millions in a business allied with health care. Those are not credentials that in my day would have allowed him even to think of running for office. Indeed, each aspect of his curriculum vitae would have been used against him. What are today his strengths would in those days have seemed his weaknesses.

No change is a complete blessing, and I am, of course, torn by some of the implications of all this change. I accept that more people are living better than in the time I lived here. But there is a part of me that liked some aspects of the past—a past that was rich and in certain ways quite comforting. I liked the sense that people knew one another and had known one another a long time, and I liked some of the mutual courtesies that that kind of connecting tissue seemed to create. I liked some aspects of the smallness and slowness of the pace of life: I liked being able to walk the ten blocks or so from the paper where I worked to the downtown and do my interviews there, talk to friends, and then, on my way back to the paper, to shop leisurely at Zibart's Bookstore on Church Street. There was a part of me that liked going to parties at night where everyone was from the region, and where the feeling of a rooted place was part of the pleasure of the evening. But that is gone, along with the old dinky highways and my old TR3. And, since I do my rental transactions ever faster at the airport, I accept the change.

KATHLEEN SPIVACK

As Animals

Green New Hampshire
on the road and the radio playing.
Behind each thicket
crickets like irritation

part the air.
This car divides the road.
I drive the uncombed side:
the grasses waver,

little splashes of gravel sprout.
Blue car in the blue air,
I am hurrying somewhere
fifty miles an hour while,

roadside, from each stalk of grass.
a microcosm watches, wondering.
Each froth of spittle
on the vetch hides complex

AS ANIMALS

compound eyes.
Each gall, inside, is star-
shaped, cancer-weird:
a smug worm, cradled, watches.

Trees along the shoulder
stand up beside the road,
slim organ pipes,
their water driven upward.

It is soundless for them, fingering
the wind, like practicing.
And I am practicing
being independent, greedy

through the country,
swallowing the green of it
and speeding—
Where's the stop?—

to some unproven mountain top
as if to choose one view
while the ground breathes,
heaving upward,

and a sweet sunlit smell
rushes in the car windows
like small strawberries, wild,
like lying in the meadow,

parting the leaves, and finding
them. Now the mountains
bump against me,
the hills tumble together;

the trees are racing me
to the waterfalls
and the road cuts the edges
of gulleys

and the radio is twanging:
be American.
Drive forever!—
I downshift at the curves.

Live forever.
The mind is suspended.
Driving is a sensation
unending, cool as sunset,

slowing finally by some
unnamed meadow, the clover darkening,
the sun finishing, the car huddled,
watching, inert: silent as animals.

Sound and Fury

DENIS JENKINSON

A Fascination That Was

The human being has always been a competitive sort of animal so it is not surprising that, when the motor car was invented, the idea of motoring competitions soon arose. In the very beginning such competitions were more in the nature of tests of endurance for the new-fangled motor car. The French liked the idea of motoring competitions and no doubt somebody took on a wager that they could get from point A to point B quicker than the next man, and soon contests were evolved from Paris to Rouen, Paris to Dieppe, Nice to Marseilles, and so on. Town-to-town racing became the thing, until it got out of hand and was suppressed by the French Government in the early 1900s. The Italians took to this form of racing as well, and they developed it into a wonderful series of events that grew bigger and bigger and, although comparatively out-of-hand for many years, it was not until 1957 that Italian legislation put a stop to town-to-town racing.

Whereas the pioneers for this type of racing had run their events from one town to the next, the Italians enlarged upon the idea and went on to the one after that and worked their way round various parts of Italy until a circuit was completed. Ultimately the open-road racing became highly organised in Italy, and many of the various provinces of that country arranged their own races from town to town, the events being known as "Giro's," or circuits, and thus there were such events as the "Giro di Umbria," "Giro di Sicilia," "Giro di Calabria," "Giro della Dolomite," and the most famous of all, known as the "Mille Miglia"—though it might well have been called the "Giro d'Italia." All these events were run annually for many years, the Mille Miglia first being held in 1927. They started from the most important town in the district, which was also the headquarters of the organising club, and passed through numerous other towns, ultimately arriving back at the starting point, and their lengths varied from three hundred miles to a thousand miles. They all conformed to a pattern, whereby the race was open to the most standard of family saloon cars, through various categories right up to specially-built, two-seater racing cars, for it was a rule that a co-driver or mechanic should be carried.

Entries for these events ranged from 150 competitors to as many as 500 or 600 and in all cases they were started at one-minute intervals, so that the contest was against time rather than personal rivals, the winner being he who completed the "Giro" in the shortest total time. The route to be followed was clearly marked, and virtually closed to normal everyday traffic, and at each big town a "Control" was set up and the driver had to stop and have a route-book stamped by an official, before racing on to the next control town. With such a variety of cars competing the form was for the slow cars to start off first, allowing perhaps thirty minutes between each category, so that public interest was maintained right to the last moment when the big factory cars and star drivers set off. This meant that the drivers of fast cars had to overtake many other competitors, but it was all part of the fascination of Italian open-road racing.

I have enjoyed some of these events both as a spectator and a competitor, and the multitude of ways in which they appealed to me would need a book in itself, but part of the fascination of these races was the "atmosphere"—not only at the start, but all round the course, running as they did along ordinary everyday Italian main and side roads, through villages and towns, over mountains and across wide open plains. The "Giro di Sicilia" was typical of these events, starting in Palermo and running anti-clockwise round the coast of Sicily and back to Palermo, some six hundred miles of winding, twisting Sicilian roads. In this event, with perhaps a hundred starters, the first man would leave at midnight on Saturday, and the start would be in the main square of the town, brilliantly floodlit, with a large wooden ramp some five feet high, in the middle of the road. The first car would drive up the ramp to where the starter and time-keepers were waiting, and a board would be hoisted on a pole giving the names of the driver and co-driver and the racing number, and on the stroke of midnight away they would go amid the cheering and clapping of a wildly enthusiastic crowd. The route led across the main square to turn sharp right into a tree-lined avenue leading out of the town, and many a competitor would rush across the brilliantly-lit square forgetting to put his head-lights on and turn the first corner at 60 mph or more to plunge into total darkness; shining brake lights would tell a story as the driver groped for the head-lights switch! As the cars left at minute intervals, so the tempo grew, for the more powerful cars could be heard assembling in one of the side streets, drivers awaiting their turn to drive up on to the starting ramp, and when the last few competitors were gathered with the factory-entered cars, from which the winner was almost certain to come, excitement would rise to fever pitch, even though it was 2:00 A.M. or later.

Finally the last competitor would leave, and as the sound of his open exhaust dwindled into the darkness a strange empty feeling would come over the centre of Palermo, broken only by the hum of the crowds going home to bed. As the populace began to turn in for a few hours' sleep it was strange to think of all those drivers racing along through the darkness, head-lights piercing the way ahead, tyres screaming and exhausts roaring. Although Palermo retired into relative quietness, the rest of the island was being rudely awakened as the fast-moving cavalcade went from town to town. For the drivers the greatest relief was dawn arriving, and all through Sunday they would drive on, some falling by the wayside with broken engines, others crashing, but always someone driving on to win. If you stayed in Palermo while the race was on, you could hang about in the square, drinking *cappuccino* and listening to broadcasts from the loudspeakers festooned on all the lamp-posts, giving reports from the various controls, and after lunch you could take up your position near the finish line, the wooden ramp now having been dismantled. During the afternoon the hot sun would lull everyone into a torpid state, the air dry and dusty, the swarthy iced-drink vendors doing a roaring trade, until around 3:00 P.M. when the shrilling of police whistles would indicate that something was about to happen. The last few miles of road into Palermo would be barricaded with straw bales and guarded by police and military, and when a lone mobile policeman arrived at speed on his Moto-Guzzi you would know that the first competitor was not far away. Sure enough a little cloud of dust in the distance heralded the arrival of the first man home, not necessarily the winner, for he may have started an hour or two before the fastest man. The crowds would come awake instantly, waving and cheering as the car tore through the polished streets of the town, tyres screaming, drivers tired and dirty, often the car showing signs of contact with rocks and walls, but everyone happy that the first arrival had returned to Palermo. One by one the cars would come in, some having made a very fast time, others limping along very late, but finishing nevertheless and for the next two or three hours the square would fill with competitors, every one of them deserving the cheers of the crowd, for to finish the course was an achievement, while the winner would receive an extra big ovation. As the time-keepers did their calculations the various class winners would be announced, and the drivers presented to the crowds from a raised dais, both weary men garlanded with flowers, photographers running in all directions to get pictures. Slowly but surely the tempo would die down, until at last all those who started were accounted for, and then the barriers would be removed and life in Palermo, and all round the island, would return to normal.

The greatest of all Italian open-road races was undoubtedly the Mille Miglia, starting from Brescia in the north and covering a thousand miles down the Adriatic coast, across the mountains to Rome and northwards up the Apennine chain back to the plains of Lombardy. Having ridden with competitors in this event for a number of years, and being fortunate enough to have been passenger to the winner in 1955, I have a thousand wonderful memories of that great race, and a badge of which I am really proud, for it is inscribed "Club Mille Miglia—Denis Jenkinson" and that means only one thing, namely that I have completed the thousand miles of that great race. Membership to the Mille Miglia Club is very strict—the only way to become a member is to have completed the race within the time limit, whether you finish first or last. Having done that seemingly simple thing you can then join the Club, but there are people who have started in that race more than a dozen times before being able to join the Club. There are no honorary members and a standing joke in Brescia is that Renzo Castegnato, the chief organiser, is not a member; even though he has organised every race since the first one in 1927 he has never competed. With the true sporting Italian motorists it was a point of honour to attempt the Mille Miglia at least once and if successful the small lapel badge is worn with pride, no matter how long ago it was won. I remember a brush with the traffic police in Rimini which eventually led to an "interview" with the top man of the police force. My Mille Miglia badge saved the day for he had competed once, in a tiny 750 c.c. sports car and sadly told me how he had broken down at Rome. None-the-less he was proud to have attempted the Mille Miglia, and said that an Italian motoring enthusiast is not a true Italian until he has driven in the Mille Miglia. Having partnered the winner of the 1955 race I was obviously beyond reproach! On another occasion the manager of an hotel I was in approached rather meekly to say he had competed in the race in 1952 in a Fiat saloon, and proudly showed me his "Club Mille Miglia" badge.

Those are personal memories as a result of that epic race. What of the event itself, the strange feeling as you get up at dawn on Sunday morning, to leave the start at around 5:00 A.M., knowing that while you have been sleeping, competitors have been leaving Brescia since 9:00 P.M. the previous evening, or being in the last car away and conscious that your shattering exhaust note will be the last to keep the town awake until competitors begin arriving back during the afternoon. A friend who watched me leave on one such occasion said it was rather like watching a trans-Atlantic liner leave the dock. For many hours the starting area was alive with activity, the excitement rising as the competing cars got faster and noisier, until, with the departure of the last car, you felt that the great "liner" had cast off its last rope and there was nothing you could do except wave good-bye. As a competitor the great feeling was that at last the roads were clear of traffic and all yours, and the driver could give the car everything it had got. Having practised round the route for weeks beforehand, getting up at dawn each morning in order to leave the start on a practice run at the same time as on race day, and having driven amidst the ordinary Italian traffic in a car capable of 170 mph dodging scooters, horses, lorries, and heavens knows what, for the roads cannot be closed for practice, it was sheer bliss to start the event proper with a clear road ahead.

Starting at one-minute intervals meant that you might never see any of your close rivals, for you would all be travelling at more or less the same speed, but if after an hour's motoring, during which time you would have covered more than a hundred miles, you saw a speck in the distance you got a wonderful feeling of achievement, while if after the same time you found another car catching you up, you felt depressed and determined to go faster. One joy of being last away was the knowledge that nobody was going to catch you, and every car you saw during the day would be a rival vanquished. Then there would be the tension of an approaching control town, the first break in the high-speed motoring for perhaps two hours or more, and knowing that the break must be kept to a matter of a second or two. The officials would be standing in the road beneath a black and white chequered banner, bearing the welcome word "Controllo" and, as the driver braked heavily down to a walking pace, the passenger's job was to hold an arm high in the air to indicate to the officials exactly where the route-book was going to be, so that they might stamp it without wasting time. As the speed would drop from 150 mph down to 5 mph you would hold the card firmly on the side of the car with one hand and point vigorously at it with the other—but not too soon, or a 100 mph gale could easily wrench your arm and take the route-book out of your hand, though to safeguard this we had it tied to the car by a length of strong string. As you rolled past the control point at a walking pace and the rubber stamp descended on to the white card you would signal the driver and he would accelerate furiously back to a racing speed. Sometimes the stamp would not be quite square, and sometimes part of it would hit your finger, but speed was of the essence and seconds wasted at a control could add up to minutes during the thousand miles. Having seen second place in one Mille Miglia lost by a mere nine seconds after more than ten hours of racing, we were determined to save every second possible at control points, and practised and perfected a routine so that during our record-breaking run we did not come to rest at any of the Stamp Controls.

Taking on petrol and changing tyres is another big problem in such a long race, and practice and briefing took many hours so that seconds gained by the driver should not be wasted at a pit-stop. Food and drink were another problem, for ten hours is a long time to go without them, there being no time to stop for picnics by the wayside, and little room in a racing cockpit for hampers. The odd piece of fruit we were able to carry was in itself a problem, for shortly after midday on Sunday, after some seven hundred miles of racing, the driver felt in need of a nice refreshing orange. By the time I had peeled it with my oily, sweaty, dirty fingers, it resembled a piece of coal, but nevertheless tasted wonderful in that roaring inferno of a cockpit. The noise of a racing-car engine is pretty devastating as it passes you, but to sit behind one is quite a strain on the system, and even though I wore ear-plugs and a helmet my ears were ringing for two or three days after ten hours of continuous noise, while the heat generated by the engine, gearbox, and brakes all combined to make the cockpit of that racing car a real "hell on wheels." Added to this heat was the burning Italian sun that shone down unmercifully the whole day, first in front of us, then to one side, then straight down and then from in front again, always pouring into the open cockpit with nothing to deflect its rays. Having started just after dawn I considered it best to wear a jersey and waterproof skiing jacket, so that by midday I was more than over-heated, an open-neck shirt would have been too much, but the pace was so fast that no seconds could be wasted in stopping to peel off jerseys, so the heat just had to be endured.

Year after year these fantastic road races round Italy became faster and faster, and with the increasing tempo of everyday life the disruption to the nation became more serious, so that the organisers had to battle hard to keep permission to close the roads, stop all the trams and buses, disrupt train services, bring whole communities to a complete standstill, hold up farm work and transport and generally cause a day of chaos and pandemonium. The more sober-minded citizens began to object, though the public loved every minute of it, and it caught the enthusiasm of young and old. In one town you will meet old men who recall memories of the stirring pre-war races with harshly-sprung open Alfa Romeos, of Nuvolari, Varzi, and Biondetti; in another I met two fourteen-year-old lads who "borrowed" their mother's Fiat 500 and, having painted a number on the car, joined in the race from a secluded side-turning. They ran out of petrol and were "found out" by officials. After being reprimanded and delivered back home they were later invited to the local motor club and introduced to the great Fangio himself when he was attending a luncheon party. What a wonderful thrill for two small boys and what a wonderful example of what the Mille Miglia meant to the Italian people. Slowly anti-sporting interest on city councils and in provinces took less kindly to these great sporting contests, and political parties took up the cry with newspapers, pretending to be speaking for the public, until the Government took action, after a bad accident had occurred, and put a stop to all such events. Naturally the loss to competitors was enormous—a chapter of motor-racing history was closed—but above all it was the public who were the real losers, in spite of what biased newspaper reports said. Gone was the excuse for an extra holiday, gone was the happy *fiesta* day of the Mille Miglia, gone was a whole day of profit for the restaurant and café proprietor, for the populace had no option but to stay and work on the annual weekend that was Mille Miglia time.

DENISE McCLUGGAGE

Juan Manuel Fangio

The last time I saw Juan Manuel Fangio, before my recent trip to Argentina, he was wearing a plaid-trimmed dark blue Tam O'Shanter. But then so was I. And so were the likes of Pedro Rodriguez, Innes Ireland, Masten Gregory, and Dr. Dickie Thompson, among others. The tams were provided by the British Motor Corp., the occasion being BMC's introduction to its U.S. dealers and the American press of its new Austin and Morris 850, a.k.a. *Mini*. We drivers had all been engaged by BMC to stage Mini races for the guests. Then we drove those who cared to ride around the courses, impressing them each in our own way. Stirling Moss, not Fangio, had been among us at Marlboro (the course near Washington, DC) for the first program. He was not with us at Lime Rock. It was 1962, and between Marlboro and this clambake Stirling had suffered his rending, career-ending accident at Goodwood.

As a replacement for Stirling, Fangio was brought up from Argentina, along with Juan Manuel Bordeu—a promising young Argentinean driver. And here he was: Fangio. The five-time world driving champion—a little portly with retirement— wearing his BMC bonnet and cheerfully racing and giving rides in these Toastmasters on wheels. And enjoying it with his usual equanimity.

When I say *stage* races, I use the word well. For instance, at the start, which had all cars abreast across the track, Innes and Pedro and I (every other one in the line up) conspired to put our Minis in reverse, so when the flag was dropped and all the cars roared off—tiny front wheels a-claw—we three shot off in the opposite direction. Our little jest left the on-lookers with a momentary sense of incredible acceleration.

Twenty-three years later, Fangio remembered this when I visited him in his Buenos Aires office. "You, Innes, Pedro." He mimed our shift to reverse and back-wards departure and laughed. I was astonished that in all the memories of this sin-gular man's experience with automobiles that tiny moment would be one of them.

The record: In two decades Fangio drove some 200 races in nineteen countries in a dozen different makes of cars. Of the 147 races that he finished he won 78 times. He won five world championships, four of them in a row, driving for four different teams: Alfa Romeo, 1951. Mercedes-Benz, 1954, 1955. Ferrari, 1956. Maserati, 1957. He retired in July 1958.

Nobody has done any of it better. It had begun in his native Argentina, which was first known for its trying long distance races, and then (as the Europeans were imported to party and compete, and a new race course was built in a Buenos Aires park) for the opening of the world championship racing season with one week de-voted to Formula One and another to sports cars—the famed *temporada*, a festival of speed.

In Buenos Aires January is summer, *serious* summer. It can be hot, humid, and over-powering. I remember tales the Englishers told about racing in a steam bath. But then Brits think eighty degrees Fahrenheit is an oven. And Mike Hawthorn was so fair of hair and skin he blistered if someone said *sun* twice in the same sentence. Stirling, on the other hand, strode shirtless around the pits, had a house in tropic Nassau, and always looked fit.

I asked Fangio how he, older and supposedly more vulnerable, so consistently took the measure of the visitors in the Buenos Aires races. "I prepared for the heat," he said, delighted in the memory of being one-up on his young colleagues. "I would go to Mar de Plata and run and play soccer. When they come from Europe where it was cold I was already used to the heat."

Although the heat nearly felled him, too, in the scorching 1955 Grand Prix. That year, only two cars—Fangio's one of them—completed the race using only one driver. (One car had as many as *eight*.) Moss collapsed. Fangio seriously burned his leg on the superheated frame of his Mercedes, but pressed on to win. Fangio had another advantage over the visitors. "They came to have fun—to dance, to eat—I was concentrating on the race."

So Fangio had been into physical fitness! Running, exercising—training of any sort wasn't that common then. And certainly unknown were training gurus, like Danny Sullivan has had. "Yes, I trained," Fangio said, "but never with a professor." He chuckled. "When we [the Argentinean contingent] went to Europe we each bought a bicycle and rode thirty kilometers a day—uphill and down."

That first full season in Europe, such a year it was for Fangio. It was 1949. (He had been to Rheims the year before to drive one race for cars under two-liters and had not finished.) His first full season he won at San Remo, then at Pau, then at Perpignan, then at Marseilles, then at Monza and then at Albi. Then he went home to a tumultuous welcome from his countrymen. From his first race abroad, whatever Fangio did made headlines in Argentina and the races he drove were broadcast at home.

In spite of the successes there had been disappointments that first year: races not finished, and financial troubles. But his showing had earned him a place on the Alfa Romeo team for 1950. The 1950 Alfa team was the team of the three *Fa's*: Fangio, Farina, and Fagioli. And the three of them battled throughout the season for the championship—first one then the other with a narrow margin in points. Fangio led most of it.

It came to the last race of the season, the Italian Grand Prix. Fangio's car broke. Then the one he took over from Taruffi also broke. Farina won and was champion.

In a book called *My Twenty Years of Racing* by Juan Manuel Fangio, in collaboration with Marcollo Giambertone, published in 1961, there are confessions of bitterness at the loss of the championship, even hints of hanky panky by the Alfa Romeo team because the public wanted so much to have an Italian champion.

I asked Fangio about this nationalistic feeling, how it had affected his relationship with the mechanics, with his faith in his car. He hadn't any idea what I was talking about. "I am Italian, son of Italians. Although I am Argentinean, in Italy they considered me Italian," he said.

"I had no trouble with the mechanics. In 1950 at Monza when two cars broke we had two or three problems, mechanical questions. In 1951 [the year of his first championship], the Alfas were perfect." When I told him I got my information from his book, he laughed. "That is *Giambertone's* book, not my book," he said. And he said, not unkindly, that Giambertone (although long associated with Fangio as secretary, manager, general factotum) was simply *poco loco*. Fangio had not wanted to have a book, but a woman, who was a friend of his, kept urging him to cooperate with Giambertone so finally he gave in. "I found out later," Fangio said, his voice dropping, "that she was paid money to convince me." Fangio is now working on his book with a respected Argentine journalist. It might be translated into English, as well.

Then also suspect was what was related in "Giambertone's" book about Fangio's differences with Ferrari? "*Claro*," he said. "The problem with the Ferrari: not just *one* mechanic was responsible for the car. When I asked Ferrari that *one person* be responsible for my car, I got it. To Giambertone, everything had some special motive behind it, but I know they were always trying to give me the best car to drive. Ferrari didn't have any preferences. He made all the cars equal for everybody."

The Ferrari year was 1956 and Fangio had just come from two championship years with Mercedes-Benz. "At Mercedes-Benz we had three mechanics assigned exclusively to each car," he said. (I smiled, having had experience with Italian pit crews I could guess at the culture shock moving from a German crew to an Italian crew must have been—even for an Italian.)

Perhaps Fangio's being a mechanic himself is why the rapport between driver and mechanic mattered so much to him. "It is very important to have a good working relationship between the driver and the mechanic," he said. And the absence of that rapport might be one reason he did not run the Indianapolis 500, though he did pass his driver's test.

Before I get to the Indy story understand what the oval racing community was like then. *Provincial* sums it up. Road racing was considered effete. "Sporty cars" was meant to be a stinging epithet. And there was no little resentment that the World Driving Champion never ran the *real* race, Indy. (Which, for political reasons, offered world championship points.) All that my-brother-can-lick-your-brother talk wasn't really silenced until Jimmy Clark and Graham Hill won Indy in 1965 and 1966 respectively.

As for Fangio, there was even a $500 bet by an Indy partisan that he couldn't as much as pass his driver's test. He passed it with ease, the bet was paid and donated to charity. OK, so Fangio—winner of the last four World Championships—was offered an Indy car in 1958. A Kurtis Offy. He said they told him it was a brand new one. He saw it—Indy cars always were impressively "sanitary" in appearance—and agreed.

"It seemed OK," Fangio said. "I went to try it out. But when I saw other Indianapolis cars—much more advanced—I knew they had not told the truth. It was not a new car. It was two, three years old." But even more important to Fangio: "The mechanics were not good. Also, I don't know English. l couldn't understand them. I have to have an affinity with a mechanic to work well."

So he decided not to run and went home.

I was at Indy that year, covering the race for the *New York Herald Tribune*. It was the year they had a terrible ragged start and a disastrous crash on Turn 3. Eight cars were involved. Pat O'Connor was killed. If Fangio had stayed at Indy. If he had made the field. Who knows? He might have been in the midst of it.

Fangio has always had a way of dodging the bullet. Maybe simply missing the race was a variation on that. If so, Cuba is another example. And there he missed the race because he was—*kidnapped*.

A road race in Havana, through the downtown streets, along the Malecon. It is 1958. Batista rules with an iron hand. Castro is in the hills. Fangio is there to drive a Maserati. But the car, raced recently in Caracas, had crashed there. "The frame was bent," Fangio explained. "It was not good in the curves."

He was in the lobby of the Hotel Lincoln discussing the matter of handling with his mechanic. "Bertocchi, Ugolini, deTomaso were with me. This young man came in and pointed a gun at me. He told me they were looking for me and I was to go with him. If anyone moved I would suffer the consequences.

"I went with him."

The young man was a member of the 26th of July Movement, Castro's group. In Buenos Aires when Fangio was telling the story he said "26th of June." Politics, anywhere, held no interest for him—which accounts in part for the longevity of his popularity. (But I had a particular reason to remember the details. I was in Havana for that race and I broke the story of Fangio's kidnapping to the world. A front-page byline in the *Herald Tribune*.)

Fangio continued: "I asked the young man, 'Why are you doing this?' He said, 'We are fighting for the future of Cuba.'" Fangio shrugged. "Always the young fight for what they believe. They are idealistic. They want to save the world." The Movement's intention, by absenting Fangio from the Grand Prix, was to draw attention to the increasing strength of those who opposed Batista. At night, after the race, they released Fangio at the door of the Argentine embassy. "They treated me very well," Fangio said. "Always very polite. I had food, drink. We watched the race on television."

It was an accident-strewn race. The course was unduly slippery and cars spun and crashed with regularity. Four people were killed when a car went into the crowd. Said Fangio: "When I saw this terrible accident on television, I told my kidnappers,

'It is possible that you have done me a favor.' I believe in destiny and maybe they helped me by keeping me out of the race."

I asked Señor Ross, the interpreter in Buenos Aires, if there is an equivalent phrase in Spanish for "dodging the bullet" because Fangio seems to have been particularly adept at doing just that. Fangio laughed. (He has a husky bark of a laugh—like a movie Mafioso don.) "*Sì, sì*," he said. "I am here, the bullet goes here," he indicates just past his right ear.

How does he account for all these narrow escapes? His voice roughened: "*Destino*," and he pointed heavenward. Then laughed. "I don't know," he said. "It is a mystery."

One of his first drives at the fringe of catastrophe was in 1938 in a Ford V-8 at Tres Arroyos, the town where his mother was born. Scheduled for three hundred miles, the race was desperately flagged to a close after only sixty-four. Thick dust hung motionless in the still air, destroying visibility, and driving was by guess and by God. Five people died in collisions and flames, accidents Fangio had no notion of until he was stopped.

The dodged bullet several years later was in one of the long distance road races, Argentina's specialty. At night plunging at speed through the dust and darkness he flicked his lights up to see two looming bridge abutments, one on either side. "Just by chance I was in the middle between them," Fangio said in wonder. "A little to either side I would have hit one."

At Monte Carlo in 1950 he was leading. Just after he had passed Tobacconist's Corner a crazy series of events began behind him. Cars spinning and crashing into each other, like a pile-up on a fog-bound superhighway. Flagged warnings were received too late and eight cars were involved in the melée by the time Fangio was due around again. Fangio's ability to draw on all his senses and synthesize the information—to instantly sort it for relevancy and act upon it—again served him well.

"I noticed the people in the stands," Fangio said. "They were all looking at the same spot. That warned me." He was braking hard before the flagman was even visible. He did not become the ninth victim. (Nor did he win the race—the car broke later.)

Even away from racing Fangio has carried his mysterious shield. I asked him about a story I had heard of a narrow escape in a movie house. Ah, he was glad I had reminded him. For the new book.

The story: In England he and his countryman, Froilan Gonzalez, had gone to a movie, Fangio recalled, hoping it would be a Western or something with more action and less talk, but it wasn't. "After a while I said, 'Come on, Froilan, let's go. We can't understand this.'" Again, his voice hoarsening: "We had just left when the chandelier fell out of the ceiling right on the seats where we had been."

The most famous of all of Fangio's close calls came just thirty years ago. "I just happened to slip by with luck," he said. "A lane opened up and I slipped past." He was speaking, of course, of Le Mans—June 11, 1955—when a teammate's Mercedes cut a hellish swath through the spectators. Eighty of them died as well as the French driver, fifty-year-old Pierre Levegh. Fangio barely escaped.

The Twenty-four Hours—flagged off at 4 P.M.—was nearly two and a half hours old. Complete were the thirty-two laps required before the first pit stops and cars were beginning to call at pit lane. Those first stops are always dramatic at Le Mans when the established pattern of engine sounds—a roaring swell past the pits then droning off under the Dunlop bridge—changes for the first time. Now engines' throats are cleared—gearing down for the stop. A flurry of refueling. Drivers hastily swap places and the gears stair-step back up to race pitch.

In those days in racing there was no one entry to the pits at most courses, no walls separating pit lane from the race course. Pit lanes were more a long, wide shoulder to the raceway—a "lay-by" on a British motorway. A driver could dive into his pit—wherever it was—directly from the race course. And pull back into the fray as his whim and discretion directed.

And at Le Mans the race course was little more than the two lanes of an ordinary French highway. The pits rose on one side and on the other was a thick earth retaining wall with a spectator area and a grandstand immediately behind it. In the years since the disaster many have speculated how that dark day at Le Mans happened. I was not there, but in the years following I talked to all the surviving principals as well as to many eye-witnesses.

Theories aside, facts do exist.

Such as: Mike Hawthorn in a D-type Jaguar and Fangio in the 300SLR Mercedes with the wing-like airbrake had been having a dice worthy of a sprint race for more than two hours. This was a continuation of the heady rivalry that had begun when Hawthorn nipped Fangio on the last turn to win the French Grand Prix at Rheims two seasons before.

At Le Mans, the silver Mercedes and the British Racing Green D-type passed and repassed each other—Hawthorn setting a lap record in the process. The two had blown the rest of the field away leaving only four other cars—two Ferraris and two Mercedes—on the lead lap. And Hawthorn lapped the latter two—Karl Kling's and Levegh's—on the lap of the accident. Fangio, too, had passed Kling and was rapidly closing on Levegh on the pit straight.

Hawthorn's pit had him ahead of Fangio by eight to ten seconds. They were expecting him to stop on this lap to turn the car over to Ivor Bueb.

Fangio, coming out of White House, the last turn before the pits, could see before him the tail of the D-type, no more than a hundred yards ahead. Also in the picture was Levegh's Mercedes and Lance Macklin, driving an Austin-Healey.

Le Mans is famous for the great disparity in top speeds of the cars allowed to compete. Macklin's car was, at best, twenty-five miles an hour slower than the lead cars, but was still far from the slowest.

Macklin was in the right lane. Hawthorn in the left lane, to pass. Levegh following more or less in the middle. Then Hawthorn was cutting across the right lane, heading for the pits.

Macklin—for whatever reason—swerved toward the left lane where Levegh was now closing rapidly. Levegh tried to go left, too, but had neither the time nor the room.

Levegh hit Macklin. His Mercedes rode up over the left rear of the Austin-Healey, taking off like a thrill-show act. It crashed in an explosive burst on the top of the protective earth barrier. The heavy engine and burning body parts tore loose and mowed a long and deadly path through the crowd.

Macklin's car, spinning like a game wheel from the impact, slammed against the pit wall at the right (injuring three people) and ricocheted back across the track, coming to rest against the earth barrier on the grandstand side. (Macklin was to leap out and run back across the track to the pits, barely hurt.)

Now imagine Fangio's view, moving at speed into this developing scene. Sensing trouble, he begins to brake. He sees his teammate Levegh—just before the impact with Macklin's car—throw his left arm into the air, further alerting him. Yet stopping is out of the question, even with the condor wings of the airbrake—new and highly effective—on the Mercedes.

Fangio has only fifty fast-disappearing yards left and he is moving at 120 mph.

Fangio sees the fated car airborne. Feels as well as hears the explosion. The fire ball. In the smoke and debris somewhere is Macklin's car, spinning. "Instinctively, I go to the right," Fangio said. The gate is open. The gate is closed. Happening faster than thought. Fangio slips through—slipping between the carnage to his left and to his right the pits. *Destino.*

Then the speculations. The French press—Levegh was a local favorite—blamed Hawthorn. It was said that Hawthorn had chopped Macklin off, thus lighting the fuse of the entire incident. Hawthorn insisted that in his judgment he had allowed adequate room for Macklin and made a normal approach to the pits.

A grandstand spectator's home movies and footage from a film crew, preparing to shoot Hawthorn's pit stop, bore this out to the satisfaction of a board of enquiry. It was judged an accident—a dreadful interweaving of events. No one's fault.

Several years later I summoned the nerve to ask Mike about that horrible day. Having myself raced in slow cars mixed in with faster company I knew that the rear-view mirror is lavished with attention. In a slow car most of the race comes from behind. Could it be that Macklin's attention, having seen Mike pass and knowing Fangio must be near as well, was on his rear-view mirror? Then, looking forward again, found Mike not where he had expected him to be but, indeed, in front of him?

If Lance had been looking in his mirror, he would have, at best, lost reaction time. At worst he might have—startled—over-reacted when he saw the Jaguar before him.

Mike agreed that was likely. And he agreed that Levegh was probably also looking in his mirror, watching for Fangio so he could tell how much time he had to clear Macklin's car and make way for his faster teammate.

We were not talking about fixed stares in the mirror—only normal information collecting. But at racing speeds even a glance means a diversion in which critical yards are covered while something else goes unattended.

After the crash, the race continued. It had to. Releasing all those spectators to the narrow roads around the race course would have delayed ambulances and hampered rescue efforts.

There was another traffic jam, though, that affected Fangio: the phone circuits. But Mercedes-Benz officials in Stuttgart finally did get through on the jammed lines and ordered their remaining cars withdrawn. Fangio (Moss was his co-driver) was leading at the time.

That was as close as Fangio came to winning—indeed even finishing—Le Mans. But those races with shared responsibility were not his favorites. "Races like Le Mans you have two or three drivers," he said. "You may go along very well, but then the other driver might do poorly." He shakes his head.

But Fangio truly regretted that he had never won that storied chase around the Italian boot, the Mille Miglia.

In 1953, in a *Disco Volante* Alfa Romeo, he did everything right *except* win. He did not lead at Rome, considered bad luck in the fabled Italian road race. But at Florence he was in first place. "I was three minutes ahead when a steering arm broke," he said. "From Bologna to Brescia, 250 kilometers, I had just one wheel steering.

The other going like this [he waggled his hand like a fish tail]. I came second. It was very disappointing."

And the experience probably qualifies as another bullet dodged. Averaging 100 mph with just one wheel steering is like flying a twin-engine plane through the mountains with one prop feathered. Just what happens if the other goes out, too?

Fangio's shield was not impregnable. He did not go through two decades of racing unscathed. Emotionally, there was the frequent trauma of friends lost and injured. In twenty years thirty of his colleagues—some very close to him—died in racing. He is a sensitive man. I remember him at the Sebring hospital in 1957, his face grave, his voice tight with care. Charley Menditeguy, the charming Argentine polo player who had turned to racing—his friend—had crashed a Maserati in the esses and now was seriously injured.

Photographs had shown the same face when the promising young Onofre Marimon, another countryman, the son of an old racing friend and rival, died in practice at the Nürburgring in 1954. The press had called the young Argentine "Fangio's protégé." Word was Fangio had considered quitting after that crash. I asked him about it. "No," he said solemnly. "No. Because I knew that Marimon had made a mistake."

Only once since he began to race, Fangio said, had he considered giving it up. In 1948 in a Grand Prix of South America (Buenos Aires to Caracas and back) he crashed in Peru and his good friend riding with him, Daniel Arrutia, died of injuries.

"I had two accidents in my life," Fangio said, "and both were caused by the same thing—I was physically tired. In Peru I had an accident with my Chevy. On a curve at night. We had already driven all day and were supposed to stop to sleep. But there was a revolution going on so we could not stop. They made us go on. My friend was killed."

The first time a revolution, the next time bad weather. All flights between Paris and Italy had been canceled but Fangio had to get to Monza where a Maserati awaited him for the Italian Grand Prix. It was 1952. He had won his first world championship the year before, then Alfa Romeo pulled out of Formula One.

He refused to accept being stranded in Paris and borrowed a car and drove all night, arriving just two hours before the race. Without practice, he started in the rear. Barely two laps into the race Fangio's car somersaulted at Lesmo and dropped him, free of the wreckage, in the grass. A broken vertebrae in his neck put him in a plaster cast and out of racing for the year. It also left him with a distinctive way of turning his upper body as he turns his head. "I said, 'No more driving when I am tired.' Not even on the highway. When I am tired I stop," he said.

"You have to have all your senses clear when you race." He refills his glass of mineral water. "You cannot think of anything else but the race. Any moment can be fatal. You have to be 100 percent. You cannot think, 'If I don't win, I don't eat.' No, when I race I have no financial problems. After the race, yes, but during the race my mind is strictly on racing—not the consequences."

Fangio, known for his smooth driving, has even had some rough days on the circuit. Maybe two, by actual count. Whispers in the pits. The Old Man hit a wall, he hit a barrel. The rarity of it.

At Silverstone he sent more than one course-marking barrel flying. He was driving the new streamlined Mercedes. "The wheels were covered. I couldn't see where they were, so I hit the barrels," he said simply. (Needless to say the Mercedes' wheels were uncovered before the next Grand Prix.)

At Monaco, the Ferrari year, he tagged a wall with the rear end of the car.

I asked Fangio if these incidents angered him, these departures from his usual perfection. *"Claro,"* he said. "Because I was at fault. When it's a problem with the car, bad luck. When it's my fault, I get angry."

But onward to a more pleasant subject. Fangio's greatest victory of them all, the one that gave him the most satisfaction of his career.

As we talked, every mention of the Nürburgring was followed by its description as *"muy especial."* Special with its length and its many twists and turns, yes, but particularly special to Fangio who won the German Grand Prix there three times—once with Mercedes, once with Ferrari, and once with Maserati. It was the race in the Maserati in 1957 that has become a motor racing classic.

"I knew the circuit very well and I had a car with great capabilities—strong, very stable—but there was one problem: It used a lot of rubber," Fangio said. The chief competition came from the two young Britishers, Mike Hawthorn and Peter Collins. The Ferraris they drove were much the same car Fangio had won the championship in the year before, so he knew their capabilities, too.

Fangio's Maserati team decided on a strategy. They would plan to stop for a tire change midway in the race and so would start with less gasoline, too, so he could, traveling light, build up a cushion of time. He wanted thirty seconds as a margin. "We practiced a lot. We found the crew could get me back on the road in thirty seconds." So he needed a thirty-second cushion.

With ten laps gone—the race mid-point on this long circuit—Fangio had the thirty seconds in hand and came in as planned. Out of the car, taking on his own mineral water, he calmly watched his crew. But suddenly all was not going as practiced. "I don't know if they were nervous, or what, but they had trouble," Fangio said. "I heard the Ferraris go by. The crew was taking not thirty seconds but an *additional* thirty seconds."

Fangio knew that he would need time at less than maximum speed to scrub in the tires. His thirty-second lead had turned into a forty-eight-second deficit, then by the next lap it was fifty-one seconds. "Almost a minute!" Fangio said. "Then I began feeling out the car, looking for the places on the circuit where I could use a higher gear to my advantage and gain time." He found places where he had once lifted but now he stayed hard on the throttle, where he had once used third gear but now he was comfortable—and faster—in fourth. He was transcendent.

"It was thus possible to overtake them and win in the last lap of the race," Fangio finished simply. Then admitted: "That was the most spectacular race of my life."

Tavoni, Ferrari's team manager, had signaled his drivers to take it easy with Fangio nearly a minute behind. So Fangio was gaining in great leaps by the time they got word of their true plight.

With the 'Ring's long laps some nine or ten minutes elapsed between pit signals. I asked Fangio if in those days there had been radio communication between driver and pit, if Peter and Mike might not have been alerted to their danger in time to do something about it. "That's logical," he said, "but the 'Ring is very special. Sometimes a driver who thinks his lead is safe loses the rhythm of the race and he cannot get it back."

As it happens so often with Fangio a story in which he is the star—in which he has been victor—is immediately followed by one in which someone else vanquished him. It is not that Fangio is without ego—he is a proud man—but rather that his sense of self is so secure it needs no petty bolstering.

So he immediately told me of a time involving Ascari and Farina and himself. "I got a little careless," he said, after Ascari had stopped because of trouble. "Farina who was following me, came and passed me. Then I could not catch him. I had lost the rhythm of the race."

His victory at the 'Ring had, indeed, been spectacular, but what meant the most to Fangio was that the two young English drivers—Hawthorn and Collins—he had beaten were as elated as he was. They came and embraced him. "The biggest joy a driver can feel," Fangio said, "is when the competitors come with congratulatory hugs."

Fangio felt particular warmth for Peter Collins. "He was a special man, a 'gentleman.'" (Fangio used the English word.) The year before, 1956, they had been teammates at Ferrari. "Twice Collins gave me his car—once in Monaco and once in Monza." The points earned made Fangio champion that year.

That matter of teammates turning cars over to other drivers was ended in rule changes a few years later, but such swapping of cars would be practically impossible in today's cars, anyway. "Today's cars are designed for the driver," Fangio said. "They are a *suit* for the driver. They cannot fit anyone else."

What did he think about the modern race car?

"There have been many technical advances. There's no stopping progress," he said. "We had a 2.5-liter engine with 430 hp. Today, with the turbo, a 1.5-liter can get *800* hp. Today, cars have better stopping power and with the wide tires can take the curves faster. Wider tires are even used in regular cars, nowadays."

Would he like to have driven these cars?

"*Claro.*" He laughed: "I would like to be twenty or thirty years younger. But all things have their time. If I were to get in one of these cars I would have to start all over and learn everything from scratch."

Engineers, designers, have made the great differences, he said. Technology. "In those days it was important for the driver to have some mechanical knowledge, but today—no. Now everything is computerized and electronic. The driver must be attentive to the suspension, but not the motor."

I asked Fangio which was the best of his championship cars. He answered immediately: "Mercedes-Benz." Then added: "But all the cars I had were good— Ferrari, Maserati, Alfa Romeo. All of them were good. All good for their time.

"The Mercedes-Benz was the most secure. It was the most advanced technically—desmodromic valves, inclined engine. All the cars at that time had some critical part—the gearbox, the engine, the rear end, brakes. You had to know which was the most critical aspect of a car and use it less," he said.

"Only Mercedes had no specific fault—except the first year. The first year it was the brakes. The brakes were inboard and when the car got hot—no brakes! I asked the engineers to move the brakes. The second year they remedied the situation and moved the brakes out next to the wheel where they could cool better."

Perhaps for stars in any field knowing when to quit is the hardest part. They hang around for one too many arias sung, one too many curve balls swung at. Fangio quit the moment he felt he was behind the power curve. It was July 1958, at Rheims in Champagne country. The Grand Prix of France. Fangio had a new, though not particularly impressive, Maserati. Hawthorn, Collins, Musso, and von Trips had the new V-6 Dino Ferraris. Moss, leading in championship points at the time, and Tony Brooks were in Vanwalls and Jean Behra had a BRM.

The race was also notable for the presence of two Americans: Phil Hill, fresh from a victory at Le Mans, was driving his very first Formula One race. His car: a Maserati that belonged to Joakim Bonnier. And making his first (and last) Grand Prix drive: Troy Ruttman, one-time Indy winner, in another privateer Maserati—*Scuderia Centro Sud*.

Fangio was particularly dissatisfied with one component of the Maserati, I couldn't figure out exactly what in the translation, a spring of some sort, but it doesn't matter. He said: "When I complained about it they told me: 'We have to use that kind, they pay us money.' I said, 'But I am the driver!'" Perhaps that conversation set the thought processes in motion. Certainly more food for thought was added when, after a dice with Moss, he stoically called at the pits to hand the mechanic the clutch pedal. The entire thing had come *off*.

He re-entered the race and finished fourth. And quit. He was forty-seven years old. "Rheims has long straights," he said. "I had a lot of time to think and I thought and I made up my mind."

In the race, Musso, pressing hard behind the leading Hawthorn, went off the road and was killed, the first Formula One fatality since Marimon's death at the 'Ring three years before. But that had no influence on Fangio's decision. "I didn't know Musso's fate when I decided."

It was a neat ending—exactly ten years before on that same circuit Fangio had raced his first race in Europe. The curtain descended where it first was raised.

But the name of Juan Manuel Fangio has not disappeared from racing. It lives in records, in memories. And also in the flesh of a new young Argentinean—the son of Juan's younger brother, Toto.

The uncle is proud. "He is a good person, a good driver," Juan Manuel the elder said. "His name, by the way, was given to him by the doctor, not the family. It is a custom in the villages that the doctor name the child. The doctor said if it is a boy it will have to be Juan Manuel." And so it was.

A very good name, indeed.

KEN PURDY

The Man Who Could Do Everything

Don Alfonso Cabeza de Vaca y Leighton, Carvajal y Are, Conde de la Mejorada, Marquis de Portago, was twenty-eight when he died at Guidizzollo, a few miles from Brescia and the end of the Mille Miglia, on the twelfth of May, 1957. Portago had been a flier, jai-alai player, poloist, steeplechase rider (the world's leading amateur in 1951 and 1952), Olympic bobsledder and record-holder, remarkable swimmer, and he was, at his death, one of the dozen best racing drivers in the world. He had never sat in a racing car until 1954, but he believed he would be champion of the world before 1960—and most of the men he ran against every week thought that he very well might be. If he lived.

Certainly, Portago was uniquely gifted. An athlete all his life, he was not a big man, not heavily muscled, but he had unusual strength, great endurance, abnormal eyesight, and a quickness of reaction that was legendary among his friends. He was highly intelligent, courteous, and very much aware of the world around him.

Gregor Grant, editor of the British weekly *Autosport*, said just before the Mille Miglia, "A man like Portago appears only once in a generation, and it would probably be more accurate to say only once in a lifetime. The fellow does *everything* fabulously well. Never mind the driving, the steeplechasing, the bobsledding, and

48

the athletic side of things. Never mind the being fluent in four languages. There are so many other aspects to the man: for example, I think he could be the best bridge player in the world if he cared to try; he could certainly be a great soldier; and I suspect he could be a fine writer."

Portago's death, I suppose, proved again the two old British aphorisms: "Motor racing is a sport at which you get better and better until you get killed" and the other, less optimistic, "There are two kinds of racing drivers: those who get killed before they get good, and those who get killed afterward." But whether they die at the wheel sooner or later or not at all, most men have to serve years of apprenticeship before they make the big leagues: the racing team of one of the major factories. They drive sports cars, stock and not-so-stock, in rallies and dreary airport events; they cadge rides in scruffy hand-me-down racing cars, hoping to attract a wealthy sponsor's eye. When—and if—they are invited to Italy or Germany or France or England to sign a racing contract, they have behind them thousands of miles of competitive driving in dozens of makes of cars. This is standard, this is usual, and, as with most of the other rules, Portago was the exception. Driving relief in his first race, the 1000 kilometers for sports cars at Buenos Aires in 1954, he did three laps so badly that he dropped the car from second place to fifth—because he had never learned how to shift gears! To the day he died he had driven few makes of competition automobiles: Maserati, Osca, Ferrari. He never drove the usual sports cars, MG's, Jaguars, and so on. For personal use—before he began to compete, he usually drove American cars: Fords, something else that may have been a DeSoto, he wasn't sure. Explaining this, the last time I talked with him, he said, "Automobiles bore me, I know next to nothing about them, and I care less.

"I have no sentimental attachment for a car," he said. "I can hardly tell one from another. Sometimes I make a little scratch in a car, in an inconspicuous place, so I can recognize it the next time I'm in it, so I can remember its defects. I'm not interested in cars. To me they're a means of transportation, or a machine for racing.

"When I have a racing car that I'm going to drive, I walk up to it, and I look at it, and I think, 'Now, is this son-of-a-bitch going to hold together for the next five hundred kilometers?' That's the only interest I have in it. And as soon as the race is over, I couldn't care less what happens to it.

"I think some drivers are not only indifferent to their cars, but hostile to them. They look at the car before a race and they think, 'Now, what is this thing going to do to me today—how is it going to let me down, or make me lose the race—or perhaps even kill me?'"

Portago's forthright disclaimer of interest in the machines on which his career was based was typical. To the outermost limits which custom and law allowed, the twelfth Marquis de Portago said precisely what he pleased and did exactly what he liked. When he saw a girl friend in the crowd lining the streets at the Rome check point in his last race, he stood on the brakes, locked everything up, waited for her, kissed her, and held her in his arms until an official furiously waved him on. The girl, of course, was Linda Christian, and Portago was probably the only man in the race who would have allowed himself such a gesture—at the risk of his life. Portago was an avowed romantic, and he had remarked that in another age he would have been a Crusader, or a knight-errant. He often dressed in black; his hair was black and curly, usually long over his neck and ears, clinging to his head like a skull-cap; he moved quickly and rarely smiled; he sometimes looked like a juvenile delin-quent or a hired killer; but more often like what he was, a Spanish grandee. The remark that he had been born three or four centuries too late was a cliché among his friends.

"Every time I look at Fon," one of them said, "I see him in a long black cape, a sword sticking out of it, a floppy black hat on his head, riding like a fiend across some castle drawbridge."

When he began to drive Portago was not the best-loved figure on the interna-tional circuit—nor was he when he died, if it comes to that. Lacking the technical skill to balance his bitterly competitive instinct, he was dangerous in his first races, and to most people he seemed arrogant and supercilious. He was reputed to be enormously wealthy, he was a great lady-killer, and if he was not pugnacious, still, he was quick to fight. Most of the other drivers preferred to leave him alone. Nobody expected him to be around for very long in any case. Many thought he was just another aristocratic dilettante who would quickly lose interest in racing cars, but the few who knew his lineage were not so sure. His mother, an Englishwoman who brought a great fortune to his father, is a firm-minded woman; and a determined lust for adventure, plus an inclination for government, runs through the Portago line. Spanish history is studded with the name. In the sixteenth century one of Portago's forbears, Cabeza de Vaca, was shipwrecked on the Florida coast. He *walked* to Mexico City, recruiting an army as he went. Another conquered the Canary Islands, another was a leader in the fight to drive the Moors out of Spain. Portago's grandfather was governor of Madrid. His father was Spain's best golfer, polo player, yachtsman; he was also a fabulous gambler, said to have once won $2 million at Monte Carlo; he was a soldier and a movie actor. He died of a heart attack on the polo field, playing against his doctor's orders. The last king of Spain, Alfonso XIII, was Portago's godfather and namesake.

Naturally enough, in the light of his background and his own propensity for high-risk sports, Portago was constantly accused of fearlessness, of clinging to a death wish, and whatnot. We talked at length about that, the last time I saw Portago. He sat in my room in the Kenilworth in Sebring. Portago had been very punctual and had apologized for being unable to keep his promise that there would be no interruptions—he had placed a phone call to Caracas, and he asked if he might tell the operator to put it on my wire when it came through. I wanted to record the interview; would he object to a Minifon? He said he would not, and then told me about an interview recording he was making for Riverside Records, a house specializing in sports-car material. We talked generalities for half an hour, and then I turned the machine on. I mentioned a newspaper article that had said something to the effect that he "lived on fear."

"A lot of nonsense," Portago said. "I'm often frightened. I can get frightened crossing the street in heavy traffic. And I know I'm a moral coward. I can't even go into a shop to look around and walk out without buying something. As for enjoying fear, I don't think anybody enjoys fear, at least in my definition, which is a mental awareness of a danger to your body. You can enjoy courage—the performance of an act which frightens you—but not fear.

"I know that my first ride in a racing car frightened me. That was the Mexican road race in 1953. I had been riding horses in competition for a long time, at least twice a week for two years, but I had to give it up because I put on some weight I couldn't get rid of. I couldn't get by no matter what I tried, and I tried most things: weighing in with papier-mâché boots and saddle made to look like leather and weighing nothing, or hiding a five-pound weight on the scale so that the whole standard of weight for all the riders would go up!

"I met Harry Schell and Luigi Chinetti at the Paris auto show in 1953, and Chinetti asked me to be his co-driver in the Pan American race. All he really wanted me for, of course, was ballast. I didn't drive a foot, not even from the garage to the starting line. I just sat there, white with fear, holding on to anything I thought looked sturdy enough. I knew that Chinetti was a very good driver, a specialist in long-distance races who was known to be conservative and careful; but the first time you're in a racing car you can't tell if the driver is conservative or a wild man, and I didn't see how Chinetti could get away with half of what he was doing. We broke down the second day of the race, but I had decided by then that this was what I wanted to do more than anything else, so I bought a three-liter Ferrari.

"I was fortunate, of course, in being able to buy my own car. I think it might have taken me five or six years longer to make the Ferrari team if I had had to look around for a sponsor and all that. I was lucky having enough money to buy my own car—even if I'm not 'enormously wealthy.' In those years I was perpetually in debt." (Portago had various trust funds, but his mother controlled the family fortune, which was of American origin and reputed to be high in the millions. In his heyday as a driver, Portago earned perhaps $40,000 a year.)

Harry Schell and Portago took the three-liter to the Argentine for the 1000-kilometer sports-car race.

"Harry was so frightened that I would break the car he wouldn't teach me how to change gear, so when after 70 laps (the race was 101) he was tired and it was my turn to drive, after 3 laps, during which I lost so much time that we dropped from second to fifth place, I saw Harry out in the middle of the track frantically waving a flag to make me come into the pits so that he could drive again. We eventually finished second over-all and first in our class. I didn't learn to change gears properly until the chief mechanic of Maserati took me out and spent an afternoon teaching me."

Schell and Portago ran the three-liter at Sebring in 1954. The rear axle went after two hours. He sold it and bought a two-liter Maserati, the gear-shifting lesson thrown in, and ran it in the 1954 Le Mans, with Tomaso co-driving. They led the class until 5:00 A.M., when the engine blew up. He won the Grand Prix of Metz with the Maserati—"but there were no good drivers in it"—and ran with Chiron in the Twelve Hours of Rheims, Chiron blowing up the engine with twenty minutes to go while leading the class. He ran an Osca in the G.P. of Germany, and rolled it. "God protects the good, so I wasn't hurt."

In 1954 Portago broke down while leading the first lap of the Pan American race in a three-liter Ferrari, and won a class, an over-all, and a handicap race in Nassau. He bent an automobile occasionally, and he was often off the road, but he was never hurt until the 1955 Silverstone, when he missed a gear shift and came out of the resulting crash with a double-compound break in his left leg.

The crash had no effect on Portago's driving; he continued to run a little faster on the circuit and to leave it less frequently. At Caracas in 1955 he climbed up on Fangio until he was only nine seconds behind him, finishing second. He was a member of the Ferrari team in 1956—an incredibly short time after he had begun to race. He won the Grand Prix of Portugal in 1956, a wild go-around in which the lap record was broken seventeen times, the last time by Portago. He won the Tour of France, the Coupes du Salon, Paris, the Grand Prix of Rome, and was leading Moss and Fangio at Caracas when a broken gas line put him out of the race. After Caracas that year I asked Stirling Moss how he ranked Portago:

"He's certainly among the ten best in the world today," Moss said, "and as far as I'm concerned, he's the one to watch out for."

In Cuba, he was leading Fangio by a respectable margin when a gas line let go again.

"I don't think anyone will be champion as long as Fangio competes," Portago told me. "If the absolute limit of adhesion of the car through a certain bend is 101.5 mph, the old man will go through at 101, every time. I may go through at 99, or 102—in which case there'll be an incident.

"Moss is, of course, better than I am, too. If I pass Moss, I wonder what's the matter with his car! But I'm learning still, I think I get a little better with every race. I hope so, anyway."

Portago ranked Collins, Behra, Schell, Musso, and himself after Moss as equals. He carefully repeated his estimate of Schell: "Harry is very, *very* fast," and then said that he considered Schell his closest friend. They spent much time together. Both appeared to be tense—more accurately, taut—something that was not in any way allied to nervousness but was instead a peculiar expression of awareness. Like Portago, Schell walks rapidly; he turns his head constantly; he seems to be trying always to see something that is just out of sight, to hear something that is just out of earshot.

I said as much.

"It sounds corny," Portago said, "but I think that because racing drivers are very near to death every Sunday in the season, they are more sensitive to life, and appreciate it more. I take it that is what you meant by what you called 'awareness' when you saw Harry and me walking together. Speaking now only for myself, I'm sure I love life more than the average man does. I want to get something out of every minute. I want no time wasted. You know, people say that racing drivers are dare devils who don't care whether they live or not, and you've seen stories about me and my flirting with death and all that. Nonsense, all nonsense. I want to live to be 105, and I mean to. I want to live to be a very old man. I'm *enchanted* with life. But no matter how long I live, I still won't have time for all the things I want to do, I won't hear all the music I want to hear, I won't be able to read all the books I want to read, I won't have all the women I want to have, I won't be able to do a twentieth of the things I want to do. And besides just the *doing*, I insist on getting something out of what I do. For example, I wouldn't race unless I was sure I could be champion of the world."

"Can you imagine yourself driving when you're Fangio's age?" I asked him.

Portago smiled. His mouth was unusually small and straight-lined; his smiles were brief, but warm enough. "Never," he said. "Certainly not. In any case I'll stop when I'm thirty-five; and if I'm champion of the world, sooner."

"And then?"

"Well, I'm very ambitious," Portago said. "I wouldn't be racing automobiles if I didn't think I could get something out of it, and not only the championship . . ." The phone rang beside me. It was Portago's Caracas call, and I handed the instrument to him. I had passed the open switchboard in the lobby an hour before, when he had placed the call, and I had overheard the operator, so I knew to whom the call was going and that it would be personal.

"I'll take a walk," I told him. "Call me."

"Please," he said. "Don't go. Please. Anyway I'm going to speak Spanish."

As it turned out, the call was a report that the party in Caracas was unavailable.

"Forgive me," he said. "I didn't mean to be rude, I didn't mean to suggest that naturally you couldn't speak Spanish. I'm sorry."

I told him that he was right, in any case. "We were talking about what you intend to get out of automobile racing," I said. "I got the impression that you thought of it as preparation for something."

"I do," Portago said. "I haven't told this to a great many people. You see, Spain has had no new national hero for many, many years. That is what the championship of the world means to me. When I give up racing I'm going to Spain and go into politics."

Later, from Paris, Portago sent me a photograph of himself and Fangio and the Pretender to the Spanish throne. But on it he had written, "With Fangio and Don Juan, the *future King* of Spain."

The rumor that Franco intends to restore the Spanish monarchy has been current for several years. Portago seemed very sure. For all I know, he may have had superior information.

His frank statement of the purpose to which he intended to put the championship amused me. A few minutes before, he had been strongly critical of another driver who has some public business ventures: "He's commercialized himself so much," Portago said, rather disdainfully.

Still, one never expects consistency in anyone who gets his head above the ruck. Consistency is one of the marks of the drudge. Portago was, of course, a cynic, and I have no doubt he thought himself skilled in the management of other people—reporters included. If he did, it was a new idea for him, a product of the past two years, because he conceded that he had during most of his life been very shy, highly introverted, and that he had occasionally covered it with action that could be interpreted as rudeness. Certainly he was enormously perceptive, and conversation with him was easy and pleasant. He obviously knew that real conversation can concern itself only with *ideas*, not *things*, and I think that, like all first-rate minds, his natural preference was for ideas; he knew that it is necessary to listen, and he could be forthright, even in response to rough questions.

Portago was married in 1949 to the former Carol McDaniel, a South Carolina girl. They have two children, Andrea, six, and Antonio, three. Two hours after he had met Carol McDaniel, Portago told her he intended to marry her. He had discovered even early in life that women respond to daring as to nothing else—to daring, to indifference, to arrogance and certainty and sensitivity. In one sense, at least, women were more important in his life than anything else.

"The most important thing in our existence is a well-balanced sex life," he said to me. "Everybody knows this is true, but nobody will admit it—of himself, that is. But if you don't have a happy sex life, you don't have anything."

"It's the first thing the historians suppress when they write the lives of great men," I said, "and it was often an astonishingly big factor in their lives."

"Of course," Portago said. "Look at Nelson, look at Napoleon."

"Well, look at George Bernard Shaw," I said. "He gave it up altogether, and married on condition his wife would never mention sex to him."

"A freak," Portago said. "A very untypical writer. Look at Maupassant. A prodigy, in more ways than one. Well, as for me, making love is the most important thing I do every day, and I don't care who knows it."

Portago was willing to back up his opinions under most circumstances, whether by debate or a right cross. I had heard that he had once challenged a man to a duel, but he denied it. He fenced rarely, he said. He was taught boxing by Edmund Nelson, who died with him in the Mille Miglia. Nelson was a British ex-boxer who was just out of the Merchant Marine and working in New York's Plaza Hotel when Portago, still in his teens, resided there. It was Nelson who taught Portago bobsledding—the first time Portago went down the St. Moritz run he went down steering, and he took fifteen seconds off the time of the then champion of Switzerland. It was Nelson who said, "I know Fon says he'll live forever, but I say he won't live to be thirty."

It is not on record that Portago lost many fights. He was always in condition. He ordered milk at most of the world's best bars. He smoked constantly, but never inhaled. His reactions were freakishly fast, beyond normal to an extent that even he apparently didn't appreciate. He once remarked after a car had spun with him, "It went very slowly. There was lots of time to think." Another time, speaking of steeplechasing, he said, "When your horse falls after a jump you look around for another horse to hide behind."

Recently in Paris Portago stepped off a curbstone as a Citroën went past, much too close, Portago felt, to the feet of the lady he was with. He flipped a cigarette at the driver so quickly and so accurately that he hit him in the face with it. The man got out and Portago knocked him down twice. He handled his own defense in the consequent law proceedings, and was thoroughly trounced by the plaintiff's attorney.

"I hate to fight," he told me. "I'll do anything honorable to get out of a fight, but I get into situations in which there is no way out. I was with some friends, shipping people, and a man called them 'a bunch of bloody pirates.' I'm afraid I hit him. Another time I suggested to a man on a dance floor that it might be nicer for everybody if he put his cigar away when he danced. He'd already burned a friend of mine with it. When I started to leave the place, later, two of this cigar-lover's friends stood in my way and wouldn't move. What could I do, once I'd asked them please to let me by? I lowered the boom on them."

We talked of a good many things that don't much matter now, in the time that we sat in that room. It had rained hard during the night, but the sun was steaming it off now. We could hear cars slowing for the corner around the hotel that led to the circuit. Two team Maseratis came past, the mechanics who drove them blipping their engines incessantly.

"Genuine Italian-type sports cars," I said, "suitable for summer touring."

Portago grinned. "This is an easy course in one way," he said. "There's only one genuinely fast bend in it. But the flat corners, the way it ruins brakes. . . . a race I don't like is the Mille Miglia. No matter how much you practice you can't possibly come to know a thousand miles of Italian roads as well as the Italians, and, as Fangio says, if you have a conscience you can't drive really fast anyway. There are hundreds of corners in the Mille Miglia where one little slip by a driver could kill fifty people. You can't keep the spectators from crowding into the road—you couldn't do it with an army. It's a race I hope I never run in."

"I have a quotation in a story, a piece of fiction that won't be published until this summer," I told Portago, "something that, I thought at the time, you might have said: Of all sports, only bull fighting and mountain climbing and motor racing really tried a man, that all the rest are mere recreations. Would you have said that?"

"I couldn't agree with you more," Portago said. "You're quite right. I've thought of bull fighting, of course, but the trouble is that you must start when you're a child, otherwise you'll never really know the bulls. And the only trouble with mountain climbing for me is the lack of an audience! Like most drivers, I'm something of an exhibitionist."

Portago and I had promised ourselves a certain length of time. We had run an hour past it when he stood up and I shut off the wire recorder. We shook hands and said good-bye. I saw him three times more, very briefly, before the '57 Sebring was over and everybody had dispersed. In April he sent me a note from Paris to say that he had won at Montlhéry, beating sports cars with a *gran turismo* car and breaking the lap record. He said he was going to run in the Mille Miglia and at Monte Carlo.

I did a draft of my story on him and sent a copy of it to him in Paris, as I had offered to do—but not before we talked. I'm not sure he ever saw it because I heard from him next from Modena. Finally, the day before the Mille Miglia, a cable came from Brescia, asking if I could use his first-person account of the race. Obviously he intended to live through the Mille Miglia now, although earlier he had written a note to Dorian Leigh, an internationally famous beauty with whom he had had a close relationship, that suggested a premonition of something happening: ". . . As you know, in the first place I did not want to do the Mille Miglia. Then Ferrari said I must do it, at least in a *gran turismo* car. Then I was told I had to do it in a new 3800-cc sports car. That means that my 'early death' may well come next Sunday . . ."

He told a reporter that he was intent only on finishing, that it was important to him to come back to Brescia "safe and sound," an obvious reference to the fact that someone was waiting for him. But when he got out on the road, Nelson hunched enigmatically beside him, Portago began to go; he was fourth at the first check point. When a broken halfshaft put Collins out at Parma, Portago began to try for second place. He was straining for a sight of Von Trips' car, lying second to Taruffi, when the tire blew at something between 125 and 150 miles an hour on the straight at Guidizzollo. The 3.8 Ferrari, a model he loathed, lifted its wheels off the road and left him helpless. The car killed him; it very nearly destroyed his body; it killed Edmund Nelson too. When I heard he was dead, I looked for a note he had sent from Paris: ". . . I don't plan to return to the States until October. Please let me know where I can get in touch with you in New York, as we must get together at least for a couple of lunches. . . . All the best, Fon."

Except for the final seconds after he lost the car, seconds that must have seemed so long to him, Portago's last hours were happy ones: Once he started running he would have set aside all premonitory fears; he was doing what he wanted to do, and doing it far better than the form-chart said he possibly could. He was surely thinking, as he screamed down the Valley of the Po toward Brescia and the finish, that he might conceivably win the race.

Most men die regretting the errors they have made in the multiple choices that life forces upon us, and Portago knew, in the fraction of time in which he could think about it, that error was killing him. Motor racing, like every other human endeavor, rigidly reserves the ultimate reward for those who are talented, lucky, and totally devoted. Portago was enormously talented, he was luckier than most, but he did not have, in the fullest measure, the vital ability to concentrate obsessively upon a single purpose. The gods, in whom he did not believe, or fortune, or fate or whatever, somehow guards those who *do* own this thing. Portago knew what it was, as many men do not. He often said that "you must have the mental strength to concentrate absolutely," but he could not maintain it as rigidly as, say, Phil Walters used to do, or Stirling Moss does today. He did not want to run in the Mille Miglia. A wiser man might have stayed out, even if it required a illness of convenience. He had not made even one practice circuit of the course, but he tried to outdrive men who could not remember how many dozens of times they had run it. Perhaps saddest of all, he overruled the Ferrari depot at Florence when he was urged to take two new tires for the run to Brescia.

In a sense, though, it is useless to think of what might have been. Portago actually had no choice. There was no caution in him. A refusal to count odds was the essence of his nature. Usually, he won, but he was intelligent and he knew that the averages would almost certainly trip him ultimately. Knowing this, he still preferred to accept the hazard. That was his nature, the core of his being, and he could do nothing to alter it. Had he been cautious, we never would have heard of him. Portago's determination to take what he wanted out of the world—on his own terms and no matter what the price, present or potential—made him what he was: the absolutely free spirit.

"If I die tomorrow," he told me that day before Sebring, "still, I have had twenty-eight wonderful years."

I cited to him the Spanish proverb, "In this life, take what you want—but pay for it."

"Of course," he said. "Of course, that's exactly it. You must pay. I remember someone who wrote about the British in the First World War, about the terrific mortality rate among young officers who had to lead bayonet charges against fixed machine guns. Most of them, or many of them, were aristocrats in those days. They had a life expectancy at the front of thirty days or something like that. And this man, he was a journalist, I can't remember his name, said, 'In war, the British aristocracy pays for the privileges they enjoy in peacetime.' You pay . . . you try to put it off, but you pay I think, for my part at least, that the game is worth the candle."

Portago was not a great racing driver, although it is certain that he would have eventually become one, had he lived—and that is not alone my opinion, but the judgment of men much more expert. He was not an artist; he left nothing of beauty behind him, nothing of use to the world. He moved no mountains, wrote no books, bridged no rivers. He saved no lives, indeed, he took innocents with him to death. He could be cruel. If he wished to indulge himself, he would, even though the act might hurt and humiliate others who had done him no harm.

Yet, it would be a flinty heart that did not mourn his death. At the very least, he was an adornment in the world, an excitement, a pillar of fire in the night producing no useful heat or light, perhaps, but a glory to see nevertheless. At most, he was an inspiration—he proved again what cannot be reiterated too often. If anything at all is meant for us, we are meant to live life, there is no folly like the folly of the hermit who cowers in his cave, a dead lion is infinitely greater than a live mouse.

The accomplishments of the twenty-eight years of Don Alfonso Cabeza de Vaca y Leighton may make only a small monument for him, or none at all, but he knew what greatness knows, and for that reason we are the poorer for his going.

JOHN WEITZ

A Letter

When I was a kid, we lived in the west end of Berlin, about ten minutes from the north entrance of the Avus, which became a racetrack a few times each year. The rest of the year, it was an express highway to the fashionable suburb of Wannsee on a large lake, where we all learned to sail. What distinguished the Avus from other public roads was the steeply banked north loop, followed by a sizable grandstands-cum-pits area. Both the banked turn and the grandstands were only open for races. Whenever our family driver would take us to visit friends in Wannsee in my father's convertible Mannheim Mercedes, I would look longingly at the empty grandstand, hoping for one solitary spectator to cheer us on our way. I would have raised my hand and waved in the approved Grand Prix driver manner, smiling while keeping my gaze fixed straight ahead. In those days, drivers sat bolt upright, close to the steering wheel, which had to be dismounted to let the driver get into and out of the cockpit.

The great German trio of those last years before Hitler were Caracciola, Brauchitsch, and Stuck, who was married to Paula von Reznicek, the German amateur tennis champion. They divorced later. She was of Jewish descent, and the racial laws came to haunt all parts of German life. Caratch, which was Caracciola's popular nickname, had a wife known by the English nickname of Baby and a terrier in the fashionable *Thin Man* style of those years. His Berlin license plate was 1A-4444. Every boy in huge Berlin, from bakery boy to high-school student, knew that number four was Caratch's lucky number.

Brauchitsch was different. We knew about Brauchitsch and his streamlined SSKL Mercedes "cigar" and his Avus victory, but not much more. He always wore a red cloth racing cap, and we tried to make some Red Baron connection, because he was titled. And rumor had it that he had a bad temper and was snobbish, which no one minded. Racing drivers were expected to be, well, gentlemen, and a bit of snobbery went with that. There were a few other aristo German racing drivers, like Prince Hermann zu Leiningen and a man called von Hasse, and Stuck sometimes called himself von Stuck, but we didn't think he was titled.

One thing we soon learned about Brauchitsch. He was a fierce driver, with lots of sliding around and sawing on the wheel, and he usually left the pits with his rear wheels smoking. Like Moss in Fangio's time at Mercedes, Brauchitsch was destined to stay a brilliant number two. Among the Germans, Caratch was number one, there was no question about that, the way Nuvolari was number one in the world. Caratch was at his best in the rain and known as the *Regenmeister*, no mean trick with the fractious Mercedes monsters.

In those pre-Hitler days, Lang was still a mechanic, and Rosemeyer, Auto Union's (and the Nazi Party's) golden boy, was still in high school.

I prattle away, unpacking the lore of those days, the things we Berlin boys knew about our racing drivers, the way that a New York kid of those years could tell you about Babe Ruth and Lou Gehrig.

For me, the whole thing came full circle during one strange and time-suspended moment, not so very long ago, at the opening of the "new" Nürburgring, the castrato racing circuit inside the famous old track. I had not seen a monoposto car at the 'Ring since my boyhood. I walked past the old garages and then through the passage under the track toward the pit area. Then came a strange moment. I was sure I could smell the familiar exhaust of the special Mercedes racing "dope," and there was no mistaking it. I also heard the howl of a W125 being "bleeped" to keep the engine from stalling just before the clutch goes up. I left the tunnel, and ten yards farther on, I was alongside a vast old *Silberpfeil* and a furious, angry red-capped Brauchitsch, who was banging his fist on the scuttle of the car. There was a grid of cars in front of him. They were all cranking up, but Brauchitsch wanted to go! They were in his way! It was an old-timers' demonstration lap, led by René Dreyfus in Caratch's old SSK and a bunch of Mercedes relics: Uhlenhaut in the Tripoli

Voiturette, a 300SLR with Fitch, and Moss in the last monoposto. So far as Brauchitsch was concerned, they were all loitering, loafing, in his way, *verdammt noch mal*, and he shook his fist and howled in anger, while his foot kept that cranky old monster under the hood from overheating. He was about eighty, I guess. Under the red cap, he looked unchanged. Forever young, forever angry.

I grinned and felt strangely at home. Some things had not changed, and that was reassuring. How many old fellows can see their boyhood gossip so graphically confirmed?

BOB OTTUM

Heck, Mes Amis, It's Only Ol' Cale

Dear Diary:

First thing, it's important to establish that Cale couldn't help crashing the car. The brakes went blooey coming around that corner and the only safe spot to spin it out was blocked by thirty or so folks standing around eating *jambon* sandwiches and drinking red wine. So he stuck it in the fence. And it was a dandy—the nose of the Chevy Camaro was slammed so far underneath the guardrail that fifteen of those Frenchmen all pulling on a rope couldn't snake it back out. That was the first pity of it all, because until then France was experiencing maybe the most unusual sight and certainly the wildest sound in all the forty-nine years of the Twenty-four Hours of Le Mans. It was a good old American stock car in there with the sporties, an outlaw car creating a hammering roar that can only be called iron thunder.

The real pity is that Cale Yarborough, at forty-one, had turned out to be a natural for that course: Right at the start he had cranked the Camaro down the Mulsanne Straight at about 210 mph—that's two *hundred* and some miles an hour—and had pulled back in to allow, "Well, I didn't come over here to poke around; I could be back on the farm, poking around on my combine."

And, of course, that's when the whole crew began to get excited and the tensions started to build, because, up until then, nobody had really figured that any of this could work. Even the cynical old-timers were getting caught up in it and then, when . . .

But wait. This is getting ahead of the story, and the best thing to do is to take it from the beginning and tell it straight. It's a sort of saga; it could be called A Yankee Goes to Le Mans.

"*Wait* a minute," Cale says. "You mean A Rebel Goes to Le Mans."

Well, either way.

Tuesday Morning, June 9, 1981

They make an arresting tableau, an island surrounded by all the urbane, continental types who are swirling through the terminal at Orly airport outside Paris. There are Cale and Betty Jo Yarborough and their three daughters, Julie, eighteen, Kelley, twelve, and B.J., ten. All of them are wary, and they're circled protectively around two shopping carts that are piled high with luggage. The most conspicuous items on the carts are the red and white Winston Cup championship garment bags with the stickers that picture a racing stock car. The stickers say CALE YARBOROUGH, NASCAR THREE-TIME WORLD CHAMPION, 1976–77–78.

Things are not going well. Everyone is stiff and creaky after the overnight flight from New York—and now Pan Am has lost Betty Jo's suitcase. Among other essentials, it contains comfortable shoes and her four favorite nighties. Little B.J. has to go to the bathroom, but she's blamed if she'll speak to any strangers. The folks around here look pretty hostile, or at least aloof. They do that in France; the French are famous for it: They see you looking forlorn and they stick it to you. Bill Brodrick, the P.R. guy for the racing team, had promised to meet them, but he hasn't shown. (It turned out that Brodrick, six feet, five inches and 240 pounds—plus another 20 or 30 pounds of neck chains, gold rings, and other jewelry—spent the entire day trying to wrestle the spare parts for the race car out of several tag teams of customs agents. "*But you do not have ze propaire papairs, monsieur.*")

Betty Jo is a brightly pretty woman, a former high school cheerleader who has matured gracefully, and she can be fiercely determined. Her South Carolina accent is a wonder; it is so purely whipped cream and honey that it turns heads when she speaks. As with many people who don't speak a foreign language, she has the vague feeling that one will be understood if one just speaks more slowly to the natives, as if to a backward child. "What ah said was," she says to a uniformed passerby who appears to be a French army general, "what ah *said* was: Surely yew-all have a ladies room around heah?" The W.C. is pointed out and she sweeps up her daughters and marches off in triumph.

Cale is absolutely unflappable, even slightly amused by all this. He has never been to France but he has been in a lot of tough spots, and anybody who has been upside down at Atlanta or Darlington a time or two isn't going to be rattled by a little French disdain. "Listen," he says to the diary-keeper, "you know how to get to Le Mans?" He even uses the French pronunciation: LuhMahn.

"Umm. I know it's somewhere southwest of Paris."

Cale had arranged for an Avis rental car—a Peugeot station wagon, the biggest car they offered but still only about two-thirds the size of Cale's Grand National stocker. We leave Betty Jo and the girls encircling the luggage and wander off to find the station wagon; the process involves a complicated switch of terminals. The Avis lady is not about to produce any upsets at this time in the morning. She's just as snotty as everybody else. The wagon is over there in the lot, she says, with a vague wave of the hand.

"Uh, Miss? Excuse me. How do you get to Le Mans?"

"*Allez sud,*" she says.

The family and luggage are piled into the wagon. There's a road map of France in the glove compartment. Um, let's see, it looks like there's some sort of, you know, like a beltway, around Paris. And then you catch good old A-11 and . . .

"You read any French?" Cale asks.

"Well, uh, not much. Maybe enough to order ham and cheese and stuff. *Poulet* means chicken, you know."

"Sounds fine to me." And the ex-world stock-car racing champion slips behind the wheel of the Peugeot and fires it up. "I'll tell you what. You read and I'll drive."

Wednesday Morning, June 10

The Camaro looks as if it might have been picked up from some raggedy-pants U.S. trackside and plopped right down in the infield paddock at Le Mans, smack in among the sleek Lolas and glittering Ferraris and some Porsche prototypes so functionally streamlined that they look like horizontal teardrops. Spectators and other drivers are strolling around to look at the Camaro. There is a great deal of Gallic shrugging and rolling of eyes. The car is, um, how you say . . .

Hurley Haywood, the card-carrying preppy sports-car and road racer from Jacksonville, Florida, has a word for it. "Junk," he says scornfully.

Haywood's absolutely right, but in a shallow way; too many European and sporty-car types fail to see the difference between junk and creative junk—the very cars that made stock-car racing great and made bootlegging a major art form in the U.S. southland.

This Camaro is a pure, direct descendant of a long racing line; it's squatty and wide-shouldered and its nose is down and its tail is up. All worthy U.S. stock cars look crooked; it's part of their rakish charm. Everybody knows you're not supposed to look at one directly; you stand off to one side and squint at it in bright sunlight, your head tilted a bit, and everything becomes clear. Cale's Camaro weighs 2351 pounds and has a 350-cubic-inch engine that's been bored out to 393 cubic inches, and it'll pound out 600 horsepower. The body sits on an "outlaw" frame; that is, a 108- inch chassis designed for small, backwoods U.S. racetracks—and that's the trick that has gotten it into Le Mans in its GTO category, right in there with the BMWs and other good stuff, all of which come up to about the door handles of Cale's car. It's a real stock car, and the only things on it that ever saw a Camaro production line are the taillights.

"It could have been a Pontiac Firebird or an almost-whatever-you-want," says Billy Hagan, who owns the car and is financing this whole adventure. "But we chose Camaro because we can get plastic body panels for replacements in case we smash something up."

At forty-nine, Hagan is mustached and seamed and grizzled, a Louisianian who made a fortune in the oil business. His company does stratigraphic readings for drillers—Bill Hagan can tell them if they're going to strike oil before they get there. And now he lavishes money on auto racing. He owns and campaigns a car on the Grand National circuit (seventh in the standings at the moment), and he hits the road- and endurance-racing circuit with his Camaro. As for Le Mans, "This is about a $200,000 trip for me," he says. "Figure about $60,000 for the car, another $30,000 in spare engines, and maybe $60,000 in expenses for the crew and hotels and meals and all. Now, for just a little bit more money, I could have bought me a Porsche or something fancy. But I want this to be an All-American operation with all by-God U.S. equipment."

Junk, indeed. Hagan shrugs and looks down at his battered cowboy boots. "This year we're gonna learn how they do this thing at Le Mans," he says. "It's tricky. They tend to make it awful tough on strangers. But next year I'm comin' back here with *two* cars and I'll blow their damn doors off." He nods toward his star driver, who is walking around the Camaro, really seeing it up close for the first time. "We were very lucky to sign Cale; that makes all the difference," Hagan says. "We got to show these folks over here that we mean bidness. Cale gives this operation credibility."

The Yarboroughs have been billeted in a sixteenth-century chateau, one of the most beautiful in all of France. The castle, as the kids call it, is Chateau de Vizé overlooking a village called Vire, and the owners, Colonel and Mme. Jean Launay, also own six hundred acres around it. The chateau, which has been painstakingly restored, has its own private chapel and dungeon, and the furnishings are authentic and expensive and rare.

Madame Launay is a handsome and imperious woman, and she is not at all keen on having guests. But the town fathers of Le Mans prevail on her to take in a celebrity now and then so that the visitors can enjoy the full flavor of rural France.

Well, if one must. But . . . Mr. and Mrs. Cale Yarborough and three kids from Timmonsville, South *Carolina*?

Coolly, Madame Launay shows them around the chateau, drawn to her full height, with her hands folded at her waist. Little B.J. looks up at her with absolute awe. And back in the giant main hall, Betty Jo looks around and says, "I swear, there sure is a lot of French Provincial furniture in here, isn't there?" She turns to a friend and adds, "But then, I guess that figures, doesn't it?"

Madame Launay sighs and looks at the ceiling.

The instructions and warnings at the drivers' meeting are spooky.

Slower cars are required to stay to the right on the Mulsanne Straight. Use your rearview mirror at all times.

A yellow flag with red stripes means that it's raining somewhere on the course—after all, the circuit is 8.36 miles around. Part of the course runs through a dark wood and parts of it are on public highways that have been closed to normal traffic for the occasion. The flag could also mean there's oil or gravel somewhere on the course.

Hold the pit speeds down to about 50 mph. The pit lane is very narrow; try not to run over any fingers and toes.

Cale sits calmly, with his muscular arms folded. He wears a sports shirt and jeans, plus tan cowboy boots with CALE stitched in a script of raised dark brown leather across the toes, and a big belt buckle, about the size of a salad plate. It's the solid silver and gold Winston Cup NASCAR championship belt.

The drivers will start their first practice session in a few hours. So far, all Cale has done is sit in the bare metal cockpit of the Camaro and shake the steering wheel a bit. The car has no niceties—no carpeting, no padding—just a tachometer, two oil gauges, water, fuel, and amp gauges, and a fire extinguisher. "It'll do just fine," Cale says. "It's not absolutely right, but, hell, it's only twenty-four hours and anybody can stand that."

Now a race official reads the names of drivers who haven't had physicals. The stewards are irritated because this vital item hasn't been completed. No physical exam, no race driving. The name Yarborough is read, with the *r*'s rolled so that it sounds especially elegant and foreign.

Then the meeting breaks up and, at the infield medical tent, the doctor looks for Cale's name on his list of drivers.

"It's not here," he says. "Your name."

Cale checks the list. "Yer right," he says.

"Write it down for me," the doctor says. He tears off a little scrap of paper.

Cale bends over the desk and carefully prints out his name in block letters.

"Fine," the doctor says. "Now the, uh, the number, please." He means Cale's age. Yarborough leans over and prints out "35," which is the number of the Camaro.

"Thank you," says the doctor. "That will be all."

"Best racing physical I ever had," Cale says outside the tent. "Just makes me feel good all over to know that I'm in such fine condition."

The drivers are permitted just two practice sessions, on Wednesday and Thursday evenings, timed so they'll stretch from daylight into twilight into darkness. Strangely, the practice also doubles as qualifying. The problem with this system is obvious: it creates pressure to get out and hammer the car right away instead of shaking it down sensibly. "I got to remind myself," says Cale, "that this here is a *ride*, not a race. That is, the main thing is, we got to keep that Camaro rolling for twenty-four hours."

He climbs in through the car window, stock-car style, although the Camaro has a functional door. Chief Mechanic Tex Powell leans in with last-minute instructions. Powell has crewed with some of the best racers in the game, Richard Petty and guys like that, and it was Powell who got the car race-ready at his shop in Asheboro, North Carolina. Tex is a racing purist; he finds the Le Mans operation a little too slapdash, but he's philosophical about it. "We just do the best we can and let the rough end drag," he says.

With the hotted-up engine, Powell figures the Camaro will get four miles to the gallon at best—or burn perhaps two gallons per lap. "Now, ever' chance you get," he says to Cale, "breathe her a little bit." In other words, ease off on the throttle from time to time so the engine can catch its breath and cool down. Cale nods and pulls on his driving gloves. Then he flicks on the ignition switch. And suddenly, there it is—the sound that shook Le Mans.

There's a heavy cough followed by a huge barrrroooooom! and the roar of it spills out on all sides. In the pits nearby, mechanics and drivers stiffen in momentary alarm, then turn to look at the Camaro. It sits there bubbling mightily, going *hoodin, hoodin, hoodin, blam, blam, blam.* Then Cale pops the clutch and it screams away, trailing pale blue smoke from the tires.

His first lap takes 6:33 minutes, second lap, 6:45—"Doggone circuit is so long that by the time you come around once you plumb forgot where to go next time." But now, flashing past the pits on the uphill main straight, Cale hunches up his shoulders and gets on it. The speed climbs dramatically and his next laps are 4:51, then 4:21. That means he's averaging better than 115 mph and hitting 200 or so down the 3¾-mile Mulsanne Straight. Next time around, the car comes burbling up the pit road at about the required 50 and slams to a stop.

Now *this* looks like old-time racing: The inside of the cockpit is coated with spattered hot oil, and Cale's face and goggles shine with it. When he grins, his teeth look whiter against the grime. "I swear," he says, "you know that long, long straightaway—the part that's actually the state highway goin' into the town of Mulsanne? Well, there's a *hotel* down there with a patio right next to the guardrail. People sitting at little round tables under big umbrellas and all. And you go past there at 200-and-something miles an hour, just inches from their noses, and they raise a toast to you. It's really something to see. It sure must make some whitecaps in their wineglasses."

Friday Morning, June 12

Something strange has happened to Madame Launay.

She is sitting in the sun on the chateau terrace, impeccably groomed, as ever, *mais alors!*, she is smiling hugely. She is surrounded by the Yarborough girls and Southern gentility has struck again. Julie, Kelley (the family pronounces it Cale-ee), and B.J. are gracious-mannered and extremely soft-spoken: each one of them can murmur a phrase like "yes, ma'am," and get about six syllables out of it. They have now seized control of the chateau. And B.J. is full of historic news.

"The madame tole me that a knot once owned this castle and that they fought real wars over it and all," she says.

"Oh, really? A . . . a knot?"

She nods brightly. "Uh-huh. You know, knots in shining armor and all like that."

"Oh. A knight."

"That's what ah said," she says—and Madame Launay nods approvingly. That's what the little girl said, *mais oui*. You do not understand ze English?

Saturday, June 13

It's Race Day, and the Camaro will start in thirty-ninth spot on the grid. Fifty-five cars will race—from 3 o'clock this afternoon until three o'clock tomorrow—and now they're all parked in a long, long row in front of the main grandstands. A crowd estimated at around 200,000 is on hand, and the air is rich with the smells of gasoline and exhaust fumes, mingled with the odors of heavy red wines and overripe cheeses and Grand Marnier crepes sizzling in the infield concession stands. The noise level is rising, and by now the Americans are excited. They shouldn't be—they're all pros—but they are. A few moments ago, the loudspeaker played "The Star-Spangled Banner" in honor of this one little old Camaro—nobody paid any attention but the raggedy U.S. pit crew, of course—and now the band is playing "La Marseillaise." The crew gathers around the car, grinning into the stands. An American flag had been flying from a standard taped to the side of the Camaro, but now it is down and draped across the hood.

Cale's isn't really too bad a starting spot. On the second night of practice-qualifying, the team had started to show its stuff. Cale's backup and co-drivers had been out: Bill Cooper, thirty-four, an instructor at Bob Bondurant's race-driver school in California; Bobby Mitchell, thirty-nine, a Huntsville, Alabama, physicist and sports-car racer; and Billy Hagan himself, cowboy boots and all. The lap times had come winding down until finally Cale had roared off to a 3:59.57, an average speed of 125.76 mph for the circuit, including a clocked 220-mph burst down the long straight. It was said to be the fastest that an American had driven there in the past ten years.

Now race officials make their way through the milling crowds around the cars for a last check of the entries. At the Camaro, a couple of crewmen quickly sit down on the track just behind the car, resting their backs against the taillights. Two more crewmen stand near them, seeming to lean on the rear spoiler. They all sport manic grins. What, me worry? The American flag has been pushed slightly askew. And Tex Powell, a dirty rag wadded in his hands, is just a touch too relaxed. Oh, oh.

"What we got us here is a tiny problem," he says, talking quietly through his clenched teeth and not relaxing his smile. "We got us a small fuel leak. Gah-*damn*. Far as I can tell, it's maybe a little bitty hole in the filler neck goin' down into the fuel cell. Now, it'll run itself down below the hole in a few minutes, we think. And it sure enough will once we get to running. But now I got our guys sort of pretending to lean on the car to tilt it out—and those guys sittin' on the track are hiding the gas puddle. And I got a couple of rags throwed down there to soak it up. And finally, we're kind of hiding all of it behind the flag."

He looks around, still grinning and nodding at passers-by. "You know how it is with these here French officials," he says. "They been on us all along: one nit-pickin' thing after another. If they see some little ole thing like this, they'll throw our ass right out of the race."

Beautiful. This is a scam worthy of a gutsy band of U.S. stock-car racers transplanted into this foreign setting and—sure enough—Tex pulls it off. The race officials, in jackets and ties, stroll past, exchanging bright smiles, and the gas-soaked rags are recovered. A team of gendarmes sweeps the course free of visitors and Cale climbs into the car through the window. And, one by one, then in groups, the drivers start their engines.

Cale sits calmly inside the Camaro, watching Tex, who is standing off to one side. A flagman walks up to the Camaro and holds his thumb up at Cale, nodding his head yes. The flagman can't hear anything because of the din, obviously; the gesture is meant to ask Cale if his engine is running. Cale shakes his head no, grinning thinly at the man, and then he looks back at Tex. They continue to wait. Finally, Tex makes a switch-on signal with one forefinger. And Cale hits it.

The timing is ab-so-lutely perfect. Most of the cars are running, producing a chorus of strained, high-pitched whines from engines not half the size of the Camaro's . . . then BaROOM! The Camaro comes to life with a shattering roar. Movies and TV film will bear this out; journalistic history will record it: there is a flicker of a moment when all heads turn toward the squatty red, white, and blue car. There is a look of collective shock, followed by purest delight. What is *this*, this wonderful banger? It is, how you say, ze stock car? Is it ever, you Frenchies.

And away they roll.

First lap, and the cars flash past the stands in a continuous blur of bright color, a long, fast-streak across the vision. And then, in the middle of the pack coming from down the hill, from *Maison Blanche*, the White House corner, comes the advancing sound. Yarborough has got the Camaro in second gear and already the crowd can hear it winding higher and higher, a sort of metallic *yang, yang, yang*—and then, *brrraaaammm* comes the iron thunder when he pops it down a gear. In the stands on both sides of the track, there is a sensation of silver fillings dropping out of teeth.

Cale settles the car into a pattern of roughly four-minute laps, as planned, and at eleven laps he makes a 2:45-minute pit stop. Nothing NASCAR about that, but with twenty-three hours and sixteen minutes to go and French slow-drip refueling, who cares? In one of the pits just down the line, the crewmen have already opened bottles of cold beer and they stand there sipping them, watching the race. Tex Powell looks at them in astonishment.

Out on the circuit, Cale finds that he can eat up some of the cars. "Hell, I had to back off to keep from running right over some Porsches," he says later. But then it happens.

He had just swung boldly out of the hairpin turn after the Mulsanne Straight and was picking up speed again, headed into a twisty section toward Arnage Corner. "On the first left-hand turn, the brakes went real mushy," he says. "And in the *next* turn, they went zero. I didn't have any brakes at all."

Like any other NASCAR veteran, Cale looked immediately for a soft spot to spin it out. There was a fine, grassy patch just off the track ahead. But, unhappily, it was crowded with spectators, and there were a couple of race marshals there as well. Cale recalls that an image instantly froze on his mind: the spectators were chewing on those long, thin loaves of bread and drinking red wine from bottles without labels. And with the fat, twenty-inch-wide tires on the Camaro, there was no way he could spin it out on the track to scrub off speed. "I tried everything," he says. "I tried grabbin' gears [translation: downshifting like crazy]. But, no. And I sure couldn't wipe out all those people. So I just aimed her toward the guardrail and slammed her in."

The car slammed in, all right, driving its nose in almost up to the windshield and pulling a few guardrail supports right up out of the ground. Cale unhooked himself and climbed out. And, in a probably illegal gesture, some spectators threw him rope. Cale tied it to the back of the Camaro. About fifteen of them tugged and heaved, spit on their hands and tugged some more. No *way*.

Back in the pits far up the track, the crewmen paced around, fretting. Cale was long overdue. It got to be 4:25 P.M. and nobody knew what had happened; for all the speed of the race, word travels slowly at Le Mans. And if he had crashed, under the rules they couldn't go out to help him, not even to yank his car free. If the driver could somehow get the car around to his home pit again, they would be permitted to build practically a whole new car if necessary, but the driver had to get there on his own. Then, finally, the report came: Cale was all right, he was just fine. But the car was an awful lot squattier than when it had left. A tow truck was winching it out from under the guardrail.

Well, uh, damn. End of race. End of the mighty thunder. They had run one hour out of twenty-four—52:54.3 minutes, to be exact. Thirteen laps. The Camaro was the second car out of the race. Tex Powell sat on the toolbox and looked down at his greasy hands, then around at the crew. His eyes were red from lack of sleep. "Y'know," he said, "I been so busy all week with the car that I haven't even had time to send any postcards to the folks back home. Why don't someone here run out to one of them stands in the infield and get us all some postcards."

Sunday Morning, June 14

Cale finishes stuffing the last red and white Winston Cup garment bag into the Peugeot. Betty Jo and the girls are crisp and fresh, as befits Southern ladies. Madame Launay stands watching; she is struggling to maintain her austere look, but regality is obviously tough this morning. And then little B.J. approaches and takes her hand and says, "We want to thank yew for bein' so nice, ma'am." And that does it: Madame Launay impulsively bends down and hugs and kisses the girls.

Off at Le Mans, over in the next valley, the race is still going on. It already has been marred by two deaths—a driver's and a race marshal's—and at the end, only twenty-one of the fifty-five cars that started will finish. The race will ultimately be won by a Porsche, of course, a 936 driven by Belgium's Jacky Ickx, with Britain's Derek Bell, each of whom had won the race before; this will be Ickx's fifth victory. They will average 125.30 mph, covering 2997.5 miles. Not a record, and a slightly slower speed than the Camaro ran—when it was running.

"But that's racin'," Cale says.

He has maintained his composure through it all. After his crash, when Cale had made it back to the Camaro compound, it had taken a worried Betty Jo several more minutes to get to him from her seat in the stands through the dense infield crowd. By then, he had his driver's uniform pulled down to his waist and his arms were folded across his thick chest. He had been standing alone, looking bemusedly at the wrecked car.

"Daddy!" she said. "What in the world happened?"

He shrugged. "Oh, I ran it under a guardrail," he said.

"You . . . under a . . . what?"

"Honey," he said, and it was the only time all week that a slight edge was to come into his voice. "Honey, ah *crashed*."

But now the station wagon is loaded and the diary-keeper/map-reader will see if they can find their way back to Paris.

Cale turns and looks out at the chateau property. "They sure got themselves a lot of farmland here," he says. "Speakin' of which, let's head for South Carolina. I got a lot of wheat to cut before the next race."

GRIFFITH BORGESON

Tragic Superhero
of American Racing

It happened very fast, faster in fact than even the camera could follow. The little car, looking more like a white, wingless airplane than an automobile, was merely a white streak against the blue Atlantic. Suddenly, horribly, it turned itself into a ball of metal and careened down the beach at nearly 200 miles an hour, finally coming to rest at the water's edge. It had been the world's most advanced automobile and it carried with it the near-illiterate genius who was credited with being the world's most advanced automotive thinker.

In his short span of years, Frank Lockhart was so busy building better machinery that he barely took the time to learn to write his own language. From childhood, Frank lived for one thing alone—speed and the ways of attaining it. Equipped with inborn and consummate driving skill, he had something else, too—an absolute and utter genius for improving the work of other men. For Frank, not even the brilliance of Harry Miller, America's foremost racing-car designer, was good enough. It was Lockhart who discovered the method of heat treating the overly brittle and fragile valves of the Miller engine, and it was Lockhart who, with Leon Duray, thought of the supercharger intercooler that made the supercharger practical and reliable.

The little white car that ended his life was to have been the culmination—the pinnacle—of a brilliant career. It was to have provided the fame and money that would allow that career to blossom unhampered. But it didn't—it merely ended a man's life on the hard sands of Daytona Beach. Had one ever asked Frank how he thought his end would come, Frank could have told him. He had already worked it out in a makeshift basement laboratory over a year before his death. As usual, he had been right!

Who was Frank Lockhart? Back in the Roaring Twenties, he was a great national hero. He was one of the greatest racing drivers the world had seen. As a kid just out of his teens, jockeying a bucket of bolts, he became famous overnight as King of the Dirt Tracks. The first time he went near Indianapolis he won the five-hundred-mile race spectacularly and decisively . . . in a borrowed car. When he rode the Championship circuit after that, he was consistently fantastic, winning races and smashing records from coast to coast. His name was almost as much a household word as that of Babe Ruth or Jack Dempsey even before he decided to become the fastest man on earth.

Then he built the Stutz Black Hawk, America's challenger for the land-speed record. Compared with the English record-holder, Seagrave's gigantic Sunbeam, the Black Hawk was a mere toy. But experts called it "the most mechanically perfect automobile ever built in the world" and predicted that what it lacked in size it would more than make up for in efficiency.

The eyes of the world were on Lockhart when, at the age of twenty-five, he *did* go faster than man ever had gone on land. In 1928, 225 mph was as unprecedented for an automobile as 425 is today. But Lockhart had done it, the papers said. They also told in their stories of how a tire had blown at that speed and how the tiny car had rolled and banged eerily down the beach until, by a cruel, ironic stroke of fate, his broken body was flung at the feet of his waiting wife.

Where the Lockhart legend survives it has a mythically heroic quality. Illiterate, the hero's intellect was awesome. Obscure, he rocketed to world fame. Penniless, he raced his way to wealth. Frail, his endurance was unmatched. What other men accomplished with a lot, Lockhart surpassed with less. Horatio Alger never dared to invent such a hero—a little guy who slew giants by virtue of nothing but guts, infinite labor, and, above all, brains.

Legend though it is, it's not far from the truth. Lockhart did all these things. But he didn't do them all single-handedly, as the myth relates. Nor were the sacrifices and heartbreaks all his own.

Frank Lockhart stood five feet, three inches, weighed about 135 pounds, and had hazel eyes and flaxen hair. He was born in Dayton, Ohio, in 1903. Three years later he was spending all his waking hours in a nearby livery stable, watching automobiles of the day being worked on. If there was an eggbeater in the house, or any other mechanism, Frank appropriated it for his own.

When Frank was six, his father died and his mother moved with Frank and his brother Bob to California She took in sewing to keep the family alive. It wasn't easy and they moved often.

Frank could not play with other kids; he had no patience with their aimless frivolity. He just worked on things, built things, and devoured all the reading matter he could find that dealt with things mechanical. He never had time to be bothered with spelling: as an adult he spelled sugar *shougar*, with phonetic logic. Even as a child he loved mathematics and felt far more at home with numbers than with words.

When Frank was eight he built a coaster—a soapbox-derby sort of thing that all the kids were building at the time. He couldn't get canvas or slats or tin to cover it, so he used tar paper. In neighborhood races he almost always won, mainly because he had the willpower to get the greatest number of kids to push him. Anyone who associated with Frank had to submit to his will. When his shoes needed polishing, Frank took care of one shoe and his brother did the other. And when Frank was running race cars, anyone who dropped in at the garage couldn't just sit and talk; he was handed a rag or a tool and put to work.

Frank had nothing but trouble in school. He had a mind that was totally his own and would work at nothing that was not important to him, personally. When automobiles still were being built with acetylene headlamps, Frank would spend his classroom time drawing cars with fully streamlined bodies. Teachers would brandish sheaves of these, demanding that his mother punish her child . . . help to get him away from this nonsense and down to serious studies. But Frank had long since convinced her that automobiles had to evolve toward the streamlined form. When he miraculously graduated from high school—to the merciful relief of all concerned —the principal told Carrie Lockhart that he had never been taken advantage of (meaning "treated as an equal") by a student as he had been by Frank.

By the time he was sixteen Frank had to have a car, family poverty notwithstanding. He lived in Inglewood then, and a vegetable peddler named Gentle listened to the kid's hopes.

"I've got an old Model T chassis in my yard over in Boyle Heights," he said. "You can have it if you can get it home."

At that time Frank felt that anyone who would build a chassis from iron rather than from light hardwood was a fool. But here was the foundation for a car that he could own, now. Day after day he and his brother made the twelve-mile trek on foot, carrying or dragging the T chassis home piece by piece.

Frank hung around all the speed shops, but his favorite was Ray McDowell's in Hollywood. McDowell—who later won fame as a builder of racing engines and components—gave him a junk T engine. Frank got it home and rebuilt it on his mother's kitchen floor.

"Our house wasn't like other people's," she told me. "That's how he started. McDowell was really a father to my Frank. He finally said, 'Bring all of your plunder to my place.' He had a pit. And they got that Ford so it would go. That was his first car. He ran it at Ascot and nobody ever passed him. He made no money there worth mentioning. He'd come home with burned feet and so tired that he couldn't get his shoes off. But that was what he had to do. He lived on grease and iron."

He lived to go fast. He never touched a drink or smoked or swore, not so much for any moral reason as for the fact that he considered these activities wasteful and pointless. He went with one girl in his life: the girl he married. In his human relationships he was fantastically stingy, but he would cheerfully spend his last cent to get a job done. That's what money was for.

Frank was no sentimentalist. "One day in 'twenty-two," his mother recalls, "he came home and announced that he had to have five new tires for the Ford. I reminded him that we didn't have the $125—we hardly had a cent. He said, 'Well the furniture is paid for and you own some equity in the house—borrow the money.' I did. Frank wasn't a boy that you could say no to. His demands were very great."

After he got out of high school, Frank continued his education at a technical night school and by a lot of reading at home. He was shy, quiet, and well-liked. "Everybody loved Frank," his mother says, "for his intelligence. He didn't have idle talk in him. When he talked you listened, because you'd never heard it before. Maybe you've known someone like that; they're rare."

Somehow Frank came to the attention of the California Institute of Technology, and he was invited to take entrance examinations. He did, and shortly thereafter his mother was called to the office of Nobel Prize–winning physicist Robert Milliken.

"Your son's score in these tests is one of the highest in our experience," he said. "He has the mind of a born scientist. Can't you find someone to back his education?"

Carrie didn't have to think for long. "We don't know anyone like that," she answered. "But I'll do all your family's sewing if that will help."

Frank did not attend Cal Tech.

Instead, he kept driving at Ascot and other small West Coast tracks. Once in a while someone would beat him, but never when there was any good money at stake. Ernie Olson, one of the finest racing mechanics we've ever produced, used to watch him there. "No one ever sat in a race car like Frank," he recalls. "On a mile dirt track he seemed to begin his slide in the middle of the straightaway; nobody ever imitated him. His skill and daring were tremendous. He wasn't exactly cool. He always got real bad butterflies before a race; he'd even vomit. In the car he'd say, 'Pat me on the shoulder.' You'd do that and it seemed to fix the butterflies. But once the flag fell he was in command of everything. I once asked him what he thought about when he was racing. 'All I think of from one second to the next,' he told me, 'is how to drive to win.'"

Hoping for a start in the big time, Frank wandered back to Indianapolis in 1926. He looked up the one man he knew there, Ernie Olson, who was then in charge of Bennet Hill's Miller. It was arranged for Frank to take a few practice laps on this course, one he had never seen before. The twenty-three-year-old dirt-tracked the bricks, taking the turns in full, controlled slides, as the birds on the outside rail cringed. "My God," said Hill, "that punk's getting around faster than I do."

When Lockhart came in Olson got him in a corner and asked how he liked the ride. "Fine, but I never was really on it" was the answer. Olson then asked how fast Frank thought he could get around the big oval if he tried. "Oh, about four seconds quicker," he said. That would have been a new track record and Olson said, "Kid, if Benny needs relief, you've got a ride in the race."

But the day before the race another Miller pilot, Steve Kreis, was taken ill and Frank was offered his car. Newspapers reported:

"The race was a quarter over and the name of Lockhart burned every wire when a fine rain swept the brick saucer clean of dirt and in its stead deposited a slippery, slimy surface that drove veteran after veteran into the pits. The pace slowed—for all except Lockhart, who seemed to drive his foot farther into the floorboards."

When the race was called at four hundred miles because of the rain, the unknown kid from the west was five miles in front of his nearest competition. It was one of the most dramatic victories ever seen at the Speedway, and Frank was the talent discovery of that or any year. Harry Miller came to him and offered him a car for the rest of the season. This was praise from Caesar, but Lockhart would not accept this fulfillment of his ambition until he had the promise of the help of the best mechanic he knew: Olson.

They made a nearly invincible team. Olson was a brainy engineer in his own right as well as being a master mechanic, race strategist, and major domo of equipment. But Lockhart needed him not so much for his exceptional know-how—Frank knew all the answers—as for his ability to keep pace with Frank's ideas and to help translate them into action. For Olson, it was an unforgettable privilege to be a principal figure in the revolution that Lockhart brought to American racing. "When any part failed or gave trouble," he recalls, "Frank would say, 'There's a reason for this.

Let's find out what it is.' He might sit and study the problem for three or four days before doing a thing. But then he'd have the answer."

Valves broke regularly in the racing engines of the day. Frank figured out why, and to him must go the credit for today's situation, in which few, if any, valves ever break. Everyone used differentials on paved tracks until Frank started winning with a locked rear end, which everyone uses today. Everyone was content with torque tubes until Lockhart discovered that rear axle housings were bending under load. Now everyone uses truss rods or radius rods, as he did. Lockhart experimented constantly and carried an elaborate machine shop with him from track to track. What Miller and Duesenberg considered their best, he refined to the nth degree.

Lockhart has been credited with the invention of the supercharger intercooler, but this was really not one of his original contributions. While working on his car at Miller's plant in Los Angeles in the summer of 'twenty-six, he became acquainted with John Weisel, a young Cal Tech engineering student who spent his vacations in Miller's employ. When Lockhart tried to interest Miller in detail improvements on his masterpieces, the Old Man was scornful. So Lockhart hired Weisel to help him with design and drafting problems and through John met his brother, Zenas, who recently had obtained his degree in mechanical engineering. His master's thesis had been a study of the supercharging of aircraft engines.

It was Zenas who proposed the intercooler. Here is how it happened: Frank had the excellent idea of building a gear train which could be bolted to the top of the transmission of his Buick road car and could be used for testing superchargers at racing revs, anywhere and at any time. Zenas proposed a refinement: design a dynamometer into the device so as to be able to tell with precision the effect of any change in blower setup. It was at this time that Zenas explained his intercooler theory to Frank. With Frank's Buick engine turning over at 1450 rpm and, through the transmission, driving the blower at the equivalent of 7500 crankshaft revolutions, Weisel asked Frank to feel the blast from the blower outlet. From eighteen inches away it was like touching a red-hot bar. Weisel said, "I can design an air-cooled manifold for you that will get rid of a lot of that heat. If it doesn't give you another 8 mph you won't owe me a dime." The first time out with the new setup, Lockhart's Miller went 8.5 mph faster than it ever had before.

That was at the Culver City board track on March 6, 1927. Frank took one warm-up lap in his 91-cubic-inch Miller, then raised his hand to signal to the starter that he was on his way, and turned in an all-time record of 144.2 mph.

The intercooler was a secret. The car's hood was kept locked and was never raised until hidden from unauthorized eyes. Frank drove the big-time circuit from coast to coast and dominated almost every race he entered. In one afternoon at

Cleveland, for example, he broke over one hundred records for the mile dirt track, including de Palma's from one to twenty-five miles and Milton's from fifty to one hundred miles. The intercooler was kept secret for almost a year.

That season Lockhart and Olson took their much-modified Miller 91 to Roberts Dry Lake in the Mojave Desert—the car long since had been purchased from Miller, who would not tolerate design changes being made on *his* car. Lockhart ran for official straightaway records under AAA sanction. Said a newspaper account, "Shattering all records for the 91-inch class at 171.02 mph—the fastest time made by any car in the world excepting the Daytona monster, thirty times larger. Lockhart's two-way average against a heavy cross wind was 164.85 mph. The new record, made by a midget with the power of a giant, is a startling achievement when compared with the records established during recent years by cars with motors many times its size."

In 'twenty-seven, Lockhart came within an ace of winning the Indianapolis 500 for the second year in a row. He held the lead for three hundred miles and then a con rod broke. After that, he redesigned Miller's rods. He finished the season a wealthy man. His lap winnings alone at Indy: $11,000.

Among the millions who had been following every step of Lockhart's blazing career with fascinated admiration was Fred E. Moskovics. His family had moved to the United States from Budapest when Moskovics was only four. His father had been a mining engineer and F.E. took a degree in mechanical engineering. He grew up with the automobile and with racing. He had managed the Mercedes team in the first Vanderbilt Cup Race, gotten Ralph de Palma his first ride in a race car and, after taking over as president of Stutz in the midtwenties, he put that marque back in the racing business both in America and in Europe.

Moskovics's enthusiasm was boundless when he learned that Lockhart had beaten the previous year's land-speed record with a tiny car of American manufacture. He sought the kid out and got to know him well.

Says Moskovics, who, in his seventies, does his commuting in a 300SL, "Frank was the greatest natural mechanic I've ever come in contact with. He told me of his ambition to win the land-speed record for the United States. I knew that if anyone could do it, Lockhart could. I agreed to give him all the backing in my power. I got a group of wealthy sportsmen together who put up about $20,000. He agreed to call his machine the Stutz Black Hawk, and I was able to add another $15,000 and put the facilities of the Stutz factory in Indianapolis at his disposal."

Olson, in the meantime, had been working hard to arrange Lockhart's participation in the Italian Grand Prix at Monza. "I had the deal wrapped up," he says, "when Frank told me he was going to build the beach car. I didn't exactly have a premonition of disaster. I just got physically ill. I felt it was the wrong thing to do and began to look for another job."

Lockhart wired the Weisel brothers, asking them to come to Indianapolis to work on the project at a guaranteed salary for a minimum of four months. The challenge was fascinating to them. They hurried east and followed Lockhart around the country as he kept up with his racing commitments.

"My brother and I," says Zenas, "traveled with a suitcase each of clothes and a big trunk filled with books and instruments and a drawing board. We landed in Indianapolis, went with Frank to Altoona, then to Salem, where we got the car pretty well in mind, then to Buffalo, then to Detroit, then back to Indianapolis. Unusual working conditions. I can still remember him sitting in a chair in a hotel room while I measured his seated posture and laid out the frame kickups so they would just clear his elbows. We built the car around him."

Lockhart's idea was to attack the record with a car running two separate Miller 91's geared together after the fashion of Milton's LSR Duesenberg. He also planned on using a bug-shaped envelope body. Zenas's engineering training had included heavy emphasis on aerodynamics as well as engine design. In this case, both were closely related, and he produced drawings of the Bugatti sixteen-cylinder aircraft engine to show how a pair of straight eighths could be joined in a very compact manner by integrating them into a single crankcase.

Concerned with the smallest possible frontal area for the car, Zenas squelched the envelope-body approach: it would sacrifice more than the meager available horsepower could afford. He held out for exposed wheels and for a torpedo shape that would enclose everything within the frame. Thus, not one square millimeter of frontal area would be allowed to absorb thrust that otherwise could be converted into speed.

Zenas streamlined the axles, of course. He also streamlined the wheels that were sitting raggedly out in the air. He had listened to drivers who had run at high speeds and were unhappy with the handling of disc-covered wire wheels. He reasoned that the effect of cross winds on their steering was not due entirely to the lateral load created by the wind acting against the area of the wheel discs and pushing them in the direction of the wind. Zenas felt that the unexpectedly strong effects that had been noted were due, at least in part, to the fact that at high speeds the disc wheel, if inclined at an angle, became a lifting surface similar to an airplane wing. He also reasoned that the center of pressure on such a wheel was well ahead of the kingpin, adding leverage to the tendency to steer in the direction of cross winds. So Weisel designed the streamlined wheel spats for the Black Hawk and made them long. He calculated their shape so that (1) the center of pressure would be well aft of the kingpins, counteracting somewhat the car's tendency to steer in the direction of a cross wind and (2) acting as air rudders, they would contribute to the car's directional stability.

That was the philosophy behind the spats, which always were essentially parallel to the car's long axis. Calculations indicated that, with an anticipated coefficient of friction on the beach of .5, the front wheels could not be turned more than 0 degrees, 6 minutes, without throwing the car into a skid. The lock-to-lock arc was fixed just short of that figure; total movement at the rim of the fourteen-inch steering wheel was just one quarter of an inch.

Efforts had been made in the past to give racing and record cars a streamlined outward appearance, hut their undersides and engine spaces were left ragged. To cut down this rather large source of wind drag, Weisel enclosed the underside of the car and sealed off the engine compartment from outside air, except for small intake and exhaust openings. He originated the idea of eliminating the conventional radiator from straightaway machines. Coolant for the Black Hawk's power plant circulated through an eight-pound ice tank.

The tiny 181.6-cubic-inch engine was supercharged, of course, and was fitted with intercoolers. The intercooler on the speedway car had been mounted under the car's hood, and its effectiveness depended upon the flow of air through the engine compartment. For the record machine, Weisel designed an entirely new kind of intercooler: a delicate, filigreelike aluminum casting contoured to follow perfectly the surface of the car's skin.

The basic idea was to enclose all parts of the machine while still avoiding the obvious tactic of wrapping it in a continuous envelope. To get the body as small as possible, while enclosing everything but axles and wheels, called for an extremely narrow frame and for springs that would also be located within the body shell. Given these conditions, the springs as well as the frame rails had to be extremely close together, a fact which would not help stability with regard to torsional action of the front axle.

To get the springs within the minimum-area body, they had to be only eleven inches apart. Weisel wanted to tie the axles to the chassis without even a thousandth of an inch of mechanical play, so that the car could be steered without concern for any movement between these elements. He designed and patented a unique suspension system. Each spring was a double cantilever machined from a solid-steer billet. The front ends of the front springs were bolted to a steel spool, which served as the center section of the front axle. The stub axles, in turn, were bolted to this assembly outboard of the springs; the back ends of the springs were bolted to bronze spacer blocks, which were bolted to the frame. Total spring deflection was three quarters of an inch, during which the kingpins remained parallel with the frame.

The rear springs were of the same unusual construction; their front ends were bolted solidly to the frame, and their rear ends pivoted around the rear-axle housing. The worm-gear final drive was dictated not by Stutz sponsorship of the project but by the fact that this feature permitted lowering the car's height by about six inches.

It seems that the Black Hawk was the first car in the United States to make extensive use of wind-tunnel testing. The base line for the record machine was Frank's 91-inch speedway car and the knowledge that it had turned 171 mph at 7200 rpm. Therefore, a precise scale model of the 91 was built, complete with radiator opening, dummy engine under the hood, hood louvers, knock-off hubs, dummy driver—all the features that might contribute to wind drag. An equally precise model of the Black Hawk was also made. Utilizing the known top speed of the 91 and the data obtained by wind-tunnel tests, the approximate available horsepower of both engines could be calculated . . . and so could the terminal velocity of the Black Hawk.

Bear in mind that the fastest car in the world at this time was Seagrave's huge Sunbeam. It weighed 8000 pounds, had a 2760-cubic-inch, 1000 bhp engine and held the world's two-way record at 203.790 mph.

Lockhart's Black Hawk weighed just under 2800 pounds. This may sound light but, because the car was a rather small one, its density-weight in relation to size— was great. Its 181-cubic-inch engine was assumed to deliver 525 bhp to the rear wheels at 7500 rpm. Thorough wind-tunnel tests were conducted by the Curtiss Airplane Company, whose engineers credited the little car with a potential top speed of 283 mph.

The models were then sent to the Army wind tunnel at Wright Field for double checking. There, the top speed was calculated to be 281 mph. But by this time Lockhart, still racing in every championship event, had his 91 turning 8200 rpm on the board-track straightaways. The horsepower estimate had to be revised upward and final calculations indicated that, on gasoline, the Black Hawk was good for 330 mph! Methanol had not yet been discovered in the United States as a racing fuel.

Naturally, no word of this fantastic potential was allowed to go beyond those persons most intimately concerned with the car. Even Moskovics seems to have had no inkling of it. But Zenas Weisel still has the records.

Standard strategy among record breakers was and is not to exceed existing records by extravagant margins but, rather, to top them adequately, reap the rewards, rest on the laurels until a new record is established, and then, if the potential of your machine has not been exhausted, go back and break the record again. Lockhart's plan was to boost the land-speed record to about 225 mph, and most of his equipment tests were based on this simulated speed, including tire tests.

Jean Marcenac was in charge of the "inner sanctum" in the basement of the Stutz plant where the beach car was built. He helped Frank run the tire tests. The test rig consisted of a big Stutz straight-eight engine, bolted to a concrete foundation, which drove the shaft on which the wheels and tires were spun. Finally, the time for the destruction test. The shop was cleared, and the test tire, inflated to 125 psi, was set spinning at the equivalent of 225 mph. Marcenac and Lockhart shrank behind concrete columns, and Frank fired at the tire with a shotgun. The tremendous, unbalanced forces that were suddenly released tore the heavy engine from the block, and its aft end disintegrated. Lockhart grimly said, "Well, I'm done for if a tire blows." He was depressed for days, but eventually accepted the gamble.

In February of 1928, less than eight months after the preliminary paperwork on the Black Hawk was completed, the car was finished and ready to go. The $35,000 with which the project had been launched did not go far, and the beach car gradually drained off a large percentage of Lockhart's massive racing winnings. Estimates of its total cost run as high as $100,000. As Lockhart's investment in the project rose beyond all expectations, his concern necessarily swung more and more from the pure challenge of ultimate speed to the financial relief and reward that would come once the record was in his hands. The project took on a definitely commercial character, and Frank and his manager would spend long hours computing the eventual take from track and vaudeville appearances, product endorsements, and awards from manufacturers.

Money became all-important to this extent: Lockhart had always driven on Firestone racing tires and had used them in his tests at the Stutz factory. But a new tire manufacturer offered him $20,000 if he would set the new record using this firm's experimental high-speed tires. He accepted.

Just before his final attack on the record, Frank's mother wrote him. "I told him that I was very ill and almost desperate. Would he send me just ten dollars? It would make all the difference in the world. A couple of days before the run I got a wire from him. He didn't mention the money. It just said, 'Ma, I have the world by the horns. You'll never have to push a needle again. I'll never have to work any more.'"

The Black Hawk was shipped to Daytona early in February, and practice runs began. Day after day they ran, but could not get above 180 mph. Frank was in a frenzy. Finally, with Moskovics' help, they found their trouble: laminar flow across the supercharger inlets was starving the engine for air. Small scoops at the inlets transformed the car's performance. But by this time the weather had become increasingly bad, and the AAA timers were ready to pick up and leave. They would stay just one more day: for Washington's birthday and the scheduled stock-car runs on the beach.

The weather was foul and the beach was miserable. But thousands of paid admissions had been collected and, in spite of intermittent rain all day long, the crowds stayed to see if Lockhart would run. Finally, late in the afternoon, the little white car was towed to the south end of the course. The next thing the crowd was aware of was the 40,000-rpm scream of the Black Hawk's superchargers. He was on it all the way, touching between 220 and 225, when he hit a patch of rain. He couldn't see and the car edged into soft sand. Then a crash, two end-over-end flips, and a flight into the sea. The car landed on its belly and then skipped like a stone over the water, making slow barrel rolls in the air. It came to rest, wheels down, nearly submerged in the surf.

It seemed impossible that Lockhart could be alive. The crowd surged toward the wreck. As the first wave lapped over the car, a hand appeared above the water. "Save him . . . he'll drown." Lockhart was pinned in the cockpit, but twenty men rushed into the waves and dragged the car to shore. Aside from shock—he had a congenital fear of water—his only injury was, miraculously, a couple of cut tendons in his right hand.

Moskovics says, "The car looked like a ruin, but actually it wasn't badly damaged. We shipped it back to Indianapolis for repair. I did everything in the world to keep Frank from going back to the beach that year. But he had made no end of commitments, and I guess he had to go."

In mid-April, Lockhart and the Black Hawk were back at Daytona with the eyes of the world on them. It was at dawn on the twenty-fifth that he made his first sally, a warm-up to the south. The beach was perfect, and he returned north a little faster. Then south again, with the superchargers' scream announcing that he was getting down to business. Then he began his fourth run, really flying. He was just about to enter the traps when a spray of sand shot from his right rear tire and the car came smashing, tumbling, thudding down the beach, and that was the end.

Officials who examined the evidence before the tide came in said that in braking at the end of his third run Frank had locked his rear wheels for about a hundred feet. In that long slide, Frank had very likely slit or otherwise weakened a tire on a piece of hidden flotsam or a sea shell. On the final run that tire had blown with just the results that Lockhart had predicted after his shotgun test.

BILL NEELY AND BOB OTTUM

Stand on It!

We were still spinning around the parking lot when they started arguing about the record.

Spinning: the entire parking lot was covered with loose, pea-sized gravel, all sprayed white, and the Ford LTD was going around in full-power skids one way and the other, and throwing up a rooster tail of little stones. The inside of the car was rattling with the sound of gravel under the fenders.

Hell of a song. I leaned my head back against the headstopper and sang a few bars:

> Oh, I've just got one leg, dear,
> And a big sack of beer here;
> But one thing is clear . . .
> DEAR,
> Uhhh . . . sure as there's a Wankel,
> I've busted my fucking ankle,
> And I'll have to hold my socks up with suspenders,
> Because: every time I see you,
> I get,
> Gravel Under My Fenders.

What the hell. I was delirious anyway and my ankle was keeping perfect time to the music. One, two, *throb;* one, two, *throb.*

The LTD came around one more time in a full, swinging three-sixty-degree turn and I finally got it figured out in my head why the car was spinning. Two reasons:

One: too much power was being applied on the loose gravel and there was no traction.

Throb.

Two: Lugs was driving it and everybody knows that Lugs is a goddam *dummy.*

Throb.

And they were arguing about the record:

Charlie had his chin resting up on the top of the front seat and his whole face filled up the space between Lugs and my shoulders. He was wearing Shirley's leopard-skin brassiere over the top of his head, with the back-snap part hooked under his chin, and the D cups poofed out on each side like big, spotted earmuffs.

"Lissen," he said, "you better get us the hell out of this here parking lot before the cops get here."

"No," Lugs said. "I'm going around here one more time. I'm not leaving this here lot until you tell me what the record is. Hold on, here we go again."

And the car came whipping around again, spraying up gravel like thunder against the chassis.

"Wheee!" Shirley said. "Sing the song again, Strokie."

Throb.

"Not until you give me another beer."

"It's right here on the seat between us," Lugs said. "You want me to drop every-thing and open you one, for chrissakes? Can't you see I'm *driving?*"

"Driving? Come *on,* Dummy. If I couldn't spin a car any goddam better than *this,* I'd get out and walk. Now, really get down on the goddam *gas,* Dummy, and crank that wheel."

Throb.

"Sing it again," Shirley said. "One more time."

> *Oh, every time I see your two knockers,*
> *I get gravel . . .*
> *Under my rockers.*

Charlie's big hands came over and opened two more cans of beer, spraying the imitation-leather dashboard. "Lissen to this," he said.

> *Oh, every time I look at your ass,*
> *I get gravel,*
> *In my GAS.*

And the car came around again.

"You going to tell me what the record is?" said Lugs. "Or are we going to spin around here until daylight?"

"All right," Charlie said. "It is sixty-three miles to Indy. And the record is thirty-four minutes. Now, if you can't beat that by at least a half-hour I'm gonna—"

"Well, hang on," Lugs said.

Throb.

We came carooming out in something of a ragged four-wheel drift just as the police car was coming in—and for just one, tiny, tiny split second there, everybody in both cars all looked into each other's eyes.

Lugs braked her hard and we did one final pirouette on the hard-top road, shaking gravel out from under the car like steel rain. And then he cranked it over tight and we came around through the Hospital Emergency entrance in a nice little circle, taking out about fifty-five feet of dahlias planted along the walkway.

By the time we hit the Interstate, just flashing under the overhead green *Indianapolis* sign, Shirley was singing:

> *Oh, who put the tire tracks in my flowers,*
> *That I worked on for hours and hours*
> *[Throb]*
> *It must have been a bunch of folks out on benders . . .*

"All together now. Come on":

> *Because now I've got uhhh,*
> *Flowers under my FENDERS.*

We made it in thirty-two minutes point sixteen seconds, sliding into the White Front parking lot in a nice, easy, long, looping drift.

"Are we going *in?*" Shirley said.

Everybody looked at her.

"No, we're just going to sit out here and insist that they open curb service," Lugs said. "Of *course* we're going in. Now, come on."

"Well, can I have my brassiere back?"

Charlie thought it over: "No. It's the first time my ears been warm all season."

So she zipped up her uniform a little bit, just up to the edge of that tawny warm valley.

Outside, the car was crackling and popping and giving off strange, helpless little clicks, trying to cool off, and little wisps of steam were curling up out of the front grill.

"The car is talking to itself," Shirley said.

"Naw," said Charlie. "What that car is doing is *praying*."

They all kept sliding in and out of focus, everybody moving wavily as if the entire White Front had been moved underwater somewhere off the Florida Keys. And little bits of conversation drifted in and out of my head, sometimes hanging there for a minute or two so I could study what was being said as though it had been printed right on the smoke over our table:

"Will you get the hell *up*? Yer sitting on Stroker's *cast*, for chrissakes . . ."

"Did you hear he was in the maternity ward?"

". . . and Lugs knocked the fireman on his ass."

". . . stole the ambulance."

Throb. Another round of beer here, Grace.

"What're you doing wrapped in a blanket, fella? You playing cowboys and Indians?"

"Who ast you? If that man wants to sit here in a blanket, it's fine, you follow me?"

"Look: I'm talking to the guy in the *blanket*. I don't like his looks, you unnerstand?"

Throb. Where's Grace with that beer?

"Uh-huh. Well, what I'm telling *you* is: leave the guy in the blanket alone."

"Yeah? Well, I don't like the looks of his fucking blanket. So I'm just going to snatch it off him and then I'm going to ram it right up yer ass, buddy-boy."

Focus: I could see Lugs sitting down, all nicely tilted back on his chair, very calm, looking up at some giant, mean hay-shaker who was standing there. The guy had big, red-knuckled hands and he was leaning over towards me.

Lugs was undoing his belt buckle while he was talking, and he was slowly pulling it out of the belt loops.

Throb.

"More beer over here?"

"Hey, Grace. Where you been?"

Throb.

Grace was all fuzzy around the edges, wavering there underwater, and she had a big trayload of beer. She smiled and the smile hung there frozen in the smoke so that I could study it.

"Maternity ward, huh? Well, here's your beer, you mother." And then she was gone, but her smile still hung there.

Throb. The bottle felt cool; the palms of my hands were hot.

"Well, I come in here for a peaceful drink, see, and I ain't gonna allow no goddam *Indians* sitting here wrapped up in blankets while I'm drinking, see?"

Focus: Lugs was still sitting easy. But his right hand had now dropped out of sight down alongside his chair. And his belt was now gone from his Levi's.

Throb. Now if I can only find a cigarette here. Must have a cigarette here somewhere . . .

Slowly, in perfect diminished four-quarter time, the two big red hands reached over for my blanket. And I looked up into the guy's face. There was a big scowl squinched down between his eyebrows and he needed a shave. He was talking to me, slowly, underwater, and I waited, listening carefully for the words to come out.

"F-u-c-k-i-n-g I-n-d-i-a-n," he said. "Gimme that blanket . . ."

I smiled up at him, trying to keep him in sight and trying to study the words he had printed in the smoke over our table.

Our faces were very close together now. And the tips of his fingers were on my shoulders. And he was looming bigger, fuzzy and bigger, very slowly, until I could see all the open pores and blackheads across his nose.

Throb. Naturally I can't have any cigarettes here because I haven't got any *pockets*, right? I wonder if this stranger has any cigarettes on him? *Throb.*

Oh, look: he's doing a nice *trick.* In slow motion.

I watched him.

His face was drawn right up close and—gently, easily, just as slowly as could be—a perfect white slash grew right alongside his right eyeline. The skin peeled back smoothly, in slow four-four time, until I could look into the new slot and see his bare cheekbone. And then, without a sound, it turned pink.

"That's *wonderful*," I said. I reached over into his shirt pocket and pulled up a pack of Pall Malls. He didn't seem to mind because he was still doing his nice trick to entertain me:

The ditch in his face turned bubbly red and, gently, a marvelous fountain of blood began to come up out of it, sparkling and frothing in the smoky light; all glistening and throbbing in perfect time with my ankle. And then his eyes grew beautifully opaque, as though he was trying hard to hold me in focus by some slow, magic force of his own will. But the fountain of red was all lit up now from the inside, just like teeny spotlights were playing on it—and he made it grow wider until part of it covered the side of his nose. Then he sort of sighed with his mouth opening just like a Walleyed Pike and he started to carefully put his head right down on the table-top next to me, in the middle of all the bottles of beer.

Throb. The beer bottles parted, smoothly and quietly tumbling without a sound; some of them giving off little foamy spurts of amber and creating neat little rivers on top of the oilcloth.

I looked at the rivers and followed their course, pretending that I was swimming in them through the red and white checks. It was easy: the foam carried me right along.

He was a big man, but now, just a little bit at a time, he grew smaller and smaller until I could just see the very top of his head. His hair was thin on top and his scalp was pretty dirty.

And then he did the final part of his trick: he vanished. *Throb.* And the only thing left was a little red road map smeared across the top of the table, pointing a trail to where he had sunk out of sight.

"You all right, Stroker?"

Hazy focus: "I'm fine. Where are the cigarettes?"

"In your hand."

"Hey, Stroker! How you?"

"Hey . . . uhhh, Demon. How you?"

"Those dumb buggers didn't close the gas cap and his car caught fire. You hear?"

"Busted his . . . look at the cast there."

"Hey, yer sittin' on Stroker's cast again. Go get another chair, he's got to have his leg propped up."

"No, wait. Here I'll put his leg up here on the table, all right?"

Throb. Where's Grace with the beer?

"Get that sumbitch out from under the table and throw him out, will you?"

"Jesus! What happened to this guy?"

"Now, how in hell would *I* know? He just came staggering over here and did a full face-down in amongst the bottles of beer here, tha's all. Grace! You got something I can wipe this blood off with?"

Throb!

"Strokie-babe. My poor baby."

Focus: it was Shirley Cleavage. Her nipples were apostrophes hidden inside the white nylon.

"Your leg hurt?"

"It's *ticking*. Can you hear it tick?"

"Well, for one thing, you got the *wrong* leg up on the top of the table. Where's your other leg? The *hurt* one?"

"Uhhh. Oh, here it is. See, right here. Look, some guy is lying down on my leg under the table."

"More beer?"

"Hey, Grace, where you been? Here, put it right down here. Wait: help me get Stroker's other leg up on the table."

"You've got nice thighs."

"Me? Where's my blanket?"

"They're carrying some big guy out in it. He hit his head on something. Hell of a cut on his head."

"Well, he wanted the blanket anyway. Anybody got a light?"

"Strokie-babe, you're all flushed. Damn, he's got a *fever*, you guys. Here, feel his head."

"Gravel Under My Fenders."

"Come on. We gotta go."

"Hey, Stroker, where's yer pants?"

Throb. And focus: Charlie was doing a ballet, an easy, quiet half-turn in the air with both hands out and his fingers all spread out like exclamation points. And then one hand dipped down just as he was completing the full swirl and when he came out of it, swinging around slowly, he had a *man* in his hand. It was nifty and graceful and I studied it through the smoke.

Throb. Charlie and the man did a half-step, except that the man's feet weren't touching the floor at all. That's because Charlie had him all gathered up right under his nose. And they spoke their lines clearly so I could hear:

"Were . . . you . . . speaking . . . about . . . Mister . . . Ace's . . . pants?" Pause. "Shithead?"

Answer: "No . . . sir . . . not . . . me . . . uh, uh . . . no . . . sir."

And Charlie gave him a little, slow twirl like they were jitterbugging and the man swirled off into the smoke until I couldn't see him any more at all.

Throb.

"I'm hungry."

"You hungry, Stroke?"

"I want a White Castle New England boiled dinner–burger."

We were tooling along in the rain and the tires were zinging. "You feeling any better?" Demon said.

His real name is Dennis Manley Daniels and he used to steal cars for a living until he got into stock car racing. And he had sense enough to know that a name like Dennis just wouldn't do. So he had changed it to D. Manley Daniels and then, after he had won his first Super-speedway race, some newspaperman had called him Demon Daniels. And that was that.

Demon is not all that far behind me in points for the championship, mostly because he drives the entire circuit and I don't. He figures to knock me over this season, which is two things. One: a lot of shit. And two: impossible.

"Where are we?" I said.

"Charlotte coming up. How's yer leg?"

It felt a hell of a lot better. I had spent two days in the Speedway Motel: one sleeping and one throwing up. And then Demon had come by and told me that he had been in the party at the White Front and that I had promised to drive down to Atlanta with him. "Besides, you need the rest anyway," he had said.

"Rest? Chrissakes, the way you drive I could get more *rest* walking down there on this cast."

But what the hell. My helmet and gearbag with the driving uniforms were in the trunk and I was resting easy in a goddam baby-blue seventy-six-dollar cashmere pullover and one very soft Gucci loafer with the gold snaffle bit on top.

And Demon was hauling right down the outside lane on his new Goodyear iron-belted radials or whatever the hell they were, and his monster goddam Chrysler New Yorker was undulating softly up and down like a killer whale masturbating in the Gulf Stream. And Demon had a bunch of stereo speakers all over the car, probably even under the seats, and we were playing Thwacker Martin's "Busted Gearbox Blues" on the tape deck, and we had two Stroker Fast Packs on the front seat between us and I was eating fried chicken drumsticks and throwing the bones out the little vent window on my side. The good life.

Demon was going to drive all the way because—even with his one big brake pedal that went practically the whole width of the car and his goddam automatic throttle—you could set for ninety-five and crawl into the back seat if you wanted to—I didn't feel like doing anything.

"You ate all the drumsticks," he said, fishing around in the boxes.

"Don't bitch to me, for chrissakes, talk to Clyde Torkle; he's the one who tells 'em what to pack in these here kits."

"And you mean to tell me he's paying you a whole bunch of money to put yer face on these boxes of chicken?"

"Uh-huh. A bunch. You see the billboards yet?"

"*See* 'em? Chrissakes, I can't even get out of bed of a morning and look out the window, but I don't see yer goddam ugly face on a billboard somewheres. Pole Position Chicken, my ass."

"Uh-huh. Well, how about Atlanta, asshole?"

He shrugged grandly, lifting his hands off the wheel for a second. "Atlanta? Lissen: I'll have you so far back in the fucking pack that you prolly won't even get in the goddam *race*."

"How far back?"

Demon turned and looked at me. "All right, then. All right. So I *heard* about yer hot new car awreddy. But I got a bulletin for you: I'll suck the doors off that sumbitch and I ain't just whistlin'."

"Look: You want to go for the pole or don't you?"

"All right: FIVE HUNNERT!" he shouted. "You sumbitch, five hunnert dollars says I beat your ass out of the pole."

"That's more like it. Now, here's a drumstick. You better enjoy that bugger because it's going to be the most expensive piece of chicken you ever ate."

Still, there was the ankle to consider. Maybe I could get Lugs to design a hinge for it, right at the ankle bone.

And there was Demon to consider: he was about as wild-assed as any driver on the circuit and he got a little bit better every year. And they loved him in Atlanta, God knows.

Well, for one thing, Demon held the all-time record for driving through downtown Atlanta and he was the only driver on the circuit ever to be banned from driving in the city for *life*, in any kind of machine, including golf carts and wheelchairs. And for two more things, he had received the only $500 traffic ticket ever issued in Georgia. And before that, he had gotten the only $400 traffic ticket. It wasn't easy.

Old Demon had worked up a head of steam just somewhere outside of Bismarck, North Dakota, for chrissakes, and he had hit I-75 going full-bore right through Atlanta. Every police cruiser in town had had a run at him and they had him figured at 140 miles an hour. So they had radioed ahead—way the hell ahead—and they had set up a roadblock. And then they had set up a series of cars with flashers on them to get him slowed down safely ahead of time and, finally, they had set up big floodlights on the road. And Demon had come purring right up to a stop, his stereo tape deck blaring.

"It's me," he said. And when the lieutenant opened the door, Demon sort of spilled right out into the street, not a bone in his body.

So they hauled him up and steered him away towards the Black Maria, between two big cops.

"What's a matter with you?" they said.

And Demon shrugged. "Well," he said. "I hadda couple of drinks, see, and I was trying to hurry back to the motel before I had an accident."

And then: about halfway back into town, the paddy wagon gave a couple of coughs and stopped dead, right in the middle of the Interstate. And one of the officers had climbed out and spent a lot of time looking under the hood and shaking his head. And finally he had come around and opened the doors and looked in at Demon.

"Awright," he said. "Yer a goddam race driver. Come on out here and tell me what's wrong with this here engine so's we can get going."

"Shertainly," Demon said. And he had fallen out into the street again and then, finally, lurched around and looked under the hood.

"Well?" the cop said.

"Ah-hah!" Demon said. "Here's yer problem right here." And he reached in and wrapped one hand around the ignition wiring harness and snatched it right off. Wiring, distributor cap, and coil all came up. And then Demon wound up and threw it all off into the darkness. "There," he said. "It's fixed."

Then he reached in and snatched all the wiring out of the two-way radio. And he was going for the air cleaner when they finally got him stopped.

That was the $400 ticket and Demon got a real nice write-up in the *Constitution*. And when his sponsors finally found him and got him back to the track, every red-neck in the crowd gave him a standing ovation.

Next time: they caught him going through town in the *other* direction in a bad-ass Avis rental car with both back doors open and beer cans falling out about every five yards or so.

And *this* time they called for the police cruiser with the prisoner setup in back. That is, it had a regular back seat, all right, but it also had this thick wire-mesh screen between the back seat and front seat where the policemen sat. And they sort of dumped him in there and locked the doors and then the two officers got in and drove off.

Demon sat there just as peaceful as could be. Then, after about ten blocks or so, he spoke up.

"Hey, there," he said.

They were so mad that they wouldn't even look back at him.

"Hey, there," he said. "How's about stopping so's I can take a leak?"

They ignored him.

"Hey, there," he said. "Lissen: I *really* gotta pee. I'm so goddam full of beer you'll never believe it. You gotta stop and lemme *whiz*, you guys."

One of them spoke without turning his head.

"No way," he said. "Yer going straight to jail."

Demon was pretty quiet for about three more blocks. And then he slowly got up on his knees on the back seat, facing the front of the car. And he unzipped his fly and he whipped it out.

"Hey, there," he said.

And he pissed right through the thick wire-mesh screen, all over both cops. That was the $500 ticket.

Demon says about the only thing he could remember about it was the scene in the station house when they were booking him. The desk sergeant had turned to one of the cops.

"Don't stand so close to the radiator, y'all," he had told him.

"Gotta stop in at Charlotte," Demon said. "Old Sam Bisby's race driving school. After I win Atlanta I'm gonna teach driving there between races. And . . . uhh, and . . ."— he glanced over at me—"and, uhh, lecture."

"What?"

"Now, come *on*, don't give me no nonsense. I'm gonna show those guys how to drive and then, well, lecture them on the techniques. You know."

I let him have that one. Those were going to be some fine lectures. Besides, Sam had already asked me about teaching and we had determined right away that he couldn't afford me.

We wheeled in at the Charlotte Speedway and one of the classes was going on and there was a pretty good size group of kids clustered around the pit wall. They all had their eyes good and wide open.

The reason was that Sam Bisby and Caleb Powell were out on the track in a brace of race cars, going very goddam fast, it seemed to me. No messing around.

And down at the other end of the pits, Hank Lewers, Sam's other assistant teacher, was strapping on a helmet while standing beside a pale green stock Dodge Charger. Demon eased the big Chrysler up and flicked down the electric window.

"Hey, Louie."

He came over and bent down and looked in at us. "Hey, Demon. How you, Stroke? I hear you busted your ass up at Terre Haute."

"Leg."

He shrugged, snapping up the helmet. "You okay for Atlanta and all?"

"I suppose. Right before the physical I'm gonna saw off this cast and tape myself right up to the balls."

He nodded.

"What you doing?" Demon said.

Louie looked out on the track. "Well, I'll tell you. Those two clowns ain't coming in, so I'm gonna take this here Hertz car and go out and chase them around a little bit. You know."

We knew all right: Hank Lewers is maybe the Number Two stock car driver in the world, present company included (which makes Demon Number Three), and he is not one to stand around when there is racing to be done.

So he popped that rascal and slewed out on the track after them. And right away, all the students could see that he was having trouble holding the Hertz car in the corners. Those skinny street tires smoked and the Aunt Nellie suspension mushed the coupe around in the groove. But he stayed right on it and, sure enough, when they came out of the Nurnber Two, he was running right between Sam and Caleb.

They both acted a little surprised to see him there. So both of them pushed the loud button a little bit harder and left Louie for a minute. And here he came again, shagging along after them.

The students loved it.

Louie caught them one more time, driving on more or less sheer guts, just as they were going into the Four Turn.

And then: Sam drove down in front of Louie and Caleb came drifting up from the low groove. Pow! Both cars caught the little Charger broadside and parts flew off like someone shaking a Christmas tree.

Poor Irving Hertz. But Louie stayed right on it—his shoulders all hunched up, no doubt—and the three cars came right on out of the turn strictly welded together. And that's the way they came down the chute, everybody waiting for everybody else to get off the damn gas.

Man, the students were laughing and howling and hitting each other on the arms a lot. Some classroom.

One of the students was a girl, no mistaking that, driving coveralls and all, and she was clearly impressed with old Sam, who once was the best in the business before he burned out. And she sidled up to him while he was explaining what just happened, with his gray old curls tumbling over his head.

"Any questions?" he said.

"Yes," the girl said. "Do you smoke cigars when you race?"

Sam said: "No, but I will."

* * *

It was quarter past ten when we got to the Kings Inn Motel in Atlanta, with Demon wearing some sort of innocent look on his face in case we passed any patrol cars.

I picked up all my mail and my laundry from the last trip: I have letters and dirty underwear at every motel along the NASCAR and USAC circuit. Sometimes it takes a whole season to get everything together.

I had:

—a check from Clyde Torkle for $7500. Expenses.
—a check from Fire Injection Carburetion Systems for $6000. Quarterly pay.
—a bill from the Holiday Inn in Milwaukee for $615.27 in damages. We had had a pretty good party there.
—a telegram from Lugs Harvey: ARRIVE WEDNESDAY. REST AND STAY AWAY FROM GREEK FOOD. AND NURSES. STOP.

Hell, telegrams don't say "stop" any more.
Do they?
"Stroker," the desk clerk said. He was half-leaning over the counter and whispering.
"Mmmm?"
He nodded towards the lobby. "There's a lady waiting over there for you. Brunette. Big jugs. You know."
And there she was: all tall and willowy, dark hair floating down over her shoulders, moving towards me with her gently shaking breasts plowing the way ahead—the silk and lace Greek.
Let's hear it out there for white underwear.
"Stroker! How are you . . . how's your leg?"
"Mmmmm, I think we better go and take a look at it right now."
Demon was standing there, kind of stunned, looking first at me and then at Nurse Polinos and then at her knockers and then back at me. Finally he took a deep breath.
"Hey, lady," he said. "I'm Demon Daniels."
She pulled her face out of the hollow of my neck for just one second and looked at him.
"Good for you," she said. And then she started kissing me again.
I nodded at Demon. "Boy, when you get a chance, drop my bags off at my room. That's a good fellow."

DAN GERBER

Out of Control!

Everything worked. He was driving to win and nothing could intrude. He had a feeling he was slightly out of control, never absolutely sure the car wouldn't fly off the road at each corner or soar at the crest of each hill. He'd had a nightmare in which the car became an airplane and he had no way to land it, exhilaration going up and terror knowing he must come down. The forces on his body were like movements in a dance danced in a space no larger than his body so it became more a dance of the mind, the road rushing into his car, the dips and bends and rises, the vibrations from the engine behind him, choreography for his toes in asbestos ballet slippers and the quick slight movements of his hands from the wheel to the shift lever and back.

The scream of the engine was behind him, pushing him as if he were trying to escape it. He imagined the twisting force, the flywheels and gears trying to drill through the firewall into the small of his back. He was more aware of vibration than sound. The fuel vapor rose from his injector stacks where the engine sucked in the air and shot it out the exhaust pipes as sound. But now it was all one, movement, vibration, sound, and the smell of heat on brake pads, rubber, and oil. The sign from his pit told him there was no one ahead and twelve seconds of vacuum behind. Three laps to go. In plain English this meant that if the car held together he'd won the race.

He didn't have a sense of it being a race anymore; he was simply trying to hold the car together, watching the oil pressure dial he'd ignored during most of the race and listening for the engine to falter. He silently apologized to the car for the abuse he'd given it and begged it not to die. He passed slower cars. He passed the pits again. Two laps to go. He braked for the left-hand bend and downshifted for the carousel right that followed. He feathered the car through the carousel and fed the accelerator on the way out. The long straight began to rush up on him. It was like driving into a green funnel. He spotted a red jacket and knew it was Frank. The red jacket was gone now and he set up for the bend in the straight.

It was the most perilous spot on the course, an almost imperceptible crick in the long straight when you passed over it slowly, but at 163 miles per hour it became a thrill. He had to place the car on the right-hand edge of the asphalt and let it drift to the left, hoping that he ran out of bend before he ran out of road. Each year the cars went a little faster and each year each driver had to find out for himself if the bend could still be taken without letting up on the gas. It could. But each time he took it, the bend was an adventure. Would there be oil on the road, would the tar be soft? The car weighed seven pounds when it got to the bend. Seven pounds distributed to four patches of rubber about a foot square each. He didn't like to think about that. He couldn't think about that when he drove. He watched the road slide from left to right under the silver of his car. He watched the green rush by and the specks of color that were the spectators. He picked his spot to shut off for the tight right-hander and anticipated the bumps in the asphalt that would make the car jump as he braked.

It seemed as if all the cars were driving themselves because the drivers were barely visible, a plastic or metallic-looking bubble of helmet protruding from the sleek wedge of the car, most of them a distinctive color or design contrasting with the body of the car; and then Roger's helmet passed, a deep metallic blue, looking really more black than blue above the silver body of the car; and nothing but the color and his name on the side of the car which he knew was there but couldn't read as the car hissed by in its pocket of air followed by the scream of exhaust as if the twin megaphone exhaust pipes were actual megaphones through which the engine was begging to be left alone. It seemed to be always on the edge of exploding, and when he had looked at it in the garage and listened to the mechanics warming it up and checking the timing he regarded it more as a bomb than a vehicle and wanted to stand clear in case it should explode and fill the air with shrapnel. The red blur on the side of the car that was Roger's name against the silver blur that was the car itself and the furtive helmet that was Roger were now gone, leaving only the scream from the black void of the megaphones rising and falling, rising and falling like a baby alternately screaming in a tantrum and pausing to catch its breath, then the steady rising pitch as he picked his apex and accelerated through the unseen corner and into the unseen straight, then lost in the sound of the other engines and erased by the cars now passing the spot where he stood.

The cars were spread out so that it seemed there was really no race, simply an undetermined number of cars amusing themselves with speed and sound, as if hurtling their unseen drivers past the crowd in an attempt to disguise them, to smuggle them past without notice as a child might scream about pain or injustice to obscure the fact that he was stealing cookies. It somehow wasn't Roger in that car, at least not the same man he had seen that morning absorbed in his own thoughts, whatever thoughts he might have before becoming anonymous in silver plastic and traffic and the stew of sound punctuated by the mention of his name from a loudspeaker as if it were the only word he could recognize in a foreign tongue, the same Roger who had eaten a rare steak and salad and drunk over half a bottle of wine the night before and overtipped the waitress because she was pretty and certainly not the same Roger who read T. S. Eliot aloud to no one who wanted to hear it and drank straight tequila when he drank it at all, which wasn't very often, and had actually claimed he didn't want to screw his fiancée until after they were married. And suddenly it was quiet as if everything in the world had been switched off except the katydids or crickets or whatever kind of bugs that hum on a summer afternoon, now overcast and looking as if it might rain, the grass and trees a deeper green against the gray sky, dense and still and the crackle of the loudspeaker and the sound of engines sounding like toys passing the officials' pagoda where the announcer stood. Maybe it was Roger's car he was hearing through the speaker like a sound effect on a radio drama he remembered as a child or a Memorial Day broadcast of the Indianapolis 500 he'd heard years ago while driving to a beach on Lake Michigan.

The man was standing on the apron of the track in front of the pit wall. He was a small man in a lavender suit. He seemed contemptuous of the cars passing a few feet from the crease in his trousers. He chewed an unlighted cigar and held a long stick in his hands. There was a piece of cheap muslin, dyed black and white, stapled to the stick and furled around it. He was looking down the track in the direction from which the cars were coming, watching for a silver car with the number 7 on the nose. Actually the car was so low that he wouldn't be able to see the number on the wedge-shaped nose from the level of the track, but the men in the tower would be able to see it and would announce it over the public address system. The man on the track would see a thin silver wedge with a dark blue helmet growing out of it. He unfurled the flag and held the loose end of it in his left hand. He began shaking the stick, still holding on to the loose end, a quick up and down motion, a motion of excitement. He was about to perform. Now he could see the silver car. It appeared out of a mirage, vague and shimmering at first, then distinct, then it was past him and he felt the vibrations in the ground beneath his feet. He continued to wave the flag and to leap into the air again and again. To the spectators he looked like a Milanese flag dancer. To Roger he looked like a blur of black and white that meant he could slow down, that meant he didn't have to listen to the engine anymore, that it didn't matter if it faltered now, that meant he'd won the biggest race of his life.

He'd won many races in the seven years he'd been driving, but never a Can-Am. The win would open a lot of doors for him. His picture would be in all the newspapers and magazines that regularly covered racing and he'd appear in advertisements endorsing tires, oil, brake pads, spark plugs, gasoline, and maybe even a certain brand of sport shirt. Years ago racing drivers had endorsed hair tonic, but not many drivers used hair tonic anymore. When his helmet was off, Roger's dark hair hung almost to his shoulders. He couldn't imagine himself endorsing shampoo.

Now the man with the black and white checkered flag was behind him. Roger let off on the gas and coasted the remainder of the straightaway. He lifted his right hand from the steering wheel and waved to the spectators and corner workers who cheered back. Roger couldn't hear the cheers, he could only hear the engine popping and sputtering as it loafed through the carousel and began to smooth out as he picked up speed down the back straight.

He cut the engine and coasted to a stop at the startfinish line. Sam Dandy, his mechanic (everybody kidded him about his name), was waiting there, so was Walter Ellison, the car owner, a flock of photographers and race officials, and the man in the purple suit, who was the first to congratulate him and handed him the checkered flag. Roger pulled off his helmet and the flameproof balaclava he wore under it and accepted a paper cup of tepid water from Sam Dandy.

"God damn, boss-man, you did it. You sure as hell did it," Sam said. He said it again and again. Sam Dandy was from South Carolina. Walter Ellison came over and shook his hand, then turned and shook Sam Dandy's hand. Walter Ellison was happy. His car had won an important race and the Armstrong Tobacco Company would be happy because they sponsored the car, which carried advertising for Sylvan Cigarettes, and photographs of the car with their advertising would be in all those magazines and on the 11:00 P.M. sports roundup on all those television stations. Walter Ellison bent down and said something to Roger, but Roger couldn't hear what it was. He was looking for a face he couldn't find. He motioned to Sam and Sam bent down to him. "Carrie?" he shouted in Sam's ear.

"I haven't seen her, boss-man."

Carrie was Roger's wife. He'd left her at the motel that morning. She didn't come to the races anymore; at least she was never there for the start of the race, not since Roger's accident. She'd seen Roger's car stall on the grid at the start of a race several years before. There was always a lot of dust and smoke at the start, and always a lot of confusion. She'd seen one of the cars from the back of the grid crash into Roger's car and seen both cars explode into flames. Roger got out with a whiplash neck and a few minor burns, but the man in the car that had hit him died. The safety crew got to him quickly and put out the fire, but he'd inhaled the flames and there was nothing they could do for him. His body wouldn't hold water. They'd taken him to a hospital and kept him alive for three days, but they knew they couldn't save him. He was in the room next to Roger's when he died and his wife and his father were there. After that Carrie never came to the track until after the race had started. Usually she never came at all.

Not easy, God and Big Business and certainly Albert Russel Erskine know. Not with mobs of shiftless and ignorant factory manpower bent on sabotaging the Divine Plan, not to mention the annual profits. Melancholy is the president, at least more melancholy than normal, as, Wackford Squeers–like, he recounts the failings of his charges down in Dotheboys Hall, and reviews the measures—firings, mostly—that God and Big Business both prescribe for their humble servant Erskine to administer by way of remedy.

The joyless Erskine creed is uncannily reflected, picture after picture, in the photographs that punctuate his words. Empty assembly halls. Untended machinery. The factory kitchen. The factory dispensary. Studebaker's far-flung showrooms and offices worldwide, looking recently evacuated. There are one or two full-page views of Studebaker company blowouts in rented banquet halls and hotel ballrooms— panoramic surveys of hundreds of full-faced Babbitts in celebration assembled. Every one of them is looking at the camera, and every one is wearing a funny hat. And not one of them is smiling.

I think Albert Russel Erskine would have liked that.

KEN PURDY

The Bugatti

Ettore Bugatti was an Italian who lived his life in France among Frenchmen, and he was, they said, *un type*, or as we say, a character, an exotic, one of a kind, greatly gifted, proud, unswervingly independent, indifferent to any opinion but his own, amused, aristocratic, impractical, profligate, a connoisseur, a gourmet, a *bon vivant*.

He died in 1947 after sixty-six years of life full of frenzy and creation. There are many photographs of him. He is in one of his racing cars in 1925, his two sons crowded into the cockpit with him, one fourteen, one three, Bugatti is smiling at the photographer and waving, his hand gloved in what looks to be immaculate chamois. Another, he is sitting, six feet off the ground, in a car he built for the Paris–Madrid race of 1903. Another, he is wearing goggles and a helmet. The helmet is odd looking. M. Bugatti has been amusing himself. He has taken a knife or a scissors to the brim of a bowler, and made a helmet of it. He didn't cut it all off: he made a neat little bill in front, to shade his eyes. Another, he is twenty-five or so, and apparently about to go riding. He's wearing a cap, a flaring short coat, pipestem breeches he must have put on barefoot, a hard collar four inches high, on his left wrist a watch and a massive bracelet showing under an inch of cuff, altogether a figure of shattering elegance and *sang-froid*.

THE BUGATTI

Bugatti made about fifty different models of automobile. One that he liked particularly was the Type 46. It wasn't his most inspired design, and nagging little things often went wrong with it. A Parisian brought his 46 back to the factory time after time. One day M. Bugatti, *Le Patron* as he was known in deference, came upon the fellow in a corridor.

You, *monsieur*, I think," he said, "are the one who has brought his Type 46 back three times?"

The man admitted it, full of hope.

Bugatti stared at him. "Do not," he said, "let it happen again."

King Zog of Albania, visiting in France, wanted to buy a Bugatti Royale, a ducal motor carriage priced at $20,000—for the bare chassis. The body came separately and expensively. Bugatti did not care to sell a Royale, a Type 41, to anyone who merely happened to have $30,000 or so, even if he was a reigning monarch. The aspirant customer was always invited to spend a little time at the Bugatti château in Molsheim, in Alsace, so that *Le Patron* might, covertly, estimate his character. Zog came, saw, was seen, and heard, in due course, that there was not, alas, a Royale available, nor could one say, unfortunately, when the factory would be able to make one.

"Never!" Bugatti told one of his assistants. "The man's table manners are beyond belief!"

"My dear fellow," Bugatti told a customer who complained that his car was hard to start in cold weather, "if you can afford a Type 55 Bugatti, surely you can afford a heated garage!"

Ettore Bugatti had earned the right to be arrogant. The Type 55 might not start first push on a January morning, but it was the fastest two-seater on the world market in 1932, and the most beautiful, and while its 115 miles an hour is no great figure today, half-a-lifetime later, it's not slow, and its fender line is still the loveliest ever put on a motorcar. No one else ever attempted anything like the mammoth Royale, its dashboard fittings of solid ivory, a Jaeger stopwatch in the center of the steering wheel, where men of lesser imagination put a horn button.

Bugatti's Type 35 Grand Prix car appeared in 1924. In 1925 and 1926 it won the incredible number of 1045 races. In 1936 a Type 57S ran 135.42 miles in sixty minutes, and it was twenty years before any other stock passenger car went faster. And then there's the Type 50, and the 44, the 37, the 51, the 57SC . . . there have been 4000 makes of automobiles, and of them all, is the Bugatti the most intriguing, the most enchanting, the farthest ahead of its time in its own day, and the most venerated now? Very probably.

Enter the devotees:

The man whose notepaper carries, not his name or his monogram, but the scarlet oval Bugatti radiator badge, engraved in miniature.

The man who wears the Bugatti Owners Club tie seven days a week.

The man who was suddenly presented, in 1957, with an opportunity to buy a brand-new Type 46, miraculously preserved through World War II, seventy-five kilometers on the odometer. The only way he could raise the money was to sell his house, so he promptly sold his house.

The young lady of Paris, whose boyfriend swore he'd go out of his mind if he didn't have a Bugatti. The year was 1934, and money was tight. Her father had it, though, and in cash. She killed him, took it, and bought the car. Her name was Violette.

It's just a car, surely?

No, it isn't, in the sense that it is very like other cars. The Bugatti was so unlike most other cars of its day as to become, almost, a different kind of object. This is true almost in equal measure of the Ferrari today. It's no use trying to convey to a man who has been driving a new Cadillac for six months the experience of driving a 250GT Ferrari. He won't understand because he doesn't have the frame of reference. Even people who did have the frame of reference were startled by exposure to some Bugattis, as Mr. C. W. P. Hampton, a British connoisseur, writing in 1937:

"I had a trial run up the Barnet bypass with Williams, the Bugatti works demonstrator, who had brought over a Type 57S electron coupe Atlantic. It was simply terrific: 112 mph still accelerating over the crossroads past the Barn—and the roads cluttering up with usual Friday evening traffic. Along the next stretch we did 122 mph, and I thought, under the circumstances, that was enough . . . thereafter we cruised along at a mere 90–95 mph, once doing just over 100 in third gear . . . the speed constantly maintained was prodigious . . . along almost every yard of the crowded thoroughfare. . . ."

("Williams" was never called anything else during the years he spent with Bugatti as a demonstrator and a team-driver. No one knew anything about him except that he was young, British, seemed to have spent all his life in France and could pass as French. When World War II broke out he dropped into the Resistance, worked successfully for a long time, then disappeared at the hands of the Germans. It is now known that his name was William Grover and that he held the rank of captain in a branch of the British armed forces, presumably Intelligence.)

The truly creative make their own worlds and populate them with people of their own choosing. Ettore Bugatti did that, and most of the people around him were, like "Williams," anything but ordinary.

THE BUGATTI

Says René Dreyfus, champion of France and Bugatti team-driver in the 1930s, "It was easy to believe, in those golden years, that we were not living in France at all, but in a little enclave, a little duchy, Molsheim, quite independent . . ."

Bugatti came to Molsheim, now the department of Bas-Rhin, then in Alsace-Lorraine, in 1906. Thereafter he worked in France, and thought of himself as French to the bone—he called his Italian birth "that accident"—but he did not take French citizenship until the year he died. He had been born in Milan, in 1881, son of one artist, Carlo, brother of another, Rembrandt. He first intended to be an artist as well, but he judged his brother's talent superior to his own, and it was not in Bugatti's nature willingly to be second to anybody in anything. Bugatti was apprenticed to the firm of Prinetti & Stucchi of Milan, and in 1898 he built a motor vehicle of his own, and raced it, probably a modification of a Prinetti & Stucchi motor tricycle. In the same year he made a four-wheel car from the ground up, and then another, which won an award given by the Automobile Club of France and a gold medal at an international exhibition in Milan in 1901.

Bugatti's gold-medal car so impressed the French firm of De Dietrich that they hired him as a designer. He was still a minor, so his father had to sign the contract in his stead. For the next few years Bugatti designed for De Dietrich, for Mathis, for Deutz, for Isotta-Fraschini, and, later, for Peugeot. While he was working for Deutz, in Cologne, Bugatti designed and built, in the basement of his home, the small car which he called the Type 13. He left Deutz in 1909 and on Christmas of that year he came to Molsheim, with Ernest Friderich, a mechanic who had been his friend and associate since 1904. He rented an abandoned dye works, Friderich installed the machinery and staffed the place, and in that year five cars were made. By 1911 there were sixty-five employees, and Friderich, driving a tiny 1.4-liter Bugatti, won his class in the Grand Prix du Mans and was second overall, just behind a mammoth 6-liter Fiat. The disparity in size between the two cars made the victory most impressive, and Bugatti was famous from that day onward. His cars were to win so many races, rallies, sprints, hill climbs that no one now remembers them in their thousands, but this was the first one and it mattered the most.

Fantastically, Bugattis are *still* winning races, although the last of *Le Patron's* own designs was built in 1939. Of course, twenty-year-old cars can't compete with brand-new ones, but there are many races for old cars today. For instance, the famous circuit at Bridgehampton on Long Island schedules such an event every year. There were seven Bugattis entered in the last Bridgehampton, among many other makes contemporary with them. They completely dominated the event, coming in first, second, third, and fourth. Indeed, when the winning Bugatti, D. H. Mallalien's Type

51 Grand Prix car, came down the straight, the very first time around, there was nothing else in sight behind it.

In July 1961, Mickey Thompson, who has driven faster than anyone else living today, broke six international records in a series of runs at March Air Force Base. One of them was a mile record that had stood for thirty-one years. It had been made by a Bugatti.

When World War I broke out in 1914 Rugatti had to leave Alsace, of course. He designed a straight-8 aircraft engine which was built in France and in the United States, under license, by Duesenberg. The Duesenberg engine, heart of the most luxurious automobile we have made, was clearly derivative from this Bugatti design. Bugatti was interested in airplanes, as he was in everything that moved by mechanical means. He built at least one airplane, and Roland Garros, one of the great French aces of World War I, was his close friend, indeed he named his second son for Garros. Garros was a pioneer in development of the machine-gun synchronizer which allowed firing through the propeller arc.

(The first American soldier to die in line of duty in World War I was an aircraft mechanic, part of a crew sent to France to assay Bugatti's airplane engine. The man stepped into the propeller while the engine was running on a test bed, *hélas!*)

After the war had been won, Bugatti went back to Molsheim and settled into a pattern of life extraordinary for an industrialist, indeed extraordinary for anyone. Ettore Bugatti made a small world for himself, and he lived at the peak and center of it. It was a world of many parts, which he arranged to fit neatly together. There was the factory, first. It was a model factory. The cleanliness of the place was startling. Bugatti bought soap and scouring powders and cleaning rags in such quantity that his accountant swore the firm was supplying every home in Molsheim.

"It doesn't matter," Bugatti would say. "Things must be kept clean, very clean."

He probably did come near to employing someone from every family in Molsheim, when the payroll ran 1000 individuals. Out of 3000 families he knew a great many of these individuals by name. Indeed, for a long time he knew by name every man who worked for him, and thus could deliver compliment or reprimand with proper force. He was severe with people who mistreated tools. Every machine tool in the place, vise, lathe, shaper, whatever, was polished and engine-turned, like the inside of a cigarette case, and *Le Patron*'s choler would spiral at the sight of a hammer scar or file mark on one of them.

He toured the factory on a bicycle or in an electric cart, both of his own design and manufacture. The French, among whom he lived, and the Italians, among whom he was born, prided themselves on their production of the world's lightest and finest bicycles, but Bugatti thought them all heavy and graceless, and so made his own. When he made his morning tour of the establishment he would often be in riding habit. His stables were extensive, and he had a covered riding hall. (The graceful lines of the Bugatti radiator, the most beautiful ever put on an automobile, are thought by some to derive from the horseshoe.)

He alone carried the master key that opened all the doors of the factory, all identical doors of brass-bound varnished oak.

There was one formal title on the Bugatti table of organization, and that was Bugatti's own. His subordinates had no titles. One man was in charge of purchase, another was chief accountant, another was head of the racing department, and so on, but no one had a title. M. Bugatti was chief and the rest were little French Indians. Such a system will work under one condition: the chief must be able to command devotion by reason of innate dignity, ability, force of personality, *not* merely by the fact of his being boss. This Ettore Bugatti could do. The soaring range of the man's imagination, his power of creativity, his sheer *drive* were clearly evident.

The Bugatti château was a stone's throw from the factory, and between these two places were the rest of the units that made up the establishment: the stables, the riding hall, the kennels housing thirty or forty fox terriers, the dovecots; the museum for the works in sculpture of Rembrandt Bugatti, and the museum housing historic horse-drawn carriages; the distillery in which Bugatti produced his own liqueurs, the powerhouse in which his own electricity was made. Farther away, but still definitely a part of the establishment, Bugatti's hotel, Le Hostellerie du Pur Sang, where clients of the house would find food, drink, and lodging fit for the gentry, and where one's standing with *Le Patron* could be gauged: some clients were given bills on departure, some were not, and some bills were more than others.

Each of these buildings reflected M. Bugatti's iron-hard view of the properties. The powerhouse, for example . . . Living as he did, Bugatti did not always have a great deal of cash on hand. He was not, after all, Henry Ford. His lifetime production of automobiles was a week's work for a Detroit assembly plant and not a big week's work, at that: 7500 cars. So his bills sometimes ran on. He shared the attitude of the Edwardian aristocrat: he considered reminder of indebtedness an affront. The Strasbourg utility company once made this *gaffe*. Bugatti paid the bill and simultaneously drew up plans for a powerhouse of his own. When it was completed, beautiful in white tile, mechanically *le dernier cri* in every way, he summoned the representative of the Strasbourg company and gave him a conducted tour. When he had finished he said, "So you see, *m'sieur*, I shall no longer have need of your firm's services." So saying, we must presume, he strode to the master board and pulled the main switch. Bugatti's life was full of such gestures. Indeed, his whole life was a gesture, a sweeping, magnificent gesture.

Even Bugatti's failures were notable. In 1922 he produced a team of round-bodied, tublike racing cars that were so ugly they were unreal. The next year he rolled out a team of motorcars notable only because they were uglier than the 1922s: they were slab-sided, slope-topped monstrosities of such short wheelbase that the back of the engine protruded into the cockpit, and they would not handle, besides being revolting to look upon. But in 1924 came the first of the Type 35s, then, and now, the most beautiful racing automobiles ever built, and, at least until the post–World War II Alfa Romeo and Ferrari machines came along, the most successful.

The Type 35s made Bugatti and it was of their time, and the time immediately following them, that René Dreyfus and others of the entourage think when they talk of the golden times. Every weekend during the season the little blue cars would leave Molsheim for a circuit in France or England or Italy or Germany or Spain, where they would probably win. On Monday or Tuesday they would be back, dusty and oil-stained, and the mechanics would tear them down and make them as new again. Meanwhile, the drivers, the aristocrats of the establishment, could amuse themselves as they pleased, eating well, drinking well in the company of pleasant people. Of course, there were times when there was no money, but in Molsheim one did not, if one were a driver, need money in order to live well, and if an imperative necessity *did* come up . . . René Dreyfus once wrote, in the magazine *Sports Cars Illustrated*,

"When I had not been paid for a while, and needed money, it would not occur to me to ask for it, and of course it would be unthinkable to approach M. Bugatti. If one were not paid, it meant only one thing: there *wasn't* any money just then. So I would go to see M. Pracht, the treasurer, and we would have a bright little conversation, moving around the subject for a while and then getting down to cases. In the course of the next day or two I would pick up a chassis, or two chassis, and take them to Robert Benoist, a former team-driver who had a Bugatti agency in Paris. I would sell them to Benoist and be in funds again.

"If M. Bugatti did not often reward his employees with money, he had other means. Like the head of any state, he instituted a supreme decoration, a sort of Bugatti Victoria Cross. This he conferred rarely, and it was much coveted: a wristwatch made by Mido to Bugatti's own design. It was very thin, very elegant, and the case was formed in the familiar horseshoe shape of the Bugatti radiator. When a driver had made a notable win against heavy odds he might be given a Bugatti wristwatch. Even a customer might be given one, if he were a notably *good* customer, say one who had bought eight or nine cars and made no complaint if some little thing went wrong with a couple of them. One was summoned to *Le Patron's* presence, perhaps in his château on the grounds, and there, with all due ceremony, the plushlined box would be presented. It was a great honor, and no one would have conceivably equated a watch from M. Bugatti's own hands with mere money."

Dreyfus tells, too, of a typical Bugatti *beau geste* which arose when he built his first *automotrice*, or rail car. He had conceived this idea when he found he had twenty-three huge 300-horsepower engines on hand, and the Depression of 1929 just getting under way. Why not make fast, self-powered railway cars? Why not, indeed? Bugatti ordered a big shed built on the factory grounds and began to draw up plans (the cars to have two engines, or four, to have speeds up to 120 miles an hour, running on rubber mounted wheels, and stopped by cable brakes; the chauffeur to sit, not in front, incongruous among the passengers, but in a little cupola on the roof, alone, undistracted, and with a proper view). But when the first *automotrice* was finished, it was evident that *Le Patron* had, as it were, made an oversight. The railway station was a mile distant, and there was no track. Indeed, M. Bugatti had not even had the *automotrice* built on track. It had been built on the floor. And it would by no means go through the gate in the wall that solidly surrounded the factory.

Bugatti was not disturbed. He spoke to one of his supervisors. "Knock down the wall, if you please," he said, "and ask eight or nine hundred of the men if they would be good enough to push the car down to the station for me tomorrow night."

It was done, the car riding on rollers so that the flanged wheels would not destroy the road, hundreds of men pushing, dozens carrying torches, the women bringing the wine. The *automotrices* were a great success. They really did run 120 miles an hour, their strange cable brakes did stop them, and the records they set—Strasbourg–Paris, Paris–Nice—stood for years after World War II.

They were Type 41 engines, made for the Royales, the kings' coaches. When the Depression came down on France, Bugatti had built only six Type 41s, his answer to the soft challenge of a British dowager at dinner: "Ah, M. Bugatti, everyone knows you build the greatest racing cars in the world, the best sports cars. But for a town carriage of real elegance, one must go to Rolls-Royce or Daimler, isn't that so?"

He went from dinner to the drawing board, the story goes, and laid down the first line then and there: a huge automobile, long as a London bus, seven feet from windshield to radiator cap, the engine running in nine individually water-cooled bearings, all working parts machined to zero tolerance, plus or minus nothing. Daimler, indeed!

Even at a ferocious $20,000 without a body, the Type 41 was in a seller's market, until the Depression broke, and certainly two or three of the most spectacular motorcars ever set on the road were 41s. There was a two-seater roadster, for example, a thing to dwarf every other roadster ever built. Bugatti himself used a *coupe de ville*, or *coupe Napoleon*, a tiny cabin for two, an open cockpit for chauffeur and footman, and all that engine out in front. He had as well a *berliner de voyage*, or double berline, looking something like two medieval coaches put together; there was a convertible with German coachwork, a straight limousine, a sedan, a touring car.

The Type 46 was a smaller version of the 41. It was usually offered as a sedan or a big coupe, but for that usage I think the Type 50, which has a detuned racing engine, double overhead cam, supercharged, and producing more than 200 horsepower, is to be preferred. A listing and description of all the Bugatti models is not for this place, but the most interesting, aside from the Royale and the children's racing car he built first for his son Roland and then in limited series for the get of the very rich, are Grand Prix cars, the various 35s, the intermediate 51, the Type 59, a 170–mph car with which Bugatti attempted single-handed to stem the tide of the Nazi-backed German race cars of the late 1930s, and the 185-mph 4.7-liter, the Brescia and "Brescia Modifie" cars of the early 1920s; among the passenger cars, the Types 40, 43, 44 (considered by J. Lemon Burton, an eminent British *Bugattiste*, to be one of the best of all), 50, 55, 57, 57C, 57S, 57SC.

Wide variation exists even in this truncated catalog. The 44 is supposed to have come about because Mme. Bugatti taxed her husband with the noisiness and harsh springing of his sports models. Accordingly he designed the 44 as a lady's car. A good one will do 80 miles an hour, it's reasonably quiet, starts easily, is pleasant to shift, and has the softest clutch I, at least, have ever laid foot to. The 43, on the other hand, is a detuned version of the racing 35B given, usually, an open four-seater body. It's a harsh, brutal, fast automobile. The 55 was race-bred, too, a Grand Prix Type 51 engine in a Type 54 chassis, while all the 57s were smooth passenger cars of varying speed capabilities up to 130 miles an hour, rare today, fantastic in the 1930s. Bugatti made something for everyone.

The history of the Bugatti is extensive, many tens of thousands of words have been published about it in many languages, and even the basic text, *The Buggatti Book*, runs to 375 pages. The Bugatti Owners Club, the oldest and biggest of the single-make clubs, has been publishing a magazine treating Bugatti matters for nearly a quarter of a century.

The BOC itself is unique if for no other reason than its possession of a seventeenth-century manor house as headquarters. This is Prescott, near Cheltenham in Gloucestershire, ninety miles from London. The house is a big one, built of Cotswold stone. It was, until 1871, the seat of the Earl of Ellenborough. The driveway leading up from the public road is more than a thousand yards long and has been made into one of the most famous hill-climb courses in the world. In 1949 a wrought-iron gate was installed in the garden wall at Prescott as a memorial to Ettore Bugatti and his son Jean. Jean, who showed signs of great brilliance as a designer, died in 1939, at twenty-seven, in avoiding a drunken postman who had come, on a bicycle, onto the Molsheim circuit. Bugatti came around a corner at high speed and elected to go off the road rather than hit the man. Ettore Bugatti died, in 1947, at the end of a victorious struggle to retain control of the factory in the upheaval of postwar France. Because he was still an Italian citizen during World War II, he had been able to bluff the German occupying authorities to a certain extent, but still he was technically an enemy alien when peace came. And there had been, even before the war, grave labor difficulties at Molsheim. During the war the Germans made torpedoes in the factory. The Canadians seized it from the Germans and burnt much of it in an accidental fire. The Americans took it over, hid away all the machine tools and equipment before the Battle of the Bulge—and lost the papers. Pierre Marco, one of Ettore Bugatti's oldest collaborators, traveled tens of thousands of miles through France, much of it in a creaking, charcoal-burning automobile, searching for the red-monogrammed Bugatti tools. He found most of them, too, took them back to Molsheim, rounded up many of the old workers, and put the factory back to work. At first he did anything. He would make stove lids if the price was right. Ultimately a few cars were produced, Type 101s, which were not really new, and in 1955 a racing car, the Type 251, again not really new, and a competitive failure. Today the factory is flourishing, making industrial and marine engines and so on, but no automobiles. Roland Bugatti survives, his sisters survive, the second Mme. Bugatti survives, but without Ettore Bugatti, nothing marches as before.

He was a man of parts. He was marked in many ways, by his determination to live like a duke, his belief that a mechanical device should be artistically beautiful as well as technically correct—he wouldn't employ a draftsman who couldn't draw in perspective, in the round—by his ability to project himself twenty years ahead of his time. He was imperious, stubborn, supremely creative—he died holding hundreds of patents covering such things as motors, fishing reels, sail rigs, Venetian blinds—and fallible. Some details on his cars were outrageously impractical: Bugatti water pumps, for example, are hard to lubricate and keep in service, and some, indeed most, of his engines are so complex that even experienced Bugatti mechanics must quote figures like $1500 as overhaul cost.

But, taken all in all, good with bad, his cars have magic. This is not to say that there is nothing as good as a Bugatti on the world market today. That's nonsense. There are dozens of cars as good as a Bugatti, and better, cars faster, more road-worthy, more reliable, cheaper, more comfortable, and so on down a long list. But they are not the *same*. There is an indefinable, impalpable quality of *life* in a good Bugatti that does not exist in lesser machines. Of course, much of the charm of the Bugatti automobile lies in the aura of splendor that lay around its creation: *Le Patron* stalking the factory corridors in pongee and yellow corduroy, a brown bowler on his head and a Malacca stick in his hand; a champagne gala at the château; the little blue cars screaming across a finish line in one-two-three order; Benoist flying down a country road away from the pursuing Nazis in a Type 57; a reigning beauty of the Paris stage posing beside her Type 46 at a Deauville *concours d'élégance* . . .

Within the week just past as I write this, I have driven, and for some little distance, two great contemporary high-performance automobiles: a 3500 *gran turismo* Maserati coupe, $13,500 worth of Italian *mácchina*, and a Bentley Continental Flying Spur, at just under $27,000 one of the most expensive motorcars ever built. I've also driven a Type 50 Bugatti a hundred miles or so. The Maserati will run away and hide from the Bugatti, and the Bentley makes it sound like a cement mixer in full cry. Maserati and Bentley performances peak, like a needle on an instrument, and that is that. The Bugatti never seems to peak. There's nothing imperturbable about a Bugatti, it may exceed every expectation, or it may inexplicably goof off, but whatever it does, the impression that *more is* possible, *more is* available, remains with the driver. The car seems to be willing to try, and try again, and keep on trying forever.

This may be the essence of the quality that Ettore Bugatti tried to put into his cars. Thoroughbred—*pur sang*—was a phrase he liked. He believed that his cars had breeding. He said, and it was true, that from 1909 to 1939 no driver was killed or even seriously injured through material failure of a Bugatti automobile. Perhaps this was because he knew how to design an automobile to endure great stress, or because he used only the best materials on the market—special Sheffield steel, for example— but Bugatti did not think so. He thought it was an indefinable thing, really breeding. He may have been right. Who is to say he was not?

L. J. K. SETRIGHT

Car v. Bike

"You haven't got one of those have you?" said the shopgirl in a scandalised tone as she looked out through the glass door. "A nice Rudge now, a Scott or a Brough—that's what I call a motorcycle; but that thing is terribly vulgar. Does it handle?" She thrust her thumbs further down beneath the belt of her already perilously hip-hung jeans, striking an attitude obviously calculated to arrest the attention of her audience. Alas her audience numbered but one. Every other man in the shop had rushed out to the pavement to admire the Rocket 3 which stood at the kerb glittering with all the pride of 60 bhp and £615.

Later that day when I had abandoned the rain-washed, greasy London streets in favour of the sunlit slopes of *CAR*'s private proving ground the same thing happened. No sniffy, hippy girls, but a crowd of admirers around the bike. Ground staff and office types, they all wanted to have a look over the big BSA, occasionally throwing out hints that they wouldn't mind a ride. There is something special about three cylinders and a reputation for standard-shattering performance, after all. Mr. Deputy Twite's Lotus Elan (kindly loaned for the day by our friends Gold Seal) with four cylinders and a reputation for standard-setting handling, hardly got a second glance. I was conscious enough of it though when we set off in company around the handling circuit. The idea was that I should ride inches behind the camera car and Deputy Twite would bring the Lotus inches behind me—for no better reason than that Mr. Photographer Perkins apparently likes these wide-angle short focus lenses with which to perform his spectacular feats of pictorial myopia. This was rather worrying, for the line that I wanted to ride round some of the tighter corners was different from the one that would be natural in a car.

Praise be, the BSA never departed from the line to which it was committed, even when banked over so far that, as I was told afterwards, the footrests were within an inch of scraping the ground. I certainly didn't feel that I was cornering fast—but then there is none of the awful stomach-swinging, nerve-straining, conker on a string feeling that you get when cornering fast in a car. I was merely conscious that I was well leaned over, having occasionally to duck my head to avoid roadside foliage when I cranked the big 750 past the apex of a corner, its road-hugging Dunlops tracking a precise line inches from the edge.

Just once Twite got a bit mischievous and went past me on the way into a corner, pressing on with a fine flurry of enthusiasm, flying pebbles, and enough opposite lock to suggest that he was going quite quickly. I let him get on with it: when you overcook a corner in a car you merely slide and scrub off speed, but when you overcook it on a motorcycle you fall off and any subsequent sliding and scrubbing is done on your ear or your backside. You get a fine sense of responsibility when you are riding a motorcycle and a clear and precise measure of the point at which you become a coward. This is no bad thing, though if you want to be brave you can go ahead in the knowledge that it is only your own neck you are risking, not that of any passenger or passer-by. The morality of motorcycling is unimpeachable. However, likewise the fun is undeniable. Away from the known lurking points of polyphemus Perkins it did not matter if the Lotus and the BSA got a bit separated. As we emerged from the handling circuit on to the back straight I trod the BSA into bottom gear and wound the twist grip until all three carburettors were wide open.

The acceleration was the most incredible that I have ever experienced. After a couple of seconds I hooked the thing into second gear, slid my bottom back along the seat, and crouched down, hanging on like grim death to the handlebar grips. Once again that phenomenal push and that weird wailing, high baritone shout as the tachometer needle, inches from my nose, spun to register 8000 rpm and it was time to snap into third. No vibration, no bumps, nothing but that gleefully rising engine note and the wind tearing at my clothing to confirm the speedo's evidence that we were already doing a hundred miles an hour and had better either ease off or get into top gear and hold ever more tightly. The tachometer needle flickered back to 6600 as the diaphragm clutch bit again but the speedo needle was still moving on steadily round the dial.

Anchor time. Shut the throttles, sit up, squeeze the brakes, and let the eight-inch front drum bear the brunt of hauling 480 pounds of motorcycle and another 170 odd of rider down from 110 to 20 mph for our turn off the straight. At speed it had been as steady as a rock and steady too as we braked; but as we went on to the bumpy tarmac that leads back to the handling circuit the BSA shook its head very slightly. The cure was simple, a half-turn of the steering damper as we pottered along at 1200 rpm in top gear waiting for the Lotus to catch up.

The Elan was not really in disgrace. This BSA is one of the fastest production motorcycles in the world. To take it from standstill to 100 mph like that takes a quarter of a mile and a little more than fourteen seconds. This is the sort of acceleration that will pin down a Miura and leave Elans gasping.

At higher speeds the car driver has the advantage. He is sitting in a wind-shielding cocoon, aware of his speed but not feeling it. Maximum speed of the Rocket 3 is really governed by the strength of one's grip on the handlebars, as the riding position is not really in tune with the bike's performance. The footrests were too far forward, the handlebars too high, wide, and handsome in the American manner. The sit-up-and-beg riding position they enforce makes the pilot feel like a detachable air brake. For higher speed motorcycling the riding position should be more akin to a racer's: feet and seat well back, body leaned well forward, arms reaching almost straight to handlebars the same width as the rider's shoulders. At low speeds your weight is taken on bars, seat, and footrests, and as the speed rises you lean your body against the wind.

Does it sound precarious? Does the idea of speed on two wheels strike you as an outmoded fashion? Is not motorcycling a perilous, impractical, uncomfortable, and antisocial activity, whose participants turn an almost blind eye to the relentless march of progress?

Everybody who has never seriously ridden a motorcycle will agree. Those who have been motorcyclists in their time will have known that magical union of the rider not only with his machine but also with the environment through which he rides it. Such men will never condemn motorcycling. They may excuse themselves from practising it on the grounds that they are too old, too fat, that the roads are too crowded, or that it would not be in keeping with the dignity of their position; but secretly or publicly they long to be back on two wheels.

Perhaps they are just offering a touch of impractical romanticism as ageing men do. After all, how practical can motorcycling be? The quick answer is that it shouldn't matter, and that motorcycling is something that you should do because you enjoy it, not because you have to. A motorcycle is a luxury to be enjoyed, not a necessity to be endured. I would never recommend anyone to rely on two wheels for all personal transport; but for the man who already has a sports car with which to satisfy his quotidiernal needs for business and domestic transport, a motorcycle will complement it far better than most things. Except for one thing . . . remember the shopgirl and her reinforced concrete antipathies? She is typical of motorcyclists: most of the enthusiasts are constructed of solid, unreasoned prejudice from the neck up. Because of this you can never trust the judgement of a motorcyclist, and you can never rely even on something as glamorous as this triple-breasted BSA serving as bait for feminine company. Kindly remember too that a motorcycle is a vehicle for one person to ride: carrying a pillion passenger is neither fair, safe, comfortable, nor enjoyable.

Now then, assuming that you are content to rely in these matters on your own personal attractions and do not feel the need for some petrol-burning cosmetic; and assuming that along with this maturity you can enjoy the exercise of skill and judgement in staying just this side of the limits of adhesion rather than the boisterous revelry of trying to recover the loss of it—you may still be wondering about the practicality of motorcycling. What is it like in bad weather, for instance?

You must dress the part. Unless the weather is fine and warm and can be relied upon so to remain you are going to have to dress up like a deep sea diver before you ride from home. Properly clad in a storm-proof, abrasion resistant suit, crash helmet, gloves, boots, and goggles you will find yourself surprisingly comfortable when riding in any kind of weather, your body temperature never seeming too high or too low for it is so well insulated. A face mask may be a good idea too: if you have been riding fast the beat of air against your face will have chilled it and made it an immobile, expressionless mask, lips clumsy in speech and reluctant to smile. Remember these things the next time you see an apparently moronic looking motorcyclist.

For all the impregnability of proper riding togs, two-wheelers can still be something of a trial in bad weather. The car driver may rely on the grip of his four tyres on the road for steering and traction and braking, but the motorcyclist relies on the grip of his two tyres even to keep his machine upright and balanced. As a motorcyclist therefore you will acquire a hypersensitive appreciation of road surfaces and when they are wet you may be uncomfortably aware of the theoretical ease of coming a purler. Take heart from the fact that good motorcycling tyres are compounded for the utmost wet grip without concessions to any other conflicting demands. By good tyres I mean Avon and Dunlop, who rank supreme.

The other uncomfortable thing about motorcycling, especially in wet weather, is that in crowded urban streets car drivers are too selfish or inexperienced to give the bicycle rider, be he leg powered or petrol engined, the amount of leeway he would like. There are compensations, though, in the mobility and agility of the two-wheeler in heavy traffic that allows you to make appointments with the certainty of being able to keep them.

And it isn't terribly dangerous. In fact the motorcycle, provided it be sufficiently powerful and of reasonably good specification, can be a remarkable pre-server of life and limb. In the first place its brakes are often excellent. Better still there is the terrific low speed acceleration under which the motorcycle demonstrates the advantages of a higher power-to-weight ratio. The seasoned car driver will employ acceleration as the preferred means of extracting himself from a potential accident situation but this is something that the motorcyclist is better equipped to do. Up to 50 or 60 mph a good motorcycle will burn off any ordinary production car, and the sporting ones will leave even Elans behind from an initial get up and go. Only if you want to keep it up into the three figure range do you have to get one of the Magnum varieties like the BSA Rocket 3 or a Norton Commando. And if avoidance calls for a swerve as well as for acceleration the motorcycle can be swerved with remarkable speed. Dunlop established during some tyre tests that a racing motorcycle can sustain 1.3g lateral acceleration: virtually as good as a top flight Formula 1 Grand Prix car. All right, it was a racer—but there is far less difference in cornering power and control response between the racing motorcycle and the street variety than there is between their four-wheeled equivalents.

Nevertheless there may come a time when you will fall off, even a time when you will think it advisable to do so. To stay with the machine when a crash is inevitable is to invite injury; better to leave it to plough its own furrow and dissociate yourself from it. Even at 60 or more miles per hour you may get away with nothing more than an abraded backside and a few bruises. This is why it pays to wear protective clothing when riding even in fine weather. The vulnerability of the man on two wheels is best minimised by "stepping off," as motorcyclists call it, when good tough suiting and a smooth-surfaced "bone dome" are as good a life insurance as the car occupants' harness. I have fallen off four or five times at speeds up to 40 mph (a speed which can be fatal in a car smash) and the worst that I suffered was a bloody forehead.

Of course motorcycling is not entirely safe. It becomes less safe not more so if you seek satisfaction astride some footling, low powered economy bike. The motorcycle designed as a cheap substitute for shoe leather is the wrong kind, offering all the disadvantages with none of the delights. Get yourself instead a proper mount that looks like a motorcycle and goes like one—better still something that looks and goes like a racing motorcycle—and you will enjoy life as no other land traveller can ever hope to do.

There are a few cars that offer something of a good motorcycle's delicacy of control. The Lotus that played harrier to my haring BSA is perhaps the best of them, but for all the breathcatching sublimity of its steering it still demands a certain amount of rather undignified exertion. Until you have driven a good motorcycle you simply have no notion of how sweet controls can be. There is no slop, no sponginess, no inaccuracy in motorcycle steering: you may move the handlebars consciously at very low speeds but once you are decently on the move it is seemingly a matter of wishing the machine around a corner on a chosen line. Laying the motorcycle over, banking it so that it is balanced against the centrifugal force, it requires scarcely any effort, unlike the heave of the steering wheel necessary to set up a car for a corner.

It's the same with gear changes. There is not a car anywhere with a gear change as good as you can get in almost any motorcycle. The change on a two-wheeler is light, positive, and silent, yet there is no synchromesh, no awkward gate, just a little pedal that you tread down or hook up with your toe an inch or two to engage the next higher or lower gear. And the ratios are beautifully close, those of a touring bike being comparable with those of a racing car, for the modest weight and sweet finger-light clutch of most motorcycles make a high bottom gear perfectly feasible. The Rocket 3 has frankly to be excepted from this generalisation for it is a real heavyweight, but it makes up for it in sheer blasting power so its gear ratios are still close. It also has a marked advantage over the majority of vertical twins and all big single cylinder jobs in that its engine is virtually vibrationless. It is also incidentally very easy to start, requiring none of the convulsive exertion that is sometimes necessary to kick lesser engines into life. Yet it is not by any means the only manageable tarmac spurner in the business, nor the cheapest. You may want something less big and flashing, less Americanised if you like—though you should be warned against going to the opposite extreme and getting a trials or scramble bike, for these things are meant for off highway horseplay and have nothing to do with engineering or elegance or practicality or safety or even motorcycling.

Because its devotees will never agree about their gods, motorcycling cannot become a religion; but it is a philosophy and properly pursued it is a discipline. Better still it is one of those rare activities which do the participants good while doing nobody else any harm. Try it: take your pick of the best in road burners, make sure it has the grippiest tyres, the smoothest brakes, and the narrowest handlebars it will take, dress yourself properly, and then go out and get to know yourself all over again.

JEAN LINDAMOOD

One Fake Ferrari

Miami—We've come to the city of skyscraper rest homes, drug-monied banking institutions, and squalid Carib ghettos to do a little cruising with Philip Michael Thomas, the debonair detective Ricardo Tubbs of *Miami Vice*. If you don't know how important Philip Michael Thomas is, you must not have read the recent interview with him in Andy Warhol's *Interview* magazine.

"We are actually more famous right now than anybody else in the world," PMT told *Interview*. "I'm the wing-footed god."

And now—some Joe Hollywood publicist for *Miami Vice* called to tell us—Philip Michael Thomas is part owner of a company that makes the Machiavelli, another in a long line of Ferrari rip-offs. "What is a Machiavelli?" we asked. "Is it the fake Daytona on the show?" No, they're not using the fake Daytona this season, said Hollywood; this is the *new* car, and PMT drives a purple one around Miami every day. Would we like to ride around with him? At that point, we weren't sure what this guy was talking about.

"We're talking cover, darling," said our man in Miami. No lie. "What did you say your name was? Linda Lindenbaum?"

When he called back to say that PMT's agent refused to return his phone calls, we figured we were going to have to drive real cars this month. Great story idea, Hollywood. Write if you get work.

But this is one idea that refused to die. Next came a call from the public relations firm hired to promote the Machiavelli itself. They insisted that the Machiavelli's maker, Robert Henderson, was worth a story in his own right, but if we *had* to have PMT, well, they could deliver him too. And we could visit the *Miami Vice* set. And Bobby Henderson would send his Rolls-Royce and chauffeur around to the hotel for us to use as a backup camera car.

Hmmm. Philip Michael Thomas. Miami. Rolls-Royce. The occasion seemed ripe for a journey into the shadowy underworld of automobile customizers.

The wet season has come early to Florida. Massive thunderheads have been rolling through Miami all week. Though we touched down under brilliant blue skies, a monstrous black cloud bank is now spreading from west to east. It's ninety degrees Fahrenheit, and it feels like I'm breathing through wet gauze. My Haitian cab driver leaves me off at the Grand Bay in Coconut Grove, a gleaming resort stuffed with palms and staffed by gorgeous Spanish-speaking gentlemen. I and my solitary bag are handed by white-gloved hand from taxi to doorman to porter to bellhop to major-domo and back to bellhop. I wish I'd worn more *parfum* to leave in my wake.

If you want to have the staff of a fancy hotel show you the proper respect, have a white, chauffeur-driven Rolls-Royce Silver Cloud whisk you away on business. This will never happen to me again. And it would not happen to me again during this visit, because Bobby Henderson's female chauffeur is really a Chilean cab driver hired only for this afternoon. She drives with little jiggles of the wheel, right hand clamped on the outside rim in the twelve o'clock position, and left hand on the cross-spoke with pinky hooked around the rim. She scares me to death, but the radio is playing rhumbas so loud that neither Henderson nor his PR lady can hear my heart beating furiously through my chest.

Luckily, I don't have to endure too much of this, because our driver hasn't been engaged for the *entire* afternoon. We drop her off at her car after lunch, and I take the wheel. (Well, *someone* has to drive.) Bobby Henderson fills me in on his purpose in this world as we head to the airport to fetch photographer Colin Curwood.

With thinning, sandy colored hair, ruddy complexion, and blue eyes, Bobby Henderson looks a proper Scot. Only he's Cuban.

"I was a real estate developer and builder for twelve years," Henderson tells me. "I still have Henderson Development Company; today I build fertilizer plants in South America." The next step was obviously the car business.

This would not exactly be the car business according to Lee Iacocca, or even the car business according to John DeLorean. More like the car business according to P. T. Barnum.

When you decide to make fake Ferrari 308s out of Pontiac Trans Ams, there's a certain amount of huckstering that goes with the territory. And Bobby Henderson can talk a convoluted blue streak about his Machiavelli:

"GM has neglected three divisions. I'm giving Buick, Olds, and Cadillac dealers a GM sports car. My niche is between Porsche and Trans Am. It's obvious to me when I look at a Trans Am that Pontiac designers took a 308 and said, 'Let's disguise it.' I reversed what they did."

What?

"I had two Ferrari 308s. I wanted a bigger car, so I bought a Mondial. I think with the Mondial, Fiat engineers were trying to show Ferrari that they knew how to build a car. Anyway, Ferrari never built a 308 model two-plus-two. That's good for me because you can't say that I'm just making a copy. I never claimed that it was a Ferrari; I just realized that they skipped over a two-plus-two. Clearly, Ferrari has no interest."

What?

"Hundreds of guys wanted a Ferrari with an automatic. I set out for something between the sportiness and beauty of an MG and the comfort of a 500SL, a car you can drive all day. I beat the Cadillac Allanté by two years. I'm still in a market all by myself. I have a GM sports car two-plus-two."

What?

"I think the Machiavelli is superior to Corvette and comparable to the most exotic cars in the world."

WHAT?

"You know, we are making two and a half cars per day, which makes us larger than Lotus. And look at the inordinate amount of attention Lotus gets from the press, and we don't get any."

Please stop.

Collecting Curwood and his photo gear at Miami International, we head for Henderson's Hialeah Gardens facility to pick up the purple PMT-mobile, hoping to do a little evening shooting around Miami.

There are three Machiavellis in residence: the purple 305 two-plus-two we are to shoot, a red Mach II with slightly more aggressive rocker panels ("like a Ferrari 308GTS two-plus-two that got sent to AMG for ground-effects work" is how Henderson describes it), and a white polished and bespoilered Max, fitted with the Trans Am's optional port-injected 5.0-liter V-8 ("like a GTS two-plus-two sent to Koenig," continues Henderson's analogy). All three have "M-A-C-H-I-A-V-E-L-L-I" stretched across their windshields in huge white letters.

From a side glance at a hundred yards, the purple Machiavelli looks like a Ferrari 308. From ten feet, it looks like a mess. Not only is it about the most awful shade of purple you could hope to paint a car, it is trashed. We can't see through the windows, the steering wheel and the dash are coated with dirt, and there is some really yucky crud on the seats.

We are certainly *not* talking cover, darling. We're not even talking photo *numero uno*.

"No" is all Curwood has to say when he sees the car. "We can't."

Quizzing Henderson, we quickly discover that PMT is actually driving a white Max around Miami, *not* the purple monstrosity, which he has apparently used up. And we threaten to abort the mission if a white Max isn't immediately substituted. Hurried calls to the *Miami Vice* set secure the loan of PMT's transport; we will drive the purple car across town and make the switch. We scrape two places clean and perch on the seats, rub portholes in the glass, and head for the set.

The show's superstud, Don Johnson, has just come back to work after a short strike for some ungodly wage increase, and tension is a bit high on the heavily guarded set. I whip the purple pig through the gate and slide it into the number one slot, next to a white Max. (A moment of truth: I spin my head 360 degrees hoping for a glimpse of Don Johnson, but he's nowhere to be found.)

"You can't park there!" frets a small woman running toward us. "Don Johnson . . ." She changes her mind. "Just leave the keys. We'll move it."

And where is Philip Michael Thomas, we ask, as we are herded toward the exit?

"You are cleared for tomorrow," she says, with a look that plainly says we are *not* cleared for today. Feeling assured that we really will see the star of this episode, we point the white Max into the steamy city.

There is no mistaking this baby from the inside out. We are driving a Trans Am. Oh, there are a few minor "luxury" embellishments to the basic Trans Am cabin: A "hand-rubbed wood panel" has been appliqué to the familiar Trans Am instrumentation, and to the center console. Stock Lear Siegler seats are swathed in red leather. A brass plate is cemented onto the top of the ashtray lid. Pressed in the center of the stock steering wheel is the Machiavelli trademark—a prancing unicorn.

But we are blasting through the potholes of Miami with the characteristic *slam-bang-pow* of the Trans Am's hard WS6 suspension, and we are tearing down Biscayne Boulevard with the Trans Am's port-injected 5.0-liter V-8 roaring its magic rib-shaking roar. It's still a kick in the head, but the Machiavelli is such a Trans Am that, if you owned one, you'd have to jump out and look at the grilles and scoops every couple of miles to remind yourself of what you bought for your $36,900 (only $29,900 for the base Machiavelli). Today, there will be no convincing people on the street of this car's true identity. Our white Max positively electrifies Miami's Latin populace.

A Porsche 928 with *pinstriping* pulls up next to us, and its heavily tinted window zips down.

"What kind of *car* is that?" says the 928's female passenger.

"We *love* it!" enthuses her girlfriend at the wheel.

"Appalling" is Curwood's opinion. "And they're in a *proper* car." I remind him of the pinstriping.

We are waiting at a traffic light, when I spy a down-and-out street dweller stepping off the sidewalk. He spies The Car and ambles directly over to my window, stopping about two inches from my left ear.

"Look, he's got his arms full of bags. He can't shoot us," I tell the horrified Mr. Curwood as I roll down the Machiavelli's window.

"What's up, man?" I greet the guy. He's grinning a big one.

"Hey! Isn't that Philip Michael Thomas?" he asks me.

Me? His car? *What?*

"Right!" I nod, and up the power window goes.

We park the Machiavelli on top of a parking structure, the Miami night strung out around us. The Machiavelli looks like a coke dealer's ride, and the towering neon-white-lined Centrust building looming in the background looks like a stack of merchandise piled up behind it.

Curwood, rare among car photographers in his love and knowledge of fine automobiles, is mortified at this assignment. He peers through his Nikon at the lovely juxtaposition of neon, reflection, and car. Something is not right. The car. He storms away from his tripod and stares with arms folded at the night.

"Bloody *hell*," he mutters, and stomps back to shoot the charlatan. On finishing the roll, he cannot bring himself to reload his camera.

There doesn't appear to be a man in Miami who shares his opinion of the Machiavelli. We pull in to the Sheraton to use the phone, and the car jockeys crowd around to gawk. At the Grand Bay Hotel's front door, the valet parker almost rips the door off its hinges trying to displace me at the wheel. The Max completely overpowers the doorman. He's about forty-five. "I *love* your car," he says sensuously, handing me neatly into the lobby.

All that this means to me is bigger tips for everyone.

Having not gotten much in the way of automotive enlightenment from one owner, we are about to interview the Machiavelli's celebrity shareholder.

Philip Michael Thomas is holed up in his trailer, parked at a marina on Watson Island under an ominous black sky, eating grapes and waiting for his camera call. We call instead.

Automobile Magazine: How did you get involved with Machiavelli?
Philip Michael Thomas: Somebody showed me a picture of the car with this chick, and I said, "Where's the *chick*?" And when you have this car, the chicks *do* come.

AM: What's the deal?
PMT: I get two cars a year: the Max and the purple Machiavelli. And I own part of the company. As spokesman, I make six public appearances per year. I'm negotiating to use the car on the show.

AM: So you don't use it now . . .
PMT: Every day, my driver picks me up and drives me to work.

AM: Why *this* car?
PMT: I think what this man has done is incredible. I like the fact that the car is made in Miami, which is one step closer to heaven because you're in paradise. I call Bobby the Henry Ford of Miami.

AM: I'm sorry. . .
PMT: You've got two little giants in Miami. That's us. You've got two little giants in Miami who are making dreams reality.

AM: Do you own other cars?
PMT: I love cars. I have a Rolls.

AM: What model?
PMT: An old one. And I have a Mercedes-Benz.

AM: Which one?
PMT: A 1970. And I have two Volvo wagons, a '65 Mustang convertible, a BMW 321i [*sic*], a 733, and a Honda Civic. The Max is exotic to me. The response I get is amazing. The car is magnetic. Everyone who sees one wants one. A guy in an Excalibur drove up next to me and asked me what it was. I personally like the body style of the Machiavelli better than the Testarossa. I told Don any time he wants, I'll give him a run for his money.

I want to design a car in the next year. I'd call it the PMT 9000. I like the number nine. I'm also designing a jean called PMT 9000. The car would be geared to the executive—phone, stereo—somewhere between the Max and a Rolls-Royce. The comfort of a Rolls-Royce, the style and sophistication of the Max, the power of GE. It's only a dream now, but where I'm at professionally and monetarily, it's easier to make my dreams reality. Money does wonders. I have an ace in the hole: Bobby Henderson, who also makes dreams reality. Henderson Motors is an example of reality, not fantasy.

AM: Why own a fake Ferrari when you can have the real thing?
PMT: I'm part owner of this company. You promote what you own. I think it's important to start on the level of developing an industry. Ferrari is already established. I'm one of the new lions helping to develop this city. I'm in on the ground floor of industry.

What's important is the consciousness of the people behind the project. This could turn into something huge. It could create jobs, and that's important. It could go from two hundred a year to 2 million.

AM: You can't be serious . . .
PMT: Anything is possible. Everything starts with an idea.

We leave the trailer and walk to the car for photos. Curwood shoots quickly, against the threatening gale. PMT's assistant takes pictures of Curwood taking pictures. I continue to take notes.

PMT: Do you understand industry? *That's* what I'm trying to do. You're right. I could afford *ten* Testarossas. But I'm trying to create industry.

Huge splats of water hit the windshield and the ground around us. PMT makes a dash for his trailer, and we are left sitting in the car, cameras jumbled around us, the storm raging. It is clear that we are probably *not* going cruising with PMT. The GM T-roof is leaking. Curwood and I look at each other as we sit abandoned in the maelstrom, thinking about industry.

"Maybe we should tell him," Curwood says. "Maybe the guy really doesn't know."

We look at each other.

Naaahhh.

Bobby Henderson makes his last pitch as Curwood and I pack up to leave town. "No one is more disenchanted with Ferrari than a longtime Ferrari owner. Don't ask car enthusiasts. They'll lie. Talk to owners that you know well. My car is for a person who wants an exotic car that is reliable, that he can drive every day.

"A lot of these guys are not mechanically inclined. They're not looking for the things that you as a car enthusiast are looking for. They are looking for comfort and exclusivity—a custom-made, handmade car. The Machiavelli owner isn't driving an imitation *anything*. Ferrari never made that car! I think a Boxer looks more like a Trans Am than our car looks like theirs."

As he talks, it dawns on me that this guy is sincere, and that he really is a pleasant man. But Henderson has unfortunately come to believe his own hype. All I would like, before I blow town, is for Bobby Henderson to tell me he makes fake Ferraris out of Trans Ams, and that he figures he can make a lot of money selling them to guys with blow-dried chest hair who don't know diddly about cars but who think a flashy ride will help them pick up chicks. I'm going to try the direct approach.

"Bobby," I say, "your car *is* a Trans Am. You've added a new front and a new rear. You've added a Herb Adams lowering kit for the suspension and taken a quarter-turn off the front springs. You've added holes and scoops and grilles. But it is a Trans Am. It has a Trans Am engine. It has a Pontiac WS6 suspension."

Bobby looks exasperated. "You just don't get it. Firebirds sold at the dealer don't have this stuff. Try to find one with this engine and this suspension."

Okay; let's try another tack.

"You say in your press release that a 'concave spoiler covering the bottom of the car creates less drag and more stability.' Do you have numbers to support that?"

"We haven't tested it," he replies.

"Can you prove any aerodynamic benefit from the spoilers and rocker extensions?"

"This is a matter of wind-tunnel testing, and we don't have access to this facility."

"Then how do you support your claims?" I ask.

"A front spoiler is a front spoiler" is Henderson's reasoning.

"The Machiavelli weighs about the same as a Trans Am" is the answer to my next question, but the literature claims a 20 percent increase in effective horsepower over the Trans Am, thanks to a combination of "weight loss due to fiberglass components and performance gain due to an improved exhaust system."

Henderson explains: "The air intakes on the hood match the air intakes of the engine. That, coupled with the increased exhaust diameter (three-inch pipes from the catalyst back), makes the difference. This is taken directly from Herb Adams's literature."

"How about this one?" I ask, quoting a Machiavelli press release. "'A set of screens in the rear act as spoilers and give the car good turbulence arrest.' What does *that* mean?"

"We came up with that all by ourselves." Henderson laughs sheepishly. "Even if it *doesn't* do it, it certainly does look nice. We like to do everything on the car as functional as possible, but sometimes we have to take poetic license."

"And you say the side vents cool the brakes. Those vents don't go *anywhere*, Bobby."

"Look," he says, somewhat apologetically. "This car is a prop for Philip Michael Thomas. It was made in a hurry to meet a deadline for a baptism. And this is the third car we've given to him. He'd gotten his two cars. He had a Max in California, but he didn't want to drive it back to Miami, so he had a dealer sell it. When he came back, he said, 'Look, why don't you give me another one?' So we didn't have one. And with the baptism pressing . . ." He shrugs.

So how many Machiavellis has Bobby Henderson sold?

"We can make 2.5 cars per day, which makes us bigger than Lotus," he begins.

I interrupt. "Bobby, how many cars have you built since production started in September of 1985?"

"Built? We have delivered about 120. But I've got a couple of deals cooking that I can't talk about. I'm working with an American marketing organization. It's talking 3000 cars per year."

"And realistically?" I prompt.

"I can sell two cars a day or two cars a week and come out all right."

"Tens of dealers" turns into maybe eleven. A "group of German investors" is Henderson's in-laws, who have lent money to his wife, which she in turn has lent to him.

"I think Ferraris are beautiful, but anyone who owns one will say they are temperamental and unreliable. I give the people power steering, an automatic transmission, air conditioning that cools, and power windows that go up and down. That a Ferrari takes curves better—true. That a Ferrari goes faster—true. What I'm giving people is a marriage made in heaven. Between General Motors and Ferrari, I'm selling the best they've got."

"No you're not, Bobby," I remind him. "You don't use Ferrari parts."

"No, we don t sell them anymore," he agrees. "We used to use their taillights and grilles, but we wiped out their North American inventory. But there are plenty of round amber taillights around, and you can buy them from whatever source you want."

I have to go to the airport now.

The world's most attentive hotel staff people tuck me into the Rolls-Royce and wave goodbye from the Grand Bay's portico. Bobby Henderson talks as he drives.

"A guy that thinks he knows about cars is going to buy a Mercedes-Benz, a BMW, a Porsche. He's not going to buy this car. Philip Michael Thomas is a good representative of the segment of the populace that doesn't know about cars, the people who judge what they see and what they feel. The Machiavelli is for those who are interested in cars, but who are not car nuts, the person who hasn't devoted his life to cars, who looks at an auto the same as he looks at a boat or a house. Our customers buy the Machiavelli for its looks, for reliability, and for its ego-enhancing qualities. These are the main reasons.

"You *could* buy a real Ferrari, but I don't think you'd get a better car unless you were going to race it. The Machiavelli was not intended to be a race car."

And Henderson doesn't give up until he realizes that I'm stepping out of his Silver Cloud and his life forever at Miami International with my solitary bag.

"Would you do me a favor?" he asks, a little nervously. "Be kind to me, because you can make or break me. I thrive on credibility."

So this is what Morley Safer feels like at the end of the day.

RONALD BARKER

Down the Hatch

(A Cautionary Dilambic Elegy on the Mortal Perils of Concealing an Internal Cremation Engine Beneath a Saurian Hood!)

Hiram P. Aloysius Platt,
A Transatlantic Diplomat,
Swept daily into Berkeley Square
On tyres marked "Use Low Pressure Air."

His fabulously finned Conveyance
(Conceived in blotto stylist's séance)
Hid all the works and wonders on it
Beneath an alligator bonnet.
Alas! His youngest offspring was
A perfect pest to Pop because
He loved to see the things inside
Which gave the beast its easy stride;
And nightly, when Pop rolled and reeled
To home-from-home in Harrow Weald,
The wretched youth would fair create
To see the Puffed-Up Powerflow Eight.

DOWN THE HATCH

For weeks and months kind Pop complied
By opening the bonnet wide
And revving till it caused vibration;
Until in final desperation
One day he firmly stood his ground,
Tho' Junior shrieked and stamped around
And scratched the paint and kicked the fenders
(All now repaired by Motormenders)
And knocked the Six-Volt Battery flat
And poured the acid on the cat.
(Alas! The R.S.P.C.A.
Were not in time to save the day,
But found 'midst weeping family huddle
A smoking, furry little puddle.)

Now sent to bed in sore disgrace,
One would have thought, to see his face,
That he was truly penitent
About the way that pussy went,
And would perhaps at last resist
Ambitions automobilist.

Pah! Little incidents like these
Are but as molecules to fleas,
And soon conceal themselves behind
The callous corners of the mind.
Thus, at the midnight hammer-fall
Of bogus Tompion in the hall,
He stole in sneakers down the stairs
And out into the chilly airs
That sweep up from the Isle of Wight
To drift across the Weald by night.
The hinges of each garage door
Had been well oiled the day before
By Thomas (Chauffeur-handyman
Employed by the American)
And so no barking creak or squeak

Betrayed him, and the Super Sleek
Dynamic Dodgem Dude Sedan
Was his, despite parental ban!

In eager haste he searched the dash
And found amidst the plastic trash
A fancy little knob upon it
To liberate the monster bonnet.
The hungry jaws swung open wide
And in a trice he was inside,
When CRASH! They shut themselves again.
(For rust from endless English rain
Had weakened the retaining spring—
In any case a shoddy thing.)

The Powerflow Eight was none too quick
At starting when the oil was thick,
And Junior's leg, caught in the choke,
Caused clouds of black and acrid smoke;
Yet start it did, and Hiram freed
The hand-brake and shot off at speed,
The crunch of gravel on the drive
Combining with the Moto-Jive
Receiver to suppress the din
Of Junior SLOWLY GOING IN!

One leg at first, and then the other—
(What use now, child, to shriek for Mother?)
Unwitting, Pop sped on in haste
With Junior soon lost to the waist;
And less and less was to be seen
As they shot over Willesden Green,
Until at Paddington his palms
And then his elbows and his arms—
At Marble Arch his neck and chin—
All greedily digested in

and the police went potty when Beau offered a cash settlement in the cells that night. But Beau was like that—he would have paid up. To him the dishonour of being caught out on his driving was like a Grand Prix driver getting tossed out of the GPDA. Paying the draper was something that might have helped Beau's feeling of guilt and incompetence. It really hit him hard.

"Today's cars and traffic don't really lend themselves to heist driving. Certainly not in the big cities, anyway—far too crowded. And with this 70 limit you're in trouble before you start.

"I suppose today's equivalent of the Cord and the Caddy is the 3.8 Jag or the big Zephyr. American cars today are out of the question: far too big, and the suspension's too soggy to drive them quickly with any degree of precision. E-types are no good, either—no headroom and far too difficult to get in and out of in a hurry. A chap I know used one for a small country bank job a couple of years ago and it was a real disaster. Came rushing out of the bank carrying a sawn-off shotgun and a bag of loot. Getting into the car he smashed his head on the roof and the gun went off, blowing his big toe off. As he fell unconscious the other barrel went off and blew the front tyre to bits. The driver panicked and drove off unaware of the blown front tyre and smashed straight into a lamp post at 50, wrecking the car and knocking himself out. That would never have happened in a car with a running board and decent headroom.

"Gone are the days when a heist man would have his own car and keep it in tip-top trim. In the old days I'd use my own car on country jobs—switched number plates, of course—but for the town stuff I'd always nick one. I'd have it away a couple of days before the job and spend a full day giving it the once over in my own garage. New plugs, points, check the tyres and brakes and steering—the lot. The boys used to take the mickey out of me. Reckoned I was some sort of fanatic, but I never ever had a mechanical failure on a job.

"Automatics are out, too. Two blokes did a Mayfair fur job with a Super Snipe automatic a couple of years ago. Kept the car parked in a mews and at dead of night they loaded it up with furs, but as they were leaving the building by a first floor window they tripped the alarm. They panicked and in the confusion the driver popped the lever into reverse and gave it full throttle. Straight backwards up the mews they went and square into a wall. They left the car jammed in reverse undriveable with about £70,000 of furs on board for the Savile Row coppers to pick up. Now with a regular manual shift that would never have happened.

"Convertibles are quite good for specialised jobs. One young fellow I know still uses a technique perfected in the States in the '40s by German Fritz. Small-time stuff but quite effective. He'll drive up to an all-night filling station and get out with the engine still running. He sticks the attendant up and lifts the takings and then with the loot in one hand he runs straight up over the back of the car and drops into the driving seat and he's off quicker than you can blink. I suppose it's a variation on the Le Mans start. German Fritz came unstuck when he nicked a British sports car for a job in Louisville once. Out of habit he rushed over the back of the car and dropped into the left hand seat to find no wheel or pedals. By the time he'd realised his mistake and got up and over to the other side he'd been popped over the head by the pump attendant with the nozzle of the filling hose.

"I only ever got caught once, and that cost me five years. Silly thing, too. Whenever I was on a job I always wore a big slouch hat and hornrim glasses with plain glass in them—a pretty effective disguise, necessary because sitting at the kerb for up to five minutes you're quite likely to be seen by a passer-by who might recognise you later in a line-up. On this particular day (it was in Belfast) we were doing a wage snatch and one of the boys borrowed my hat. I sat calmly in the car polishing the lenses of my glasses. We were pulled in on suspicion afterwards and some stout citizen identified me on an inspection parade. Spent five years thinking about the folly of my ways and I've been straight ever since.

"Saved a few bob I had, mind you, and when I came out I set myself up with a little showroom selling cars. Still doing all right. I did a bit of racing in the late '50s—Goodwood, before your time probably. Collected a few pots but nothing outstanding. Getaway driving is very different from circuit racing. Only one man I know was ever really good at both and he's still about, so we mustn't name him.

"Twenty years ago you'd probably have made a really good getaway driver. I'd like to have schooled you. But today it's one of the lost arts. All the scope has gone. You won't make as much money on the circuits, but at least if you spin off you aren't likely to wind up behind bars.

"Must be off now. Told the wife I was at a board meeting. See you down at Brands sometime."

The Alfa engine burst into life. Wilf roared away towards the respectable West End. Diamond swore on his muvver's life that he was going straight this time. The man in the chunky blue polo-sweater rolled another cigarette. "Don't forget," cried the barman. "Keep stuhm."

HUNTER S. THOMPSON

Back Door Beauty . . . and Finally a Bit of Serious Drag Racing on the Strip

Sometime around midnight my attorney wanted coffee. He had been vomiting fairly regularly as we drove around the Strip, and the right flank of the Whale was badly streaked. We were idling at a stoplight in front of the Silver Slipper beside a big blue Ford with Oklahoma plates . . . two hoggish-looking couples in the car, probably cops from Muskogee using the Drug Conference to give their wives a look at Vegas. They looked like they'd just beaten Caesar's Palace for about thirty-three dollars at the blackjack tables, and now they were headed for the Circus-Circus to whoop it up. . . .

. . . but suddenly, they found themselves next to a white Cadillac convertible all covered with vomit and a three-hundred-pound Samoan in a yellow fishnet T-shirt yelling at them:

"Hey there! You folks want to buy some heroin?"

No reply. No sign of recognition. They'd been warned about this kind of crap: Just ignore it. . . .

"Hey, honkies!" my attorney screamed. "Goddamnit, I'm serious! I want to sell you some pure fuckin' *smack*!" He was leaning out of the car, very close to them.

But still nobody answered. I glanced over, very briefly, and saw four middle-American faces frozen with shock, staring straight ahead.

We were in the middle lane. A quick left turn would be illegal. We would have to go straight ahead when the light changed, then escape at the next corner. I waited, tapping the accelerator nervously. . . .

My attorney was losing control: "Cheap heroin!" he was shouting. "This is the real stuff! You won't get hooked! Goddamnit, I *know* what I have here!" He whacked on the side of the car, as if to get their attention . . . but they wanted no part of us.

"You folks never talked to a *vet* before?" said my attorney. "I just got back from Veet Naam. This is *scag*, folks! Pure scag!"

Suddenly the light changed and the Ford bolted off like a rocket. I stomped on the accelerator and stayed right next to them for about two hundred yards, watching for cops in the mirror while my attorney kept screaming at them: "Shoot! Fuck! Scag! Blood! Heroin! Rape! Cheap! Communist! Jab it right into your fucking eyeballs!"

We were approaching the Circus-Circus at high speed and the Oklahoma car was veering left, trying to muscle into the turn lane. I stomped the Whale into passing gear and we ran fender to fender for a moment. He wasn't up to hitting me; there was horror in his eyes. . . .

The man in the back seat lost control of himself . . . lunging across his wife and snarling wildly: "You dirty bastards! Pull over and I'll kill you! God damn you! You bastards!" He seemed ready to leap out the window and into our car, crazy with rage. Luckily the Ford was a two-door. He couldn't get out.

We were coming up to the next stoplight and the Ford was still trying to move left. We were both running full bore. I glanced over my shoulder and saw that we'd left the other traffic far behind; there was a big opening to the right. So I mashed on the brake, hurling my attorney against the dashboard, and in the instant the Ford surged ahead I cut across his tail and zoomed into a side-street. A sharp right turn across three lanes of traffic. But it worked. We left the Ford stalled in the middle of the intersection, hung in the middle of a screeching left turn. With a little luck, he'd be arrested for reckless driving.

My attorney was laughing as we careened in low gear, with the lights out, through a dusty tangle of back streets behind the Desert Inn. "Jesus Christ," he said. "Those Okies were getting excited. That guy in the back seat was trying to *bite* me! Shit, he was frothing at the mouth." He nodded solemnly. "I should have maced the fucker

. . . a criminal psychotic, total breakdown . . . you never know when they're likely to explode."

I swung the Whale into a turn that seemed to lead out of the maze—but instead of skidding, the bastard almost rolled.

"Holy shit!" my attorney screamed. "Turn on the fucking lights!" He was clinging to the top of the windshield . . . and suddenly he was doing the Big Spit again, leaning over the side.

I refused to slow down until I was sure nobody was following us—especially that Oklahoma Ford: those people were definitely dangerous, at least until they calmed down. Would they report that terrible quick encounter to the police? Probably not. It had happened too fast, with no witnesses, and the odds were pretty good that nobody would believe them anyway. The idea that two heroin pushers in a white Cadillac convertible would be dragging up and down the Strip, abusing total strangers at stoplights, was prima facie absurd. Not even Sonny Liston ever got that far out of control.

We made another turn and almost rolled again. The Coupe De Ville is not your ideal machine for high speed cornering in residential neighborhoods. The handling is very mushy . . . unlike the Red Shark, which had responded very nicely to situations requiring the quick four-wheel drift. But the Whale—instead of cutting loose at the critical moment had a tendency to *dig in*, which accounted for that sickening "here we go" sensation.

At first I thought it was only because the tires were soft, so I took it into the Texaco station next to the Flamingo and had the tires pumped up to fifty pounds each—which alarmed the attendant, until I explained that these were "experimental" tires.

But fifty pounds each didn't help the cornering, so I went back a few hours later and told him I wanted to try seventy-five. He shook his head nervously. "Not me," he said, handing me the air hose. "Here. They're your tires. *You* do it."

"What's wrong?" I asked. "You think they can't *take* seventy-five?"

He nodded, moving away as I stooped to deal with the left front. "You're damn right," he said. "Those tires want twenty-eight in the front and thirty-two in the rear. Hell, fifty's *dangerous*, but seventy-five is *crazy*. They'll explode!"

I shook my head and kept filling the left front. "I told you," I said. "Sandoz laboratories designed these tires. They're special. I could load them up to a hundred."

"God almighty!" he groaned. "Don't do that here."

"Not today," I replied. "I want to see how they corner with seventy-five."

He chuckled. "You won't even *get* to the corner, Mister."

"We'll see," I said, moving around to the rear with the air hose. In truth, I was nervous. The two front ones were tighter than snare drums; they felt like teak wood when I tapped on them with the rod. But what the hell? I thought. If they explode, so what? It's not often that a man gets a chance to run terminal experiments on a virgin Cadillac and four brand-new eighty-dollar tires. For all I knew, the thing might start cornering like a Lotus Elan. If not, all I had to do was call the VIP agency and have another one delivered . . . maybe threaten them with a lawsuit because all four tires had exploded on me, while driving in heavy traffic. Demand an Eldorado, next time, with four Michelin Xs. And put it all on the card . . . charge it to the St. Louis Browns.

As it turned out, the Whale behaved very nicely with the altered tire pressures. The ride was a trifle rough; I could feel every pebble on the highway, like being on roller skates in a gravel pit . . . but the thing began cornering in a very stylish manner, very much like driving a motorcycle at top speed in a hard rain: one slip and ZANG, over the high side, cartwheeling across the landscape with your head in your hands.

IAN FRASER

Streaked!

It wasn't until I reached the privacy of the hotel room in Austria that I was able to take off my shirt and examine the full extent of the problem. Sure enough, the yellow stripe that was previously only an inch or so wide was now practically full width. I was getting worse and I knew it. This latest expansion of the yellow badge of the cowardly, cringing passenger had happened on a German autobahn just a few hours before. Editor Nichols was threading our Jaguar XJC V-12 through the Death Race 2000 traffic at 85 to 90 mph while I examined every situation for its potential to frighten me. And most of them did, not because the aforementioned driver was doing anything awful but because I just happen to be the world's worst passenger. I spend most of my passengering time working out reasonable-sounding excuses for persuading the driver to stop, but there's a limit to how many times per hundred miles that you can go to the loo, drink coffee, eat, feel sick, buy film, admire the scenery, investigate the burning smell, read the map in the lay-by, get another map from the boot, change clothes, and jog-on-the-spot to get the circulation working. During these sneaky stops I work out a plan of action to get the driver's seat before anyone else and in that way usurp command. Selfish maybe, but it puts me in with a fighting chance of survival and shrinks the yellow streak back to containable levels. The only time I ever voluntarily give up the wheel is when sheer tiredness overtakes me. Then I let someone else have a go; of course, I don't go to sleep. Their driving automatically pops my eyelids open and I transfixedly stare at the screen, unable to forego the suspense for mere sleep.

On the Jaguar occasion I had grudgingly surrendered the helm to Nichols and was searching for my next reason for stopping when publisher Frankl, believed to be slumbering in the back, suddenly piped up with: "Mel, if this is a 140 mph car, why aren't we doing 140?" My buttocks contracted so hard that I rose two inches in the seat and the adrenaline started pushing sweat out into the undersides of my white-knuckled hands. A prickling feeling up and down my spine announced the arrival of a broader-than-ever band of yellow while on the front side of my shirt buttons were straining under the palpitations of my heart. There was absolutely no retort that I could make. Coolly and diplomatically, Nichols replied that going that much faster would be counterproductive because it would mean more fuel stops and thus a lower average overall. "Oh," said the voice of doom from the back and lapsed into untroubled sleep.

Things like that, no more than mere suggestions, are the key that lets my imagination run riot. I read into them untold horrors. I need smelling salts if I find myself in a car with a driver announcing that we are running late and that he will hurry a bit to catch up. To me, that's rather like being on a passenger jet you thought was Paris-bound and then the captain says: "Good morning, ladies and gentlemen. This is your captain welcoming you on this non-stop flight to Uganda. Immediately after take-off we will begin a sequence of low level aerobatics, starting with a stall-turn followed by a low pass, inverted, along the runway. If we survive that without the wings falling off I will demonstrate series of barrel rolls before we finally set course for our destination. I hope you have a nice flight."

Of course, this passenger-seat phobia was not a genetic inheritance. It is certainly an acquired trait, but just when it was acquired I am not sure. If I could just say: "Ah, yes, I remember exactly the occasion that turned me from a normal person into an unyielding coward. It was when the driver, who was drunk at the time, spun on a mountain road and we plunged four hundred feet into the sea. After that I was never the same." Then I would be able to avoid travelling with drunk drivers on mountain roads near the sea. But there's no single incident that could be described as the turning point. Of course, it may have been the time that I went to a party with a girlfriend in her MG. It was a heavy-drinking party (they always are when you're young) and at around 1:00 A.M. I felt the need of fresh air and quietness.

After a short stroll I went back to the MG, opened the door, and sat down in the passenger's seat. It seemed higher than I remembered it a few hours before, but while I was thinking about that problem the seat groaned, snarled, and bit. Thinks: "I'd recognise those teeth anywhere—the reason the seat is so high is that my girl-friend is asleep across the seat and I am sitting on her head." And I was. People could get phobias about that sort of happening, although I don't think that was the thing that changed me.

Nor was it the incident of the big spin in a racing MGTC, en route to a sprint meeting. While I was uncomfortably placed in the passenger seat, with cans of methanol stacked around my legs, tools and assorted hardware behind my head, and a lap full of spare wheels and tyres, my driver had an enormous spin on wet cobblestones, in front of a bus queue . . .

. . . Four of us did get the shakes about five minutes after a hair-raiser in an Austin-Healey 100/4, though (yes, that long ago). A quartet in a two-seater is ambitious stuff, but as it happened the weather was fine and the hood was down and we hardly had a care in the world until we charged over a blind crest at about 85 mph to find two acquaintances in a post-vintage Aston Martin sports/racer just as fast on our side of the double lines and only a few feet away. As luck would have it, they had already set course back to the correct side of the lines when we arrived. There was no time to brake, steer, or be frightened. The collision was averted only by time, not space or action.

Not long after that, I was actually enjoying the experience of being very expertly driven through the night in a particularly fast MG Magnette, of the pre-war vari-ety, with a six-cylinder, single-overhead camshaft engine and, in this case, six Amal carburettors. Just as we nosed into the first long left-handed corner of a particu-larly twisty section of the road, with the tachometer talking of 6000 plus rpm in top, the lights went out. The moon was between clouds at the time and after a bit of gravel-scattering we came to a halt more or less still on the bitumen, thanks to a touch of lunar illumination.

As a reluctant passenger, it's impossible not to play some role in the driving. After wearing the carpet thin with endless frightened shuffles and putting dents into the toe board as well as straining the seat backrests during moments of extreme rigidity comes the temptation of snatching at the wheel rim or assaulting the driver. I contemplated both during an incident involving a broken windscreen: forward visibility exploded into opaqueness and driver, concluding that he was dead already, figured there was no point in trying for a comeback. I tended to agree with this unspoken theory until I heard the gravel rattling under the car, in the way it does when you are rapidly departing from the road for a trip into the scenery. Since the driver didn't seem to get the message, I excused myself, leant in front of him, and punched a hole through the screen in a belief that there may still be some hope. There was and we eventually found the road again. None of the cuts in my hand actually needed stitching, but there was some blood . . .

. . . Such is human frailty that temptation too easily overcomes vows of intent. That's why I eagerly accepted Lamborghini test engineer Bob Wallace's invitation to ride in the prototype Lamborghini Urraco. I have never had any qualms about riding with Bob, for he is one of the best and safest drivers imaginable. We literally flashed through the Apennines between Florence and Bologna while Bob demonstrated the tremendous road-holding of the well-used experimental car. We were very high, I could not help noticing—high enough for one's clothes to get back in fashion again before getting to the bottom if you ever slipped over the edge—but there was no cause for more than the usual paralysing fear. All went well until we slowed down to 60 or so to search for a spot to take some pictures. There was a loud crack and the Urraco sagged slightly at the front and started making funny noises while Bob, arm muscles straining, kept it straight. One of the front wheels had broken off. Just at the right place. Just at the right speed. Just time to admire the view over the distant hills—and the view vertically downwards . . .

. . . Without a shadow of doubt there are people who live in terror of driving with me. That's only right. I am sure to have frightened the wits out of some passengers; I may even do so frequently. How I sympathise with them, but there's no way I am going to pat them on the head, hand over the keys, and say: "You poor fellow! I had no idea you were so nervous. Here, you drive for a while." When that happens, be assured that it probably means that I have done something terrible and know full well that whoever is driving the car is about to be arrested for a heinous offence or punched in the nose by an angered citizen.

JIM HARRISON

Log of the Earthtoy Drifthumper

Lake Leelanau—A few summers ago in Michigan's Upper Peninsula I walked out of my cabin well after midnight, took off my clothes, and dove buck-naked into the river, swimming and drifting downstream in the darkness, clambering over several logjams. It was pleasant, if eerie, until it was time to make my way back through the unpeopled forest and swamp. Then it became clear why shoes and clothing had been devised.

This is not generally recommended behavior, but then we like to think that life is usually lived between the lines, when we surprise ourselves, or lived while others are making plans and appointments. Mostly, though, I had to take the swim because I needed to know what it was like in order to conclude the novel *Sundog*.

This January I was having trouble with another book, because I am just another alpha manic-depressive who spends too much time in the air, with a dozen or so not very meaningful trips a year to either of America's dream coasts, to New York, which is really Europe, and to Los Angeles, which is an enticing, sunburned void. I needed to know what the Great Plains were like in the winter, and the king of information I wanted could not be extrapolated from the vantage point of 37,000 feet or from trips to the library.

* * *

At the outset you should know that I am not a car freak or maven. This disinterest can be attributed to a childhood trauma. At sixteen I bought a 1929 Model A, covered with birdshit, out of a barn and received a ghastly electric shock from something under the hood that my father described as a "magneto." Other young folks have been bitten by horses and turned to cars, but I was bitten by both, as it were. That summer I rode a balloon-tire Schwinn 128 miles in one day in reaction to horses and cars.

As a consequence I have gone through life at forty-nine miles an hour—if I were a boat, I'd be a tug. I have never run out of gas (for fear that the car won't start again), and I haven't washed a car since my teens, when I washed too many of them for quarters. Not that I am a totally slow-track guy—through the kindness and misapprehension of friends I have driven Porsches, a Ferrari, a Maserati, a 600 Mercedes, even my wife's Saab. Also a Daimler limousine in London when the chauffeur was drunker than I was. Curiously, I have never met anyone who thinks I drive well.

Late on the eve of my departure from Lake Leelanau, Michigan, I am having a heavy nightcap to steady my nerves, and listening to the wind howl. The snowdrifts have collected against the lower tiers of the windowpanes. Dimly under the yard light I can see the fully packed 1986 Subaru 4WD Turbo station wagon with manufacturer's plates. Parked next to it is my own 1981 Subaru 4WD station wagon, only mine has a skidplate, a cowcatcher, and a winch. There is a temptation to take "old reliable" and leave the new one at home. All I want in a car is reliability, just as in boats I prefer one that floats. The tempting factor is the turbo, though my wife quipped earlier in the evening that I don't know what "turbo" means. If it sounds good, you don't need to know what it means, I replied, remembering Paris, where I invariably order unknown items from the menu. Much of life seems to be a blind date.

Soon after daylight—actually, a few hours—I was on my way, double-checking for the shovel, the sleeping bag, and the big, white candles that were to save me if I became stranded—I'd read that if you light a few candles in your car, they give enough heat to keep you from freezing to death. I headed northward to the Straits of Mackinac with the snow coming down so hard I only averaged 38.5 miles per hour in the first four hours, or so said the elaborate trip computer. The trip computer was to be virtually my only sore point about the car. I was reminded of what Garrison Keillor, Lake Wobegon's celebrity, had said: "People in the Midwest don't take trips, they compute mileage and distance." I wanted my land voyage to be taken on house-cat time, with no attention paid to anything but the essentials of what I was seeing. Do you want to remember that you climbed a 10,000-foot mountain or what happened to you on the way up or down? But then I couldn't use my heel or Magnum on the trip computer because it wasn't my car. I've always felt those nitwits on the annual coast-to-coast race should be beaten across the gums.

I began to cool off approaching the Mackinac Bridge. There's no real point in getting angry while driving solo, when you can only yell into your Dictaphone. There are racers, and there are those who tour. Meanwhile, the bridge was swaying visibly in the gale-force winds. I began to have thoughts about mechanical mortality: just as a car grows old and dies, with gray hairs hanging from its mud flaps, so also must a bridge die. I just don't want to be there when it happens, when it finally gives up its bridge ghost and plummets into the bottomless straits. A few years ago, I missed by a mere seven months plunging off the bridge that collapsed between Tampa and Sarasota.

My spirits picked up when the weather cleared enough for me to see that there was barely any traffic. This was a signal thrill that was to follow me for the next twenty-eight days. By summertime standards, the progress was unimpeded by other cars. To be sure, there were trucks, but then they are somewhat predictable and reliable. There must be folks heading south to Florida, I thought, drawn there for the vermin-ridden night flowers, and for the clothing and pharmaceuticals on display in *Miami Vice*. I punched on cruise control and opened the sunroof, standing on the seat and steering with my fingertips.

I was headed west on Route 2, and now the sun glistened off the storm-tormented northern Lake Michigan. It was like driving a two-ton motorcycle without a wind visor. An oncoming car beeped, suggesting perhaps that my method was reprehensible. I forced myself into a more serious, mechanical mood. My '81 Subaru, with four forward gears, required 3300 rpm to go 58 miles per hour, while the '86 Subaru in fifth gear required only 2400 rpm to maintain the same speed. Any fool could figure out that if you were a skater or a dancer, 900 fewer twirls per minute would make a big difference.

I had planned my first night's stop for the House of Ludington in Escanaba, my favorite Midwestern hostelry. When I got out, I gave the car a friendly pat for a good day's work. Despite some harrowing moments, I felt much better than I would have arriving at La Guardia, or on a jam-packed flight at Los Angeles International with a dead woman and bizarre but friendly Siamese twins connected at the head, as had happened in December. Besides, no terrorist or member of the criminal element was likely to stick a bomb in the car. And I didn't have to pull up at this wonderful hotel and restaurant at 170 miles per hour, which has always been an enervating way to retouch earth.

Not knowing where the next good meal might come from in the hinterlands, I treated myself to fresh oysters and soup and a bottle of Graves. I was torn between the roast duck and the roast smoked pork loin, so I ordered them both, accompanied by a Châteauneuf-du-Pape. This normally might have put me to sleep, but I walked a mile up the street to see the kindly dancing girls at Orphan Annie's, somewhat as a soldier might do on the eve of battle, or a sailor before a voyage that might very well take him off the edge of the earth. The Great Plains were not known for nude dancing girls, and it would be best to take a look now. There were to be no flesh colors in future landscapes, or so I thought.

At daylight, or soon after, I adopted a slightly higher sense of purpose. At the current rate, what could I discover through red eyes and 10,000 lost dollars, a bilious stomach in a land without rest stops? I had worked the bugs out to the point where I comprehended the entire, intricate instrument panel of the car—except, of course, the trip computer. There were a few bugs left in my head, but they would presumably pass with the miles.

The trip through Wisconsin and Minnesota (the weather was nasty, but it was a garden-variety nasty) illustrated the central weather fraud current in America: Everyone brags about his bad weather. I've even had Texans tell me that I had "never lived through a Texas winter," a winter so severe that most northern Michiganders wouldn't bother putting on their winter coats. The fact is, the Leelanau peninsula had 108 inches of snow by New Year's, and much of the Upper Peninsula had half again as much. In Michigan I had humped through drifts about the size of a low-slung ranch house. Naturally you pause to check for oncoming traffic before you crank up toward the redline.

Route 64 through northern Wisconsin was a good choice, an improbably beautiful landscape with frozen forests and clearings, Scandinavian barns with frozen white, shimmering haystacks, an immense field with thousands of bright, frozen thorn apples catching the morning sun, the breath of Holsteins rising in steamy wisps in the still air. Hooking to the left on 73 and 95, you descend into the upper Mississippi River basin, moving down toward La Crosse through a rural landscape pretty much unequaled, somewhat like the hills of Kentucky. A well-tended hill farm owns a pure but functional beauty. Nearing a town or city of any size, you are reminded again of the implausible junkiness of mankind—I don't mean, in the anal-compulsive sense, that everything should be beautiful, but that ninety-nine percent of our artifacts are ugly, and strewn around so haphazardly that we are forever pausing to figure out why we feel so badly about what we are seeing.

At a service station near Sioux Valley, Minnesota, I flipped out my Dictaphone, determined to get at some troublesome questions concerning the average weight of heartland ladies, also whether any of the assembled had ever named their vehicles. The consensus was 150 for the ladies (the respondents were truly big ole boys, upward of 200 apiece). All of the men admitted to having named cars and trucks anything from Bullet to Bob to Fireball to Myrna (after a girlfriend). They liked the idea that I was going no place in particular for as long as cash and credit cards lasted.

"How long would that be?"

"About thirty days west of here," I answered.

"Too bad you can't drive to Hawaii. You should go to Vegas." (Everyone in the Midwest wants to go to Vegas or Hawaii.)

"I'm going to end up in Arizona to track mountain lions and track a Mexican wolf known as a white lobo. I night shoot some quail to eat too."

There were long faces at the station when I pulled out. Everyone wants to go someplace and the comparatively rare idea of a trip without a plan was even more attractive. As the days passed, I came to think that the finest thing about a long solo car trip is that you get to forget who you are, if anything celebrated or negotiable beyond the normal bounds of ego. Every place you stay is a place you never stayed before. Everyone you talk to is new, and no one can get you on the phone unless you call home. The bottom line is that you are free, however temporarily, and you return to the exhilaration of those childhood myths of Robin Hood or the lone cowpoke.

I'm heading through a hellish Minnesota storm toward a corner of Iowa, and the closest thing I have to a destination, Nebraska. The radio announces that all local schools will close because of the storm. I come upon the aftermath of a truly nasty truck–snow plow collision. I feel like I'm driving in a dentist's chair during an unsuccessful root canal. This weather is why I've had two Subarus for a total of seven years—there was only one trip to the garage, and that was caused by a caroming trip down a steep hill through the woods. Suddenly there's a bit of ugliness caused by a jackknifing semi that overshot an exit. I'm forced over a bank onto a cloverleaf in a split second. In another split second I think, "I'm not getting stuck here this close to lunch," punch the four-wheel-drive button, downshift to second, and fishtail in big circles to gain speed, throwing a roostertail of snow that I pass through before leaping a bank back onto the shoulder.

I am rewarded by a grotesque pork fritter and canned gravy at a truck stop where the assembled Knights of the Road all look like they need a resident nutritionist. On the road, breakfast is the most reliable meal. When I'm settled into my motel in the early evening, I invariably call the local radio station for a hot dinner tip. I figure disc jockeys are layabouts like writers and they would likely know the best place to eat. This works pretty well if you're willing to settle for a little less and can develop the uncritical state of mind that is required if you're ever going to get out of bed in the first place. In Alliance, Nebraska, I had a fabulous two-pound rib steak, watched a soft-core porn film on TV, and went to an American Legion country dance, where I jumped around like a plump kangaroo to work off the protein rush, or whatever.

I suppose if the country I had been driving through held anything in common from state to state it was that it had changed less as time had slipped by than it would have anywhere else in the United States. I mean outside the cities of Sioux City or Omaha or Lincoln. Iowa owns a charming lack of differentiation. If you lived there, you would seek out the extraordinary tuft of grass or mudhole, the most beautiful pig. Only one bird nests in all of Iowa, and it is called, simply enough, "brown bird." Iowa has a fifty-by-fifty-foot national park called Wild Thicket. The Iowa Writers' Workshop visits this place every year to write an annual nature poem— "how thick the thicket/where Brer Rabbit lies." There are no Sierra Club–type articles called "Hiking across Iowa."

I spent a number of days wandering around Nebraska. At one point, the January head wind was so strong my car seemed to hold in one place, a land Cessna passed by crows. Not incidentally, the sunroof is a splendid vantage for the road-side bird watcher, just as in Kenya and Tanzania; birds, especially hawks, and coy-otes are less disturbed if you stay in the car. Near the Wyoming border I was able to study at close range a golden eagle on a fence post and, one morning just after dawn, a big coyote with a blood-wet muzzle settling down for a stint of car watching. We exchanged deeply meaningless glances, the same as one does with a porpoise at sea. Much of the Great Plains will return to being a sea of grass when we stop overpro-ducing beef, and when the Bureau of Land Management decides to stop disastrous overgrazing. The Sand Hills themselves, an area of some 150 by 100 miles between Broken Bow and Alliance, Merriman and Lemoyne, will be largely abandoned by agriculture because they share the same diminishing Ogalala aquifer as Houston, Texas, far to the south.

Without question the best place to begin exploring Nebraska is the Stuhr Museum of the Prairie Pioneer, in Grand Island. I spent a full day there and will return this summer to finish my research. It isn't a place readily admired by yuppie nitwits, but it will deeply satisfy anyone with an interest in how we used to live and, consequently, why we live the way we do now. I was mostly studying the lay of the land, the windbreaks and shelterbelts, the possible soul history of the Dismal, the Middle Loup, and the Niobrara rivers. I am reminded that these concerns are not everyone's and shouldn't be. I'd like New York better if I could see it with the spirit of George and Ira Gershwin. I imagine if I lived out here, I would have to take R & R in Omaha every few months. For inscrutable reasons, there are some very good Chinese restaurants in Omaha.

One evening up near Whitman I had an urge to frighten myself. The moon was nearly full, and I had stopped along the creek bed after a large bird had swooped across the road. I was sure it was a great horned owl, so I walked up the creek bed in the direction the owl had taken. I circled up and over a hill with the air icy and metallic and the moon visibly moving as I walked. Far off I could see a small herd of ghost buffalo, though they were probably cattle. Now I could hear the owl from the creek bed, and he showed his lack of curiosity about me by staying there. I felt fine and undramatic, though a little lightheaded. Unlike the train I heard in the middle distance, I could make a right turn and do something different.

And I continued doing so. I woke up in the morning in Alliance after the kangaroo country hop and watched the news on CNN, which was dismal, unlike the Dismal River. I had finished my research in Nebraska and felt it was an even bet that I'd end up living there, because I like to live at the end of the road. Despite the fact that it was zero outside—the car gives the handy exterior temperature—I spread the map against the steering wheel while listening to Aretha Franklin sing "Spanish Harlem." I would hook a left outside of Alliance and reach Colorado Springs in time to watch the Super Bowl. Then on south through Taos, where my Zen master, Kobun Chino Sensei, owned a blue '84 Subaru 4WD. He liked my Turbo but was no help on the unruly trip computer, which he gazed at serenely. Then south to Tucson and Patagonia for a week, turning left to drive three days to Point Clear, Alabama, for sailing on Mobile Bay and quail hunting in Baldwin County with my friend Tom McGuane. Another left turn and it was north toward home with a day's stop in Oxford, Mississippi, to visit Rowan Oak, the home of my dead mentor, William Faulkner.

I liked being home for the first forty-eight hours; then the urge to drive returned. May seemed like a good possibility. A little green would be a nice alternative to black trees, white snow, the brown frozen prairie grass. I would call Lincoln, Nebraska, and get a set of county maps and log a couple of thousand miles on gravel roads. Maybe rig some foot pedals so that I could steer while standing through the sunroof of my motorized prairie schooner.

Suddenly I have decided to admit that I came within a few inches of losing the car on a two-track in Arivaca Canyon in Arizona. As the car slid toward the precipice on the frost-slick dirt, I undid the seatbelt and opened the door, under the assumption that a car is easier to replace than a novelist. Perhaps I'll order another Subaru this summer, if only because the car is foolproof.

DAVE BARRY

Slow Down and Die

I think it's getting worse. I'm talking about this habit people have of driving on interstate highways in the left, or "passing" lane, despite the fact that they aren't passing anybody. You used to see this mainly in a few abnormal areas, particularly Miami, where it is customary for everyone to drive according to the laws of his or her own country of origin. But now you see it everywhere: drivers who are not passing, who have clearly never passed anybody in their entire lives, squatting in the left lane, little globules of fat clogging up the transportation arteries of our very nation. For some reason, a high percentage of them wear hats.

What I do, when I come up behind these people, is the same thing you do, namely pass them on the right and glare at them. Unfortunately, this tactic doesn't appear to be working. So I'm proposing that we go to the next logical step: nuclear weapons. Specifically I'm thinking of atomic land torpedoes, which would be mounted on the front bumpers of cars operated by drivers who have demonstrated that they have the maturity and judgment necessary to handle tactical nuclear weapons in a traffic environment. I would be one of these drivers.

Here's how I would handle a standard left-lane blockage problem: I would get behind the problem driver and flash my lights. If that failed, I'd honk my horn until the driver looked in his rear-view mirror and saw me making helpful, suggestive hand motions indicating that he is in the passing lane, and if he wants to drive at 55, he should do it in a more appropriate place, such as the waiting room of a dental office. If *that* failed, I'd sound the warning siren, which would go, and I quote, *"WHOOP WHOOP WHOOP WHOOP."* Only if *all* these measures failed would I proceed to the final step, total vaporization of the car (unless of course there was a BABY ON BOARD!).

Too violent, you say? Shut up or I'll break your legs. No, wait, forgive me. I'm a little tense, is all, from driving behind these people. But something has to be done, and I figure if word got around among members of the left-lane slow-driver community, wherever they get together—hat stores would be my guess—that they had a choice of either moving to the right or turning into clouds of charged particles, many would choose the former.

It is not entirely their fault. Part of the problem is all those signs on the interstates that say SPEED LIMIT 55. I am no psychologist, but I believe those signs may create the impression among poorly informed drivers that the speed limit is 55. Which of course it is not. We Americans *pretend* 55 is the speed limit, similar to the way we're always pretending we want people to have a nice day, but it clearly isn't the real speed limit, since nobody, including the police, actually drives that slowly, except people wearing hats in the left lane.

So the question is, how fast are you *really* allowed to drive? And the answer is: Nobody will tell you. I'm serious. The United States is the only major industrialized democracy where the speed limit is a secret. I called up a guy I know who happens to be a high-ranking police officer, and I asked him to tell me the real speed limit, and he did, but only after—this is the absolute truth—he made me promise I wouldn't reveal his name, or his state, or above all *the speed limit itself.* Do you believe that? Here in the United States of America, home of the recently refurbished Statue of Liberty, we have an officer of the law who is afraid he could *lose his job for revealing the speed limit.*

When things get this bizarre, we must be dealing with federal policy. Specifically we are dealing with the U.S. Transportation Secretary, who is in charge of enforcing our National Pretend Speed Limit. The Transportation Secretary has learned—you talk about digging out the hard facts!—that motorists in a number of states are driving faster than 55 miles per hour, and she threatened to cut off these states' federal highway funds. So, to keep the Transportation Secretary happy, the police have to pretend they're enforcing the 55 limit, when in fact they think it's stupid and won't give you a ticket unless you exceed the *real* speed limit, which varies from state to state, and even from day to day, and which the police don't dare talk about in public for fear of further upsetting the Transportation Secretary.

I told my friend, the high-ranking police officer, that this system creates a lot of anxiety in us civilian motorists, never knowing how fast we're allowed to go, and he said the police like it, because they can make the speed limit whatever the hell they want it to be, depending on how they feel. "It used to be," he said, "that the only fun you had in police work was police brutality. Now the real fun is to keep screwing with people's heads about what the speed limit is."

Ha ha! He was just kidding, I am sure. Nevertheless, I think we need a better system, and fortunately I have thought one up. Here it is: The state should say the hell with the federal highway funds. They could make a lot more money if they set up little roadside stands where you could stop your car and pay five dollars, and a state employee would whisper the speed limit for that day in your ear. What do you think? I think it makes more sense than the system we have now. Of course, the Transportation Secretary wouldn't like it, but I don't see why we should care, seeing as how the Transportation Secretary probably gets chauffeured around in an official federal limousine that is, of course, totally immune from traffic laws. Although I imagine it would be vulnerable to atomic land torpedoes.

RONALD BARKER

On the Horns of a Dilambda

When the metallic clangour suddenly rang out from under the bonnet, like Kipling's dry rattle of new-drawn steel, it abruptly pulled a single train of thought straight off the rails and scattered it three ways in acute disorder. For we were on a lonely back-road in the heart of Burgundy, and although it was nowhere near lunch time we were already gulping saliva at the prospect of a brief gastronomic respite. As the old Lancia slowly freewheeled to a standstill, three brains registered individual reactions to the shock of this new predicament: no lunch today, of course—a broken car in need of sympathetic shelter—a mountain of miscellaneous baggage and unpacked paraphernalia—nearly four hundred miles between us and Le Touquet. And just when everything had seemed at last to be in our favour.

For the fun had begun early the previous morning, outside the Polo Club near Turin. A mature lady of thirty-seven is never at her best for a long journey after a night out, and this one was suffering from flatulence of her battery. Perhaps, too, she was reluctant to be parted once again from the city of her birth in 1930 and from Pinin Farina, her celebrated *haut couturier* who had clothed her in accordance with the wishes of her first aristocratic gallant, Lord Berkeley.

There's an awfully dead feel about four litres distributed among eight compressions on a cold and misty morning, then that almost animate little kick on the starting-handle which tells you, "We have ignition!" Open the hand throttle and she's away with scarcely another tweak on the handle.

Artist Dexter Brown and chauffeur Steady Barker roll majestically into Turin to pick up Editor Blain, who is stowed initially in the cargo hold behind the glass division with baggage stacked so high around him that he could be crushed in the avalanche if we take a corner a bit sharpish. We need fuel and lots of it. An adept conjuror, Barker suddenly flashes a wad of magic free coupons, and being unable to understand a word of Italian in such emergencies fails to explain to the attendant how he has come upon them. "Something something buonos de benzina?" asks Antonio with a puzzled scowl. "Si, si, molto buono!" we reply in unison, concealing our apprehension behind barmy tourist grins. Then we gonfi our Pirelli gomme with his free air, delivered in hurricane gusts through a sort of outsize mercury thermometer, and depart with an impromptu farewell arpeggio from "La Scatola del Gambio de Velocita Lancia."

Next, three empty stomachs gurgling like fifth-floor bath-plugs are silenced at a little country albergo-ristorante, where we find sculptured Piedmontese grotesques in the courtyard and quite a wealth of interesting old furniture and clocks inside. Blain's Cordon Blue eyes sparkle greedily when they spy through an open doorway rack upon rack of local wine stored in black litre bottles upside down like champagne. We resist the temptation . . .

. . . At the other end of the tunnel it's France, where only the uncivilised can pass the subtle aromas of a good restaurant. After an excellent light lunch, though, at the Savoy in St. Michel de Maurienne, one of our regular haunts, there is an ominous ticking like an army of deathwatch beetles from beneath the Dilambda's rear floor, so the head chauffeur removes all the luggage to tinker with the twin SU pumps—a post vintage afterthought. Blain takes the wheel; it is dusk, so he switches on the sidelamps. Almost immediately they go out. We stop again, and the chauffeur miraculously finds a spare fuse in a door pocket while two helpful gendarmes look on.

Editor Blain continues, evidently completely at ease with the car and handling it so sympathetically that the owner can relax completely in the back except for keeping a wary eye on the tottering baggage: that is until somewhere deep in the Tunnel du Chat, in total darkness, when the engine begins to splutter and the lamps to flicker ominously. The chauffeur bangs frantically on the glass division. "Keep the revs up, for God's sake!" he shrieks, which Blain does, and we keep going somehow, but only just reach the first well-lit cafe before coasting to a stop. Blain orders brandy for three while the chauffeur, with no understanding of total loss electrical systems, fiddles with the voltage regulator. A vivid blue flash, and the main fuse expires. With silver paper from a Gitanes packet to bind it, all systems are suddenly go and we go. The chauffeur is now smugly optimistic, and Blain drives impeccably to Bourg en Bresse and the Grand Hotel de France. Life is good again—until next morning.

Which brings us back again to square one and THE NOISE. A dropped valve or broken rocker, possibly? Off with the rocker cover, and nothing obviously wrong there. Remove plugs, and find water in two adjacent cylinders, so decide chauffeur will hitchhike to get help and artist guard car and contents while editor tramps through autumnal lanes to nearby village in search of food and wine. A 403 pulls in and its driver volunteers to help find a friendly garage. We pass several which do not have quite the right ambience, and decide to make for Louhans, where the 403 driver knows just the man . . .

. . . At the garage we remove the cylinder head and with a valve sucker extract one piston plus a short length of its connecting-rod. There are fissures at each side of the bore through which water is seeping rather quickly and trickling down into the crankcase. M. Creuzenet telephones an engineer friend in Chalon, who pronounces the cylinder block irreparably damaged. He will take us to the railway station in Chalon to catch a train to Paris . . .

. . . On the train we engage in a shuttle contest with the ticket inspector because, like most rail travellers, we prefer living above our station, and so take turns to scout his whereabouts until it's time to pass through interminable crowded coaches to the dining car. Here the meal is taken vibrato, which turns our chateau Batailley into neo-lambrusco, but it makes us feel alive and well and living in a French rattler. What next? A late flight to LAP? The Golden Arrow? We are not really rich enough for a night in Paris. First, though, we must claim our baggage at the Consignee Arrives, where two Gallic loons wearing wooden clogs and cardboard suits do a sort of music hall pas de deux, delighting in our discomfort when our consignment fails to appear.

Do they know if there is another train for London tonight? No, but they do know there is a plane leaving for Morocco at 5:00 A.M.; they giggle in unison. True, there is no train till midday tomorrow (a Sunday) so when the luggage arrives we hasten to the Aerogare. No more planes to London either until midday tomorrow; we take a taxi to the Hertz car-hire office and rent a Renault 10, after payment of a monstrous deposit. Blain drives, Brown chats to keep him awake, Barker sleeps aft with the luggage, but is awoken five times at road-blocks where riot police wearing Day-Glo Wimpey jackets inspect us to see if any of us look like an escaped prisoner. We all do, but they aren't looking for three. We notice they have spiked mats like Fakirs' beds of nails, ready to pull across the path of any car that fails to stop.

A few hours' kip at a small Le Touquet hotel—the Moderne, which is cheap and always open, in case you are ever stuck—and we motor up to the airport. There is no Hertz man around to return our deposit, so we leave the car in the charge of the AA rep there and fly BAF to Lydd, with no extra charge for the ten pieces of baggage. If we take a taxi to Ashford, they say, we can easily catch the eleven-something to Charing Cross.

We move with unparalleled deliberation and concentration in the direction of Ashford. Our taxi driver points out places of intense interest such as the deep ditch from which a farm tractor has extricated him only a few weeks ago. Under the circumstances it seems wise not to press him to hurry; as we unload at Ashford Station we actually watch our train depart.

Nothing for it now, of course, but to suffer buffet char and wads until BR send up another. Blain buys a paper. Eventually another train arrives and once again we shoulder our burdens.

"All we need now, just to round things off nicely," suggests Barker cheerfully, "is a damned good train crash with us inside." Well, it didn't quite happen that way. But there was an almighty train crash late that afternoon, and on that very line.

CALVIN TRILLIN

On the Road

September 29, 1979

There I am, bombing down Interstate 95, thinking my usual six-lane interstate kind of thoughts. I am wondering how much larger the pyramids might be if there had been a pyramid construction industry lobby for the Pharaohs to contend with. I am considering whether those in charge of the next gas-crisis allocation plan might be made to see the wisdom of a system that allowed people with even-numbered license plates to buy gas on even-numbered days, people with odd-numbered license plates to buy gas on odd-numbered days, and people with their names or initials spelled out on their license plates to buy no gas at all.

The children are in the back seat, continuing their odd custom of not arguing about who is encroaching on whose side of the seat. I know that in the view of some of my Eastern analytical friends I should worry about this. It is true that as children, my sister and I covered thousands of miles of the Great American West ignoring mountains and mesas and buttes (if they are different from mesas) and Indian-moccasin stands and roadside zoos and Burma-Shave signs and whatever else was visible out the window in order to give our complete concentration to guarding our territory. I imagine one of my Eastern analytical friends asking me if I'm worried about the possibility that our girls might be sublimating natural sibling hostilities that should be expressed. I imagine another of my Eastern analytical friends asking me if we feel guilty about not imbuing our children with the sort of contentiousness that will allow them to persevere in a world dominated by delicatessen lines. I think of myself telling both of my Eastern analytical friends to buzz off, and I keep bombing down Interstate 95.

Alice is sitting beside me in the front seat, watching me glance nervously at the state-police car in the rear-view mirror, and asking me again why I am so afraid of policemen. Alice, being a romantic, used to think that my feeling that all policemen were after me came from my experience as a reporter in the South, but I finally admitted that it comes from my experience as a teen-ager in Kansas City. Talk about traits imbued during childhood! Every teenage American boy knows that the police are lying in wait to catch him going three miles over the speed limit (posted on a smudged sign behind a thick hedge)—allowing the viciously anti-teen-age judges to strip him of his God-given right to drive. Every teen-age American girl who doesn't look like a teen-age American boy knows that the policeman who stops her for an illegal left turn that snarled traffic for six blocks is likely to put on the stern look that he has been told makes him resemble a slightly heavier Gary Cooper and say something like, "Well, you promise me you'll be real careful in the future, little lady, because we sure wouldn't want anything to happen to you."

It occurs to me, bombing down Interstate 95, that pressure on police forces to hire women and gays will eventually change all of this. A female motorcycle cop will stop a teen-age girl for a bad turn and say, "Don't give me that helpless-little-me smile, sister; I wrote the book on that one." A gay state trooper will stop a teen-age boy for going 80 in a 50-mile-per-hour zone and let him go with a warning—asking the teen-ager, while returning his driver's license, if anybody had ever told him he looks a lot like James Dean. For the time being, I am still glancing nervously at the state-trooper car in the rear-view mirror.

I pass a Cadillac Seville and feel a twinge of envy—not for the Seville but for the trip computer that I know, from an article in the *Times*, may be ticking away inside of it. When Cadillac announced that the Seville's options would henceforth include a computer, I naturally belittled the entire project. A computer, we are always being told, is only as good as what is programmed into it, and I figured the Cadillac folks could be counted on to apply the same corporate wisdom to computer programming that they once applied to the need for fender fins. Sure enough, the *Times* said that one bit of information that could be conjured up from the computer at the press of a button was how many miles the Seville was getting to the gallon—a figure that these days is likely to traumatize a Cadillac driver to the point of making him a danger to navigation. The *Times* said the computer could also calculate "speed in revolutions per minute" and "engine temperature in degrees"—just the sorts of things I have no interest in whatsoever. I was once told of a squeamish man who liked to envision his insides as being very much like the inside of a potato, and I prefer to envision the inside of automobiles exactly the same way. The Cadillac folks, I said at the time, never seem to have me in mind when they make one of their little improvements. Their market research people have never captured my profile, or, more likely, their market research people know my likes and dislikes precisely and also know that I am fated never to trade up from a Volkswagen Rabbit.

I have to admit, though, as I bomb down Interstate 95, that I covet the Seville's computer. There is no reason, after all, why the computer's program could not be varied. Instead of calculating the estimated time of arrival, "based on the variables of speed, stops, etc.," it could calculate when I will next have to stop to let my younger daughter go to the bathroom, based on the variables of 7-Up intake, nagging, and parental insensitivity. It could be of great comfort to me if it were programmed to tell me the next time we could, according to the percentages, expect to have our luggage rack fall off the car—surely a date blessedly far in the future for a family that has, the computer knows, already had its luggage rack fall off the car once. Having fed the computer statistics gathered from the Law Enforcement Assistance Administration and the American Civil Liberties Union, I could punch a few buttons and see what my chances were of encountering a gay state trooper. Thinking of the possibilities of a properly programmed computer, I am bombing down Interstate 95.

JOYCE CAROL OATES

Night Driving

South into Jersey on I-95, rain and
windshield wipers and someone you love asleep
in the seat beside you, light on all sides
like teeth winking and that smell like baking
bread gone wrong, and you want
to die it's so beautiful—
you love the enormous trucks floating in spray
and the tall smokestacks rimmed with flame
and this hammering in your head,
this magnet drawing what's deepest
in you you can't name
except to know it's there.

Man versus Machine

Of course he has moments of triumph, as when he first owns a Delusion-Demountable. But the Delusion-Demountable is three hundred dollars cheaper than a Complex Collapsible, and the Browns have just purchased a Complex. The Complex is a good car and it is a far cry to the first motor. He is a changed man, for a man changes with his cars. He is making much more money, too. He has to or face bankruptcy. In fact he is so successful that one night after dinner the Mrs. broaches the subject of a Pierced-Sparrow.

Going from even such a car as the Complex Collapsible to a Pierced-Sparrow is only comparable to the initial jump out of the Fordowner class. A Pierced-Sparrow is the insignia of success. In our modern system of civilization the Pierced-Sparrow takes the place of the heads that our ancestors used to dry in the smoke of their hut fires. In the Pierced-Sparrow are concentrated all the scalps of his business competitors. It is better than the accolade. He thinks that if he has a Pierced-Sparrow it will mean that he has arrived in the elect.

So he buys a Pierced-Sparrow, unhappy man! As soon as he has the Pierced-Sparrow he discovers that a great many other people have them too. Then one day at the club he overhears this conversation:

"What kind of a car has he?" asks the first gentleman.

"Pierced-Sparrow," replies the second, blowing a cloud of smoke.

"Upper Middle Class people, eh?" says the first comfortably.

It is the beginning of the end. The ex-Fordowner has achieved business success. He has raised a son who knows more than his father. He has a daughter who smokes cigarettes and has been a successful debutante for eight years. He has enough servants to make him uncomfortable. You would imagine that he would be happy. But he is not.

He makes one last desperate effort to escape from the Other Half. He buys a Rice-Rolls. He can't afford it, of course. But it is necessary for his self-respect. The Rice-Rolls is the ultimate.

Now if this were comedy we would leave him in happiness riding through life in his Rice-Rolls, having attained the true happiness of success. His chauffeur might even let him drive his Rice-Rolls sometimes. Nothing would be lacking. His son would know more every day and his daughter would learn to roll her own. But this is tragedy.

There is no peace for him this side of the sepulcher. We have reliable information from England that a super-car is being brought out which will cost at least four times as much as the Rice-Rolls. The curtain falls upon the tragedy of How the Other Half Lives.

JAMIE KITMAN

My Brave New Face

Edgewater, New Jersey—The twentieth day of March marked a special anniversary for me this year. It would for you, too, if one night exactly ten years prior you'd driven your 1967 MGB into the back of a big ol' Chrysler—stalled, lights out, in the passing lane of the George Washington Bridge eastbound into New York City—while traveling at 55 mph. Ten years ago, I bought myself a brave new face.

Although this story has a happy ending, those who tend to squeamishness may wish to consider signing off right here. For them, I will briefly summarize my thoughts on the subject of violent car crashes: They're a genuine learning experience. But I don't recommend them. My advice? Don't die.

There may not be a lot of cosmic truth to be gleaned from an account of a single automobile accident, but events of that far-ago evening and their aftermath sure taught me a lot. For instance. pulling out to pass a semi-trailer blind is not the smart driver's money choice. At the ripe old age of twenty-four, I had yet to learn that. Now I know. Sometimes speed doesn't kill. Sometimes it just hurts.

Fortunately, I was alone when my plans changed unexpectedly. I was going home to meet some friends in Brooklyn. It's fair to add I was wearing my seatbelt (a three-point harness I'd personally installed three weeks earlier) and was soberer than the judge himself, an irony of some sort as I was driving to town in preference to attending a Friday night self-criticism session in Jersey with some co-workers and their stern Old Grand Dad, he of the 86-proof variety.

Don't you hate it when people park in the left lane of busy highways at night with their lights out? I don't remember seeing the car I hit until after I'd hit it. That was after my mug had clocked the sharp-edged aluminum spoke of an aftermarket steering wheel squarely in the upper jaw above the right middle tooth. A doctor later described it as the type of injury you would see if you really pissed off Joe Frazier and he took a sledgehammer to your face.

The author and critic Susan Sontag has written of her personal Vietnam. Ground zero for my personal Hiroshima was the borderline between New York and New Jersey, a mystical spot denoted on the lower level of the George Washington Bridge by a grimy overhead sign. If my case had ever gone to court, this geographical oddity might have made for an interesting question of state law, but for me at the time, the relevant state was shock.

Whatever you've heard about shock, rest assured that it's great stuff, a kind of limited-slip diff or traction control system for the brain when the going gets tough. For a guy who had just driven into the back of a full-size car at speed, I didn't feel half-bad. Kind of fuzzy and warm. I knew I had the definite option of passing out, but didn't. Although exhibiting the presence of mind to hit the kill switch for the electric fuel pump and climb out of the car, I otherwise held a deeply uncertain tether on reality.

I knew some teeth had gone down, and I had become aware that my lower lip had been sliced by the wheel and was now dangling around my collar, which troubled me, but not inordinately. I suspected that blood was being lost in greater than paper-cut volume and felt an Excedrin-strength headache a brewing. But mostly I was cranked at the people in the Chrysler. They'd messed up my car, and I was going to be late to meet my friends.

Holding my lip roughly in place with cupped hands, I set off to tell them. Staggering past the steaming MG—a rust-free example I'd gone all the way to California to find—I stuck my head through an open window and found six startled but miraculously uninjured Puerto Rican Americans.

"You #@%*ing idiots!" I thought I screamed as I uncovered my mouth. "Do you have any idea how much it's going to cost to fix my car? It needs two fenders and a grille. At least $600!" (In fact, both cars were totaled.) As I was ranting in this vein, some teeth fell out. I looked into my new acquaintances' eyes, and it dawned on me that I was not looking my best. I stepped back for a second, and they rolled up their window in horror.

Hmm, not a good sign, I thought to myself, standing about in a surreal but not unpleasant fog while three lanes of traffic stopped around me and people got out of their cars to help. An ambulance arrived. "Who's been injured here? Who?" the EMT barked. I uncovered my face and attempted to offer an unbiased analysis of the relative blame of the parties to the accident. He recoiled. "Let's go."

The EMT's reaction and the tracheotomy they gave me in the ambulance on the way to Englewood Hospital should have clued me in to the serious nature of my condition, but I still clung to the hope that I'd be in my own bed before the evening was out. At the hospital, as I waited for surgeons to arrive and X-rays to be taken, I gave nurses contact telephone numbers of some friends in New Jersey.

Some time later, a couple of compadres arrived. They were much the worse for wear, the hour being late, but their honorable intentions were undoubted. "Where's Jamie Kitman?" I could hear them demand of a duty nurse as I lay in a nearby room, barely conscious and unable to speak.

"He's in that room. But you can't see him."

"Why not?"

"He's been injured," the nurse explained. "Seriously."

WHAT?! I thought. Me? Seriously injured? Why haven't I been notified? I have places to go.

"We *have* to see him," they bellowed. "We're his friends."

"You can't see him."

"We must. We're going to," they announced bellicosely, barging past the duty nurse. Directly outside my door, they were halted by another nurse.

"We must see him. Why can't we see him?" they persisted.

"How about because he's in critical condition with a split palate, a jaw broken in eight places, an eviscerated lip, two broken eye sockets, a broken nose and cheekbones, and some fractured ribs?"

"Right. Well . . . er, just, ah, tell him we stopped by," the newly courteous well-wishers allowed, beating a hasty retreat and leaving me to process this shocking medical bulletin privately. Man, I'd certainly cracked the executive coconut this time. Recalling a line from David Lynch's nightmarish film *Eraserhead*, I thought, Gee, I really am sick, and passed out.

Twenty-four hours later, I awoke in the intensive care unit to learn that I was not dead, just incredibly ugly. Three surgeons had labored twelve hours to put me back together again.

"Fifteen minutes more and you'd have been outa here," one of my pinstriped saviors told me proudly as he fingered a Phi Beta Kappa key and ran down the basic facts of my new circumstance.

The face—minus four teeth and a piece of upper jawbone, R.I.P.—was held together by an elaborate infrastructure that wired the unbroken lower jaw shut to the temples in a sort of stressed Jell-O mold arrangement. Wires exited through the temples to form the hideous Frankenstein plugs I was just noticing. These would begin to hurt shortly, but not to worry because they couldn't be removed for twelve weeks. On account of shattered cheekbones and eye sockets, the whites of Master's eyes were understandably green and red, but the eyes themselves were more or less intact, although a Silastic implant had to be installed permanently to hold up the left one. Rubber gloves filled with ice were strapped to the presidential noggin on the hour to reduce the massive swelling of a black and blue visage. The beloved sinus cavities were history, hundreds of stitches were holding the lower lip crook-edly in place, and a pulverized facsimile of what I had liked to call my nose was in a splint. In other words, they told me, things were going great.

My little sister came to visit, took one look at me, and ran out crying. A doctor continued working on me.

A plastic tracheotomy tube was the device jutting painfully from my neck, those were IV units jacked into my arm, and the thing residing uncomfortably you-know-where was called a catheter. Sixteen weeks' downtime in the hospital seemed reasonable to expect, and the strong possibility of ongoing neurological and vision impairment existed. Recurring headaches and a lifetime of head colds were also dis-tinct possibilities. Beginning law school in the fall as planned might not be realistic.

By the way, the doctor asked, how many fingers am I holding up? Sixteen is not right, he told me, but nice try. Hugely good news was an X-ray that showed a bone splinter from my nose had missed my eye by about 1/164th of an inch. My luck was picking up, it seemed, but only temporarily.

Responding to a scrawled question by a son with an unshakable grip on the bottom line (i.e., me), Dad reluctantly confessed that the Chrysler had turned out to be uninsured and unregistered. Its driver gave police a false address and license and—surprise, surprise—disappeared. Said son had no medical insurance, and his automobile insurance company advised (in error, it would mercifully transpire) that medical bills, promising to total more than $100,000 in good-time 1982 dollars, would not be covered. In short, he and my mom might have to sell their house.

Things were pretty grim all around and might have gotten me badly depressed if it hadn't been for my faith, my native optimism, and regular doses of hard drugs.

By allowing me to assume an ultrarelaxed state, one that seemed to blend the essential consciousness of William Burroughs with that of a Maryland blue crab, morphine and Demerol put real wrenching pain and my family's impending bankruptcy on hold. It was a cozy time.

Lest I become a crazed dope fiend or a communist, though, they took me off the hard stuff after about a week, and I was able to reacquaint myself with reality, headfirst. Believe me, you feel awful and you look awful when you try to eat a Chrysler. You think things will never be the same. By turns, you get mad and sad. But then nature takes over. To hasten the body's healing, the mind switches to autopilot. You are a finely tuned machine, with one purpose—getting better. Denial, the most useful human faculty, takes care of most of the recent past. A sense of perspective takes care of the rest.

For a short while after an accident, you become incredibly stoic, heroic even. I feel bad calling myself a hero, but the days and months after my accident stand as one of the few times in my life when I can remember behaving admirably for any sustained period, and I don't remember having any choice in the matter. I believe that inside every idiot who goes around whining about the petty and bemoaning the relatively decent lurks a tough mutha who knows that it could have been a lot worse. It's just that some of us need this realization kicked out of us.

Of course, it's easy to summon perspective when people are dying around you in an intensive scare unit. You have to be a pretty big jerk not to realize that they're the ones with the problems. It turns out you're not blind, deaf. or impaired. You're still young. Rather than horribly unlucky, you've been incredibly lucky, narrowly missing an early curtain in life's grand theater. Or a lifetime impaired. That would be tragic.

Dwelling on the bright side is infectious, too. The more I thought about it (and I had plenty of time to think), the more the continued viability of my corporeal being proved conclusively to me that my number had come up, that I had been tested by the divine puppet master and spared. Death had pulled up to my doorstep in a British sports car, and I had declined to take the final ride. I was invulnerable now. Upon release from the hospital, I would be free to drive Morris Minors backward down mountain passes blindfolded while smoking banana peels, without fear of mishap or great bodily injury.

Ever hopeful that I would find religion, my mother wondered whether a brush with death had brought me any closer to the Almighty. Yes, it has, I told her. And I realized that I am He.

A newfound spirituality was the best part about arranging to rearrange my suave good looks for all time. But almost as satisfying was the knowledge that I'd also inadvertently pulled off one of the rarest feats an American can achieve, and that is: beating an insurance company for its dough without dying in the process. If I live to be one hundred, I'll never pay enough in premiums to be anything other than a net disaster for the insurance industry. To a frugal, cranky Yankee like me, that's a hell of a meaningful achievement.

I used my recovery time profitably. With mouth wired shut, I quit smoking and shed excess blubber. With calendar free and the distractions of enterprise and commerce out of mind, I could further explore my spiritual side, catching up on my TV sitcom viewing and thinking about what kind of car I'd buy when I was fixed.

Did you realize that in the series *Get Smart*, Don Adams drove successively a Sunbeam Tiger, an Opel GT, and a Karmann Ghia? Surely, it's no coincidence that the show's ratings tracked its star vehicles' downward performance spiral. As for my own wheels, parental types advocated a Volvo or preferably an experimental safety vehicle or an armored personnel carrier. In the end, a diminutive 1981 Fiat X1/9—a leftover that must have entirely escaped Fiat quality control because it proved stone reliable—got the nod. Don't forget, the laws of physics mean little to someone convinced of his own immortality.

Others described it as a miraculous recovery, but, being immortal, I almost expected it when I was ready to leave the hospital in sixteen days, two and a half months ahead of schedule. Two weeks later, I'd be ready to return to work. Five months later, I'd attend law school. One year later, a piece of my rib would be implanted in my jaw. Another six months of dental work, and it would all be over with. The vision and headache problems would never appear, although I would be consigned to a lifelong postnasal trip, a tedious mélange of colds, sinus trouble, and many new and strange allergies. I'd also look a little different—worse, really, but not so much that people don't recognize me. As my friend Joe Ranker liked to observe, surgeons have options that auto body men don't. Doctors merely have to put the parts near one another and they'll probably grow back together and it'll probably look okay. Try doing that with the rear clip of a Monte Carlo.

Over the years, some friends have speculated that I might have been better off had I not been wearing a seatbelt. I've had a lot of time to think about it, but I still can't see any good coming out of allowing one's person to continue to observe the national speed limit once one's car has stopped. Because I don't think I'm immortal anymore, if I had to do it all over again, I think I'd stick with the seatbelts.

When it was time to remove all the dressings and bandages and stitches, the surgeons arrived and assembled around my hospital bed. First, they removed the stitches from my temples, and they liked what they saw. "Doctor," one of them enthused, "this is most assuredly some of your best suturing ever, I must say. Truly quite remarkable."

The medical men's delight continued unabated as they removed the stitches from below my eyes. Inspecting the scars closely, one doctor said aloud to a colleague: "Virtually undetectable. Sir, I've said it before, you are so talented." Things, it seemed, were going swimmingly. The exultations ensued as they examined the stitches joining the parts of my severed lip. High fives and kudos were dispensed all around. "Genius," one of the docs whispered.

This left only for them to remove the splint from my nose. Strangely, as they lifted the contraption from my proboscis, their smiles abruptly faded. They appeared flummoxed and bewildered and glanced nervously away. Finally, one of them gathered his composure.

"Listen, son, these things happen. We're not happy with the nose, but there really is no cause for alarm. This is New Jersey. We're in a no-fault state. Money is no problem for necessary surgical procedures arising from car accidents. So, whenever you feel up to it, you book yourself in here, we'll fix up that nose of yours in a jiffy, and it won't cost you a cent. Robert Redford's, Bobby De Niro's—you name it, we'll give you the nose you want. Tell us when you're ready."

Cripes, I thought. Just my luck. Here I am thinking I'm making a wondrous comeback, only to discover that I'm totally disfigured, and these clowns are being friggin' cheerleaders about it. "Let me see it for myself," I barked rudely, grabbing for a hand mirror on the bedside table. Surveying the schnoz, unsheathed after two weeks in traction, I couldn't help smiling. "Sorry to disappoint you, fellows," I said, "but that's the same nose I've always had." Talk about adding insult to injury.

ALLEN GINSBERG

Hiro Yamagata's Holy Ghost XX Century Automobiles

I never learned to drive—how do people overcome panic at intersections, or speeding freeways & superhighways, autobahns, bridges? Thousands of motors on wheels revving up noisy crisscrossing cloverleafed borders at 80 mph? What would I do, Thump, a bloody body dangling over my hood, skull crushed, intestines dripping over the fender?

Meanwhile the Sphinx is losing the rest of his nose, the Acropolis' columns are pitted, David's been taken indoors in Florence, cars hoot up alleys by the Bargello, the Bible says brimstone falls from heaven at Apocalypse time, sulfuric acid rain eats away Notre Dame's gargoyle mouths, petrol exhaust rises to Paris' skies, a thin brown layer of gas floats over every city in the world, Mexico, New York, Denver, Beijing, Los Angeles, Kyoto.

Persian Gulf, reefs clogged with petroleum, more than a hundred thousand teenagers bombed to death in Baghdad, desert sands, Ur, Sumer—Petrochemical Nightmare! The planet revved up on fossil fuel, bigtime wars pivot round Middle East's petroleum "Concession States." Israel Iraq Iran Saudi Yemen Bahrein Kuwait Lebanon are battlegrounds for rights to subterranean oily lakes that power the Metropolises of the world. We continue our dirty work, colonizing every continent, reducing the mass of humanity to "underdeveloped" fools supplying raw materials and labor while the ecosystems that bore them are destroyed. Mile by mile, hectare by hectare, forest by forest, river by river chemicall'd, gigantic cities spread tentacles of highway trucks & acid rain on subcontinents' polluted Edens.

Billions of carbon bodies, a hundred million years of trees, fireflies, liquid fish & animals' remains sucked out of Earth's hide run through energy machines that spew them out into the atmosphere. The Karma of a billion years' conifer & mosquitoes, pterodactyls, stegasauri & dragonflies, roaches, giant lizards, waterbugs, enormous ferns—all fumed into the air, cyclic eons of life resurrected & exhausted onto the thin layer of planet oxygen.

We can't kill the plant. Asteroids, moons, volcanoes, ice ages come & go, seeds sprout, mastodons freeze, tropics turn arctic, poles reverse their charges, the brontosaurus sprouts wings, the planet's got another couple billion years to breathe, clouds swirling round like TV speedup weather reports—"The sun's not eternal, that's why there's the blues." So the sun's got another 12 billion years (I once heard) before it runs down, eats itself up, sucked into its black hole, lots of leisure time to recuperate from human virus & its fossil pneumonia.

Not that I don't ride cars myself, fly jet planes, turn on the petrochemical lightswitch, or eat cauliflowers grown with fossil fertilizers & nitrates that pollute the waters—or enjoy Lower East Side apartment steamheat in freezing New York wintertime, plug in amps to read ecologic poetry Harvard auditoriums, waste huge forests to read the *Times*, or publish ravings such as this—as Gregory Corso said, "No good news can be written on bad news."

We won't kill the planet but we might well suicide the human race, wipe ourselves out with the help of the World Bank—jungle industrialization brings ecocide, ecocide brings genocide in Amazon, Borneo, Far West, Far East, USA.

We can only destroy ourselves and a lot of mammals birds & fish—maybe not extinguish the entire gene pool, just blank out portions of our own, other species', vegetable germs, whales or birdies. They'll come back, maybe we'll come back gnashing our teeth, starting fires, inventing the wheel, or taking it easy, four hours a day for hunting & gathering food shelter & amusement. Neanderthal folk had bigger brains than we have—crammed full of info on local flora & fauna, Minute Particulars re their bioregional territories. They knew more about quality leisure time than we do.

So now we're stuck with a science that doesn't know how to wipe its own half ass—witness the impossible task of cleaning out old Rockwell Corporation's abandoned Plutonium bomb trigger plant at Rocky Flats, 15 miles from this table whereon

I write. This monstrosity, a fossil remains of an "American Century," is a waste dump employing increasing thousands of laborers to contain its transuranic elements less they migrate outward in vast underground plumes to poison the soil under universities & downtowns of the Denver Rockies' Front Range region. Yes, we're stuck with a Frankenstein civilization we grew up in, that nourished our flesh & minds at the expense of billions of underclass sentient beings.

What to do? The Bosatsu Vows point a way—to do whatever's in our power to relieve the mass of sentient suffering, to dissolve the illusion of permanent solidity of our selfhood & the pains of extreme views: Eternalism (America & Japan will last Forever! Our science will progress eternally till everyone on the planet is drinking milk eating cow steak & zipping around the equator in 10 billion Mercedes-Benzes by the year 3,000 Ad!) or Nihilism ("The world's a wreck, whadda I care—might as well burn down the rest of it while I'm alive—'After me the deluge' I got mine! Screw Africa Asia South America the Arctic Poles the Future").

Middle Path, we won't wreck the planet only ourselves. Knowing that, we can look into our own eyes and calm the Anger Ignorance Disease that drives our multinational machine. Can acknowledge our own materiel lust and resentment, calm down a bit & take classic steps to purify our consciousness—recognize our own wreckage, regret wrong actions, repair what loss we can, and not repeat wreckage where we have control. Admittedly we don't have much control. On the margin we control, can relieve our bit of the great drag breakdown of false civilization. "Benevolent indifferent attentiveness," "a choiceless awareness" of our own grief & despair at what we've done gives rise to compassion for ourselves. That extends to the world's inhabitants, transforming grief to energetic action for everyone's benefit.

Catholics confess & ask absolution, Buddhists wipe out a billion years of Karma with an empty thought, Moslems lift their hands & give the grief over to Allah. Artists take nightmare & paint it up for what it is: dream, illusion, transitory Maya, flowers in the air, bubbles on a stream, rainbow clouds. How turn "Waste to Treasure"? How alchemize "Shit to Roses"?

The private automobile's the symbolic villain of this subjective essay, perhaps objectively symbolic of all East & Western hyperindustrialized villainy. This little bubble of speed on high tech gearshifts rubber wheels & fossil fuels liberates the rich to flit around Earth, escaping boredom stuck in slums bidonvilles bustees & shanty towns of the upper class. A mass of humanity howls on garbage mountains and urban ashpits, left behind.

O.K. Hiro Yamagata's taken the most brilliant of all cars— in his view—the long outmoded Mercedes-Benz Cabriolet 220A—an aristocrat of capitalist cars, luxurious toy of the tasteful racy rich—to rescue it from oblivion, alchemize the wreckage to exemplary totemhood. Cannibalizing the bodies of dozens or hundreds of such cars, he's reversed Time's ravage of these wearouts. Not quite mass produced, not quite singular & unreplica'd, with old handcraft style & artisan comeliness, sleek modish dated chic & charm—Yamagata's resurrected this mid century's last gasp of "innocent" mechanical beauty.

With an eccentric idea, the use of the "ultimate" car for floral arrangements or sky & ocean waves usually reserved for Japanese fans, screens or exquisite nightclub wallpaper, the artist's imagination's run wild on hood & fender canvas. Paint the universe itself! Paint the high class villainous machine with 1960s flowerpowered lilies orchids daisies, Fijian blossoms, porcelain bugs & butterflies, graffitian tattoos, funky hallucinatory flowers on the carapace of a finetuned Germam machine. Disney meets Hitler, Mickey Mouse wraps up the Nazis (ie, not to be chauvinistic about German politics) Free Imagination meets Naive Industrialization. In any case Japanese and German modern technologic "Idealism" is subjected to the extremest sophisticated whims of a highly competent individual artist with the Herculean means to undertake symbolic cleaning of the liquid-looking horseless carriage's Augean Stables.

Appropriately this creation & exhibition takes place in Los Angeles where over half century ago General Motors bought up and destroyed Charlie Chaplin's & the Keystone Kops' mass transit trolley system to clear the way for its car products. I saw their clean hallucinatory "World of the Future" (with no ecological fumes, made of plaster) in the New York World's Fair's 1939 Perisphere. A commercial hallucination that's turned into a material nightmare "Only the Imagination is real," said W. C. Williams.

My 88 year old stepmother still drives, that's her desperate last mobility. Not driving I ride taxis in Manhattan, as before congestive heart failure 1990 I "Put on my tie in a taxi, short of breath, rushing to meditate." In my first long poem "The Green Automobile," I imagined a motor vehicle crossing the 1953 continent to see my boyfriend Neal Cassady. I backseat drive, at age 68 I want comfort, have twice hired a limo to get from Kennedy airport to my brother's birthday party in Long Island. Guilty!

But Hiro Yamagata's got one good idea and's accomplished it: cleaned up in perfect condition, painted over with vegetation, cars don't belong running around the earth, cars belong in museums along with stuffed dinosaurs, whose ghosts they've devoured.

The Open Road

P. J. O'ROURKE

Border Patrol

Somewhere-o Mexico—The U.S./Mexican border region isn't one of earth's garden spots. Especially not now, when low oil prices, corruption, and enormous foreign debt have created the worst economic crisis in Mexico's history (and that's going some). But the truly devoted tourist likes to avoid the crowds, and the only crowds on the Mexican border are swimming across it.

Automobile Magazine said it would give me a car and a photographer if this was really where I wanted to go. I went to pick up the car at the Ford offices in Dallas. I was expecting a Bronco or a four-wheel-drive pickup. Ford handed me the keys to a Cartier Designer Series Lincoln Town Car, metallic silver with silver leather interior, silver vinyl landau top, power moonroof, and a big sign reading CARTIER on the trunk lid. Driving this through the barrios of Juarez would be, I thought, like sending Pasadena's Tournament of Roses Parade through Watts in the middle of an outdoor Run-DMC concert. Then the photographer arrived. It was Maria Krajcirovic, the beautiful Czechoslovakian whose hand-colored photos make the editors at the front of this book look a lot better than they really do. But Maria is a bit *too* beautiful—blond, tall, and emphatically shaped. Between Maria and the Lincoln, I was sure I'd attract less attention in Mexico if I brought the pope.

Czechoslovakia is a serious and orderly country. And Maria had emigrated from there to Ann Arbor, Michigan, one of America's most serious and orderly towns. It was news to her that people keep goats in their kitchens, throw soiled Pampers out car windows, and use the ditch beside the road for the family Maytag. As soon as we'd crossed the Rio Grande, Maria began calling the border the "Tropic of Dirt."

We crossed at Eagle Pass, into the Mexican town of Piedras Negras, about 145 miles southwest of San Antonio and somewhere near the bleak setting of Larry McMurtry's novel *Lonesome Dove*. I piloted the Lincoln through Piedras Negras's warren of tiny side streets, feeling like the captain of the *QEII* on a cruise through the canals of Venice. No rocks or bottles were thrown by the populace, however. I'd figured this car would earn us a life sentence in prison for first-degree gringoism. Not so. We received nothing but approving looks and profuse compliments. The Mexicans thought the Town Car was *muy bueno*, an *automóvil superior*, or, as one Pemex gas station attendant put it, *"el car boss."* This says a lot about the unenvious good nature of the Mexican people. I'm not sure what it says about the Ford styling department.

To tell the truth, I was glad to get into Mexico. Mini-mall clutter and highway strip development stopped at the Rio Grande. The Piedras Negras market was still downtown in an ancient adobe building. Music blurted from loudspeakers in the market stalls. Outside, mufflers dragged behind cars, and people were all over the place laughing and yelling. Mexico is a mess, but it's a lively mess. And, best of all, there are no Taco Bells. Mexico is the last place in North America where you can escape the horrible Mexican restaurant plague. They have great *hamburguesas* in Mexico, excellent *perros calientes* (hot dogs), delicious *quesadillas* (toasted cheese sandwiches), and wonderful *huevos revueltos* (scrambled eggs). But if you want a double dog-food taco in a rock-hard corn tortilla, you have to go back to the States.

But I used to be a hippie, so you shouldn't trust me about Mexico. Anything that reeks of natural materials and native tradition is better than anything plastic as far as I'm concerned. Of course, I might think differently if I had to choose between an artificial heart valve made of polystyrene and one made of adobe, as Maria was quick to point out.

Maria was also quick to point out the stuffed frogs. "Oh, God, oh, God, what's *that*?!" she screamed when she had her first look at three shellacked amphibians standing upright with miniature mariachi band instruments in their webbed fore-feet. Stuffed frogs posed in various clever ways were for sale in all the border towns. But for sale to whom? Even the most addled tourist isn't going to bring home a frog swinging a golf club as a souvenir. Souvenirs are supposed to evoke memories. Who would want to remember a thing like that? Stuffed frogs are one of the aesthetic mysteries of Mexico. I only bought a couple of the really good ones working out on Nautilus equipment.

There were a lot of other aesthetic mysteries in the Piedras Negras market. Who wants a sombrero the size of a hot tub? Or a forty-five-pound onyx bunny? Or a three-foot sculpture of Don Quixote made out of welded coat hangers? Maybe nobody, because vendors were throwing themselves at us as we walked through the aisles.

"Señor, a painting of Sean Penn on velvet for the lady?"

"Señorita, Aztec pottery—almost genuine!"

"The largest selection of cement burros for your yard!"

"Many fine wallets embossed with the Virgin Mary!"

Maria said this importuning was a sign of economic desperation. But I don't know. You have to remember the national sport of Mexico is putting a large farm animal into a sports arena and teasing it. I think the Mexicans just know how to get the most fun out of their tourists. And I think New York's Fifth Avenue would be a lot more festive if the salesmen at Georg Jensen ran out the door and chased you down the street yelling, "My dear man, simply observe the understated elegance of this sterling silver baby porringer, available with the baby's own future country club name engraved upon it."

We headed northwest out of Piedras Negras along the Rio on Mexico Route 2. Here my second big worry about the Lincoln disappeared. It's hard to describe Mexican pavement conditions without the use of swear words. I figured the Town Car would find its Cartier-signature self shaken to rubble in a twinkling

The Lincoln has a mush-bucket suspension in the great Buick Roadmaster–Packard Caribbean tradition. But this is a mush bucket that works. The wheels just slurped and gobbled all the heaves, holes, and whoop-de-dos. I've driven a lot of miles through Mexico in everything from off-road racers to Saab Turbos, and this is the first time I've been comfortable. It was also ninety-five degrees outside with Hiroshima-class sunshine, and the Town Car's air conditioner was still able to give us frostbite with the moonroof open. Furthermore, I'd filled the poor vehicle with horrible Pemex gasoline, which has lower octane than fruit cocktail, and the engine just purred along—not a knock, a ping, or a burp to be heard.

The scenery, unfortunately, was not as pleasant as the ride. Scattered along the highway were little ranchos made from cement blocks, wattle, corrugated tin, and whatnot—chickens and children all over the place, and yards festooned with old car bodies, oil drums, and bald tires. The North is to Mexico what the West is to the United States: the place people pick up and go to to make a new start. Except, in Mexico, they're not looking to get a bit part on *Dynasty*. They're hoping for two acres of scrub land, one cow, and a twenty-year-old-truck.

Maria was shocked at the living conditions. She looked like Eleanor Roosevelt must have the first time somebody showed her a coal mine. I didn't have the heart to tell Maria these people were doing pretty well.

Route 2 stops at the Del Rio border crossing. Beyond this are the trackless *Serranias del Burro*, the Donkey Highlands, forming the Mexican side of the Big Bend country. To continue west we had to go back to the United States.

The U.S. Customs agents took a long look at the dirt-smeared Lincoln. Its vast back seat was filled to the windows with camping gear, bags of canned goods, suitcases full of Banana Republic clothes, tubes of sun block, coolers, thermoses, and fifteen gallons of bottled water. You can't be too prepared south of the border.

"How long have you been in Mexico?" asked an agent.

"Six hours."

They went through the car and everything in it and on it and under it. I wanted to ask them if this is how narcotics usually come into the country—with good-looking blondes in a car that probably should belong to Liberace. (If so, you'd think they'd be able to stop a lot more of the drug traffic than they do.) But I restrained myself. The agents were already grumpy enough trying to figure out whether shellacked frogs are on the endangered species prohibited import list. (They aren't.)

Customs let us go after an hour, and we drove west across the Pecos River and its spectacular canyon, and into the broad, grassy basins of Val Verde County. The land was astonishingly empty, and you'd better come see it quickly, because I'm sure some new Phoenix or Houston is slated to go up here any minute.

The Lincoln was swell on its home turf. We just pointed it at the setting sun and let it go. I have a few minor complaints. The speedometer only reads to 85 mph, but the five-liter V-8 will easily shove the car to 100 and maybe well beyond. (Road manners were so good, and wind noise so minimal, that it was hard to estimate top speed.) There was a tiny shimmy up around 95, but I think this was a result of what Mexico had done to the wheel alignment. The cruise control also stops at 85, and this is not fair to those of us with lead-filled but lazy accelerator feet. On the plus side, the Town Car's trip computer is way too complicated. This didn't happen to be an advantage for Maria and me . But if you're traveling with a pesky teen, all the function buttons will keep him silent and enthralled for hours.

We stopped at a restaurant in the total middle of nowhere, and the food was so good that I bought the chef a drink. I wanted to find out what kind of person knew this much about cooking and this little about getting to New York or Paris.

He was a former marine, about twenty-eight. I'll call him Dave. Midway through his third Jack Daniel's, Dave began telling me how he smuggles drugs.

"I go down to Boquillas Canyon in the Big Bend National Park and go across the Rio with a backpack. I have a connection down there, in this little dirtball Mexican town, with *La Familia*, which is, like, the Mexican Mafia. Then I walk out, traveling at night. It takes a couple of days."

"U.S. Customs doesn't mind this?" I asked.

"They don't expect anybody to take a backpack and walk out. But it gets a little hairy sometimes. I was working with some other guys once, and I was caught in an ambush, and three of them were shot."

Maria was looking at the ceiling by now, but I'm a credulous type.

"Customs agents ambushed you?" I asked.

"No way. I think it was the guy who sold us the stuff. You know, so he could get it back and sell it to somebody else. He makes more money that way."

Maria and I continued west to Marathon, where we found a great little hotel called the Gage. We arrived just in time to see a Texas plains lightning storm, rated R for violence, from the Gage veranda. I don't know what all these first-rate travel amenities are doing out here. I can't imagine that the lightning storms attract that many tourists. Maybe people buying drugs like to stay and have a nice meal and a snooze.

In the morning, we drove south toward Big Bend National Park. I pushed the Lincoln back to top speed. This car never loses its road feel. Of course, it doesn't have a lot of road feel to begin with. But what it has, it keeps. Usually driving an American luxo car at exotica speeds is like the last half-minute of landing an airplane with the gear up. (Often with the same results.) But the Town Car hangs in there, and could almost be said to track if you don't count the four inches of on-center play in the power steering.

Big Bend is more desolate than awesome or rugged. It's interesting, if you've been very bad and want to see what the afterlife will be like. Otherwise, not. We saw some signs to the Boquillas Canyon that Dave the *soi-disant* drug smuggler had mentioned. We followed them and arrived at a small parking lot by the Rio Grande. An old Mexican was sitting on a stump. For three dollars he said he would take us across. He led us along a half-mile path through the cottonwood and canebrake to a rowboat pulled up on the bank. There were no gates or customs agents or formalities in sight.

On the Mexican side of the river, we hired two burros and rode up to the canyon rim, where we found a nasty and impoverished-looking town. The sole café was nothing but a shaded patio with a cookstove in a shed beside it. At one corner of the patio sat a dark, barrel-chested man of about fifty, in a shiny American wheelchair. His legs were covered with a blanket, although the temperature was almost 100 degrees. He wore a large Rolex watch and a freshly pressed shirt and a new straw hat with sharp creases.

We had lunch at the café, or, rather, I did. Maria took a look in the cookshack and demurred. As we were leaving, I said *"Buenos días"* to the man in the wheelchair. "Good afternoon," he answered affably enough. But he had a smile like a lizard's, and all his teeth were gold.

"I don't know," said Maria on the way back down to the river, "maybe Dave wasn't lying after all." As far as I could tell, we could have brought the treasure of the Sierra Madre, or the Sierra Madre range itself, back to the U.S., and no one would be the wiser.

Look alive, you customs people. If Americans spend all their money on crack and so forth, they won't have any left to spend on flashy cars, and then where will this magazine be?

We went west out of the park on Texas 170. The Rio Grande canyons are lovely here, but there were park ranger speed traps all over the place, so we were going too slowly to appreciate the beauty. Spectacular scenery should always be driven through at 100 mph. That way it has poignancy. It's a fleeting glimpse of paradise. But if you dawdle or stop to gaze, you'll realize scenery is pretty static stuff. There's no plot line to speak of, and Debra Winger is not going to bound through it nude anytime soon. You'll become restless and bored.

To be bored with beauty is a terrible thing for the soul, so I was anxious to return to Mexico, where I could drive the Town Car like a maniac. There are no rules on Mexican highways, at least none that a ten-dollar tip to the *federales* won't excuse you from. And there are practically no *federales* on the highways anyhow. They are napping in the towns.

We blasted out of Presidio on Mexico Route 16 south into the IUD coil switchbacks of the Sierra de la Magdalena. The pavement, such as it was, was a lane and a half wide, with no guardrails and abysmal drops on every side. Enormous trucks doing 5 mph blocked the blind curves going uphill. Enormous buses doing 80 mph blocked them coming down. Stray cows and goats wandered in between.

Here the Lincoln showed a glorious and wholly unexpected side of itself. The thing corners. It is a somewhat peculiar, slightly freight-trainish, 4038-pound kind of cornering. But cornering it is. There's plenty of understeer, of course, but no sudden shifts to insane tail-wagging or broadside death drifts. The big old fifteen-inch radial plies keep a leech grip on whatever's under them. There's none of the man-the-bilge-pumps body lean that cars this size had back when cars were this size. And the front disc, rear drum brakes work like a broomstick does when stuck in a bicycle wheel. The Town Car carried us through all the tight spots at speeds that would do a cruise missile proud. My only gripe is that the suspension isn't perfectly located. The whole chassis shifts on its wheels in the hard turns, and this is unnerving until you realize it isn't a harbinger of disaster. But I'm picking nits. Every hairpin in those mountains is decorated with little white memorial crosses. Thanks to the Lincoln, there aren't two more of them for us.

Maria may have been a sissy about lunch, but she was no coward in the passenger seat. She opened the Town Car's moonroof and, bracing herself with one foot on the trip computer, stood up out of the car and began clicking photos. The Mexican truck drivers were appreciative to the point of distraction. I refused to look in the rear-view mirror for fear of seeing what kind of accident she'd caused. "The light is exquisite," yelled Maria.

At sunset, we reached the broad plateau leading to Chihuahua City. Maria was hanging out of the moonroof again when suddenly her face swelled like a melon. "I cwan't bwief," said Maria, dropping into the car. Her eyes looked like coin slots between the great red puffs of her forehead and cheeks. She was shaking all over.

"Insect bites! Are you allergic to insect bites?!" I shrieked. "Pollen? Truck fumes?" I was panicked. If they'd given me all that trouble at customs about stuffed frogs, what would they say about a dead blond photographer?

"Nwo!" said Maria. "Mwexago! Um awergic to Mwexago!"

"You're allergic to Mexico." I mentally cataloged the first aid kit I'd brought along: whisky, extra cigarettes, and a large buck knife, in case I had to cut my leg off because of snakebite. "Would some whisky and cigarettes help?"

"Nwo!"

I drove at top speed for Chihuahua City, and just on the edge of town I saw the sign "Médico" on a ramshackle little house.

I knocked and was invited in by a smiling fellow in a doctor jacket who looked to be about nineteen. His living room was littered with clothes and newspapers just like my own, which was not reassuring. There was a desk in one corner with a prescription pad and some tongue depressors lying on it.

"*Médica emergencia,*" I said, and added, "*por favor,*" remembering that Spanish is a language where courtesy is very important. "*Mi amiga es muy* . . . um . . . sick."

"*Tiene una enfermedad?*" asked the doctor, picking up a tongue depressor and advancing on me.

"No, no. Mi amiga!" I said, running to help Maria out of the Town Car, which was surrounded by a crowd of urchins admiring its styling excesses.

"Es una alergia," said the doctor when he saw Maria looking like a pumpkin.

"Sí, sí! alergia," I said.

The doctor took out a stethoscope and one of those pointy ear and nose flashlights from an end table drawer and examined Maria's giant head. *"Alergia,"* he confirmed, and took a big hypodermic needle from the bookshelf. The doctor patted his behind and pointed to Maria.

"No!" said Maria, who had pulled a phrase book out of her purse and was frantically paging through it looking for the Spanish word for "no," which is *no.*

"What is, I mean, *que es* that?" I asked, pointing to the needle.

"Es vitaminas y antihistaminicos y cortisonas y amphetaminas y otras vitaminas y etcétera."

I wouldn't have minded a shot of this myself, but Maria was adamant.

"Just some capsules! Some *cápsulas!*" she yelled, tearing through the phrase book. *"Los capsulidads! El pills!"* Maria was getting her voice to work remarkably well.

The doctor shrugged. What could he do if the patient didn't want to be cured? With the help of the *Berlitz Passport to Spanish,* he made a list of things Maria shouldn't eat: eggs, fruit, vegetables, dairy products, meat, fish, poultry, alcoholic beverages, soft drinks, water, bread, salt, and candy. Then he wrote out several elaborate prescriptions and charged us $3.50.

By the time we were back in the car, Maria was completely well. At least, she said, "I'm fine now and don't stop at any more doctors," although she still looked a little basketballish around the face for the next couple of days.

I immediately got lost in Chihuahua, which is not the sleepy ranch town I had pictured, but a city of 300,000 people and two working street lamps. Asking directions was hard since I not only didn't speak the language, but I also had no idea where we were going. It had not occurred to us to make hotel reservations.

I asked various passersby, *"Dónde es el hotel grande?"* This met with the inevitable Mexican answer to any question about which way to go: *"Sí, sí, bueno."*

"Es el hotel aquí?" I'd ask and point up the street.

"Sí."

"Es no hotel aquí?" I'd ask and point in the same direction.

"Sí."

A Mexican will never admit that he can't understand, any more than an American will admit he can't be understood. Mexicans are, however, very agreeable about this.

We did find a hotel eventually, because eventually everything happens in Mexico. The trick is to drink enough so you don't mind if it doesn't. By the time we'd found the pleasant and reasonably priced Sicomoro on Boulevard Ortiz Mena, I'd been doing that for hours.

Don't bother to take that address down. Chihuahua is the Gary, Indiana, of Mexico, with the same charming combination of heavy industry and unemployment.

We had *desayuno*, a.k.a. breakfast, and drove north on Route 45 toward Juarez. The road took us through rolling green hills that could have been in Switzerland except for the roadside shrines full of Virgin Mary statues wearing clothing and jewelry. A good-sized rainstorm didn't show the Town Car to its best advantage. There are some inevitable handling flaws in a two-ton auto with gross front-end weight bias. But the Lincoln has an essential goodness as a vehicle, a sort of "hefty deft" that keeps it from ever turning treacherous. With one exception. A car of this caliber deserves something better than standard-issue Detroit windshield wipers. It's typical of Motor City provincialism that American windshield wipers do only one thing well. When a Michigan sleet storm freezes the wiper blades to the glass, the wiper motors are strong enough to yank the blades loose. But make the world visible through a film of wet Mexican road grit? Forget it.

Sixty miles north of Chihuahua, the rain disappeared and the land turned to flat scrub with the Sierra Madre Occidental peaks rising to our left, real purple mountain majesties stuff, but minus the fruited plain.

In Juarez, we stumbled onto a remarkable antidote to stuffed frogs and cement burros. In the middle of town, there's a government store selling Mexican folk arts and crafts. It's called Fonart—short for *Fondo Nacional para el Fomento de los Artesanos*. Here was the brilliant part of Mexico's mystery aesthetics. The place was filled with handsome rugs and blankets, beautiful pottery, papier-mâché work, wood carvings, and basketry. All cheap, with the peso going for 780 to the dollar, and all leavened with just the right grotesque sensibility. For instance, there were Oaxacan Indian ceramic sculptures of demons and dead people, but they weren't just hanging around being demonic and dead. The pottery demons were driving pottery buses or riding pottery motorcycles. Skeletons were having jam sessions, feasts, and fiestas. These sculptures were anywhere from a foot to three feet across, painted in amazing colors and fired to a brilliant glaze. Maria bought herself a huge demon mermaid playing a piano made of human skulls. I think she was beginning to change her mind about the country.

When we came out of Fonart, there was another approving crowd around the Lincoln, which brings us back to the stuffed frog side of Mexican taste. Ford has here what may be the best full-size luxury car in the world. And it only costs $25,000. You can pay that much for a damned van these days. But why do they make it look like a rolling chromed tract house? And I don't want to hear any marketing survey baloney. All the lummoxen in America think Jaguars are beautiful, and they're right. Why not steal the Jag body and blow it up to size? Or, better yet, the Bentley shell? I want one of these cars. A lot of other moderately well-off forty-year-olds like me would want one too. But we're embarrassed to be seen in the thing. Lights on in your head, Ford!

Anyway, Juarez was nice. We stayed at the El Presidente Hotel, which is quite luxurious if you don't mind some of the luxury coming off in your hand when you try to turn on the shower.

The next day we went west on the resumption of Mexico Route 2, through the desert and up into those purple mountains. At the Continental Divide, on the border between Chihuahua and Sonora states, there is the most amazing view I've ever seen from an automobile. You push uphill through the mountain passes for an hour, and suddenly an enormous V-shaped notch opens before you, and there, a thousand feet below, is the immense north Sonoran plain, stretching green and cottonwood-dotted away to three horizons. Much as I hate stopping and gazing, I had to stop and gaze at this. And I noticed that even the truck drivers and the crazed bus pilots stopped here, too.

We drove through those grasslands and up to the border and spent the night in Douglas, Arizona, at the Gadsden Hotel. The Gadsden is a splendid remnant of Douglas's days as a silver mine boom town. Huge Corinthian columns of travertine marble support the lobby ceiling. One wall is pierced by a series of windows in Tiffany stained glass, depicting the local landscape. It was the only desert mural Tiffany ever did. The broad marble staircase has a chip out of one step where Pancho Villa is said to have ridden his horse upstairs.

But, again, I was glad to return to the freedom and disorder of Mexico, where I could really let the Town Car holler. We would ultimately cover 2200 miles over some of the worst major highways north of the Darien Gap, and the Lincoln never developed a single rattle or had the slightest mechanical malfunction of any kind. Fuel mileage worked out just a little shy of 18 mpg—not bad at full throttle on Pemex and with the A/C going all the time. Only one quart of oil was needed. I defy anything, army tank or tricycle, to go through Mexico with less trouble.

We continued west on Route 2, back into the mountains, and at about four in the afternoon we came upon a fiesta in the town of Magdalena. It was some saint's day; we never figured out which. You could buy plaster images of his dead body in a glass box, and hundreds of people were lined up to go to confession. Once cleansed, they spread out under an acre of awnings, where there were a dozen beer taps and two dozen mariachi bands all playing different tunes at boom box volume. People were coming into town from every direction, walking and driving and crammed in the back of stake bed trucks. Seventy or eighty Indians were sleeping in the bushes behind the church. All sorts of gaudy things were for sale. Barbecue pits had been built in the plaza. Chickens sizzled on grills, and beef chunks smoked on skewers. And on the banks of the Rio Alisos, a traveling carnival had set up shop.

Maria and I were standing near the Tilt-A-Whirl ride. "I love Mexico!" I said, *"Yo amor Mey-he-ko!"* (I'd had a few beers.) "There's something about this place," I raved on, "a big-hearted heedlessness, a spirit of reckless life, an air of wild slap dash. There are no insurance salesmen, no retirement benefit packages, no DOT or Office of Consumer Affairs. It's one of the last mad, wide-open places in the world. Anything can happen here!"

Maria was looking intently at the Tilt-A-Whirl mechanism. There was an unoiled mangle of gears at its center, with rusty pulley wheels radiating a dirty nest of slack V-belts. "If you like Mexico so much," she said, "I dare you to get on that carnival ride."

JOHN STEINBECK

Travels with Charley

From the beginning of my journey, I had avoided the great high-speed slashes of concrete and tar called "thruways," or "super-highways." Various states have different names for them, but I had dawdled in New England, the winter grew apace, and I had visions of being snowbound in North Dakota. I sought out U.S. 90, a wide gash of a super-highway, multiple-lane carrier of the nation's goods. Rocinante bucketed along. The minimum speed on this road was greater than any I had previously driven. I drove into a wind quartering in from my starboard bow and felt the buffeting, sometimes staggering blows of the gale I helped to make. I could hear the sough of it on the square surfaces of my camper top. Instructions screamed at me from the road once: "Do not stop! No stopping. Maintain speed." Trucks as long as freighters went roaring by, delivering a wind like the blow of a fist. These great roads are wonderful for moving goods but not for inspection of a countryside. You are bound to the wheel and your eyes to the car ahead and to the rear-view mirror for the car behind and the side mirror for the car or truck about to pass, and at the same time you must read all the signs for fear you may miss some instructions or orders. No roadside stands selling squash juice, no antique stores, no farm products or factory outlets. When we get these thruways across the whole country, as we will and must, it will be possible to drive from New York to California without seeing a single thing.

At intervals there are places of rest and recreation, food, fuel and oil, post-cards, steam-table food, picnic tables, garbage cans all fresh and newly painted, rest rooms and lavatories so spotless, so incensed with deodorants and with detergents that it takes a time to get your sense of smell back. For deodorants are not quite correctly named; they substitute one smell for another, and the substitute must be much stronger and more penetrating than the odor it conquers. I had neglected my own country too long. Civilization had made great strides in my absence. I remember when a coin in a slot would get you a stick of gum or a candy bar, but in these dining palaces were vending machines where various coins could deliver handker-chiefs, comb-and-nail-file sets, hair conditioners and cosmetics, first-aid kits, mi-nor drugs such as aspirin, mild physics, pills to keep you awake. I found myself entranced with these gadgets. Suppose you want a soft drink; you pick your kind—Sungrape or Cooly Cola—press a button, insert the coin, and stand back. A paper cup drops into place, the drink pours out and stops a quarter of an inch from the brim—a cold, refreshing drink guaranteed synthetic. Coffee is even more interest-ing, for when the hot black fluid has ceased, a squirt of milk comes down and an envelope of sugar drops beside the cup. But of all, the hot-soup machine is the tri-umph. Choose among ten—pea, chicken noodle, beef and veg., insert the coin. A rumbling hum comes from the giant and a sign lights up that reads "Heating." After a minute a red light flashes on and off until you open a little door and remove the paper cup of boiling-hot soup.

It is life at a peak of some kind of civilization. The restaurant accommodations, great scallops of counters with simulated leather stools, are as spotless as and not unlike the lavatories. Everything that can be captured and held down is sealed in clear plastic. The food is oven-fresh, spotless and tasteless; untouched by human hands. I remembered with an ache certain dishes in France and Italy touched by innumerable human hands.

These centers for rest, food, and replenishment are kept beautiful with lawns and flowers. At the front, nearest the highway, are parking places for passenger automobiles together with regiments of gasoline pumps. At the rear the trucks draw up, and there they have their services—the huge overland caravans. Being techni-cally a truck, Rocinante took her place in the rear, and I soon made acquaintance with the truckers. They are a breed set apart from the life around them, the long-distance truckers. In some town or city somewhere their wives and children live while the husbands traverse the nation carrying every kind of food and product and machine. They are clannish and they stick together, speaking a specialized language. And although I was a small craft among monsters of transportation they were kind to me and helpful.

I learned that in the truck parks there are showers and soap and towels—that I could park and sleep the night if I wished. The men had little commerce with local people, but being avid radio listeners they could report news and politics from all parts of the nation. The food and fuel centers on the parkways or thruways are leased by the various states, but on other highways private enterprise has truckers' stations that offer discounts on fuel, beds, baths, and places to sit and shoot the breeze. But being a specialized group, leading special lives, associating only with their own kind, they would have made it possible for me to cross the country without talking to a local town-bound man. For the truckers cruise over the surface of the nation without being a part of it. Of course in the towns where their families live they have whatever roots are possible—clubs, dances, love affairs, and murders.

I liked the truckers very much, as I always like specialists. By listening to them talk I accumulated a vocabulary of the road, of tires and springs, of overweight. The truckers over long distances have stations along their routes where they know the service men and the waitresses behind the counters, and where occasionally they meet their opposite numbers in other trucks. The great get-together symbol is the cup of coffee. I found I often stopped for coffee, not because I wanted it but for a rest and a change from the unrolling highway. It takes strength and control and attention to drive a truck long distances, no matter how much the effort is made easier by air brakes and power-assisted steering. It would be interesting to know and easy to establish with modern testing methods how much energy in foot pounds is expended in driving a truck for six hours. Once Ed Ricketts and I, collecting marine animals, turning over rocks in an area, tried to estimate how much weight we lifted in an average collecting day. The stones we turned over were not large—weighing from three to fifty pounds. We estimated that on a rich day, when we had little sense of energy expended, each of us had lifted four to ten tons of rock. Consider then the small, unnoticed turning of the steering wheel, perhaps the exertion of only one pound for each motion, the varying pressure of foot on accelerator, not more than half a pound perhaps but an enormous total over a period of six hours. Then there are the muscles of shoulders and neck, constantly if unconsciously flexed for emergency, the eyes darting from road to rear-view mirror, the thousand decisions so deep that the conscious mind is not aware of them. The output of energy, nervous and muscular, is enormous. Thus the coffee break is a rest in many senses.

Quite often I sat with these men and listened to their talk and now and then asked questions. I soon learned not to expect knowledge of the country they passed through. Except for the truck stops, they had no contact with it. It was driven home to me how like sailors they were. I remember when I first went to sea being astonished that the men who sailed over the world and touched the ports to the strange and exotic had little contact with that world. Some of the truckers on long hauls traveled in pairs and took their turns. The one off duty slept or read paperbacks. But on the roads their interests were engines, and weather, and maintaining the speed that makes a predictable schedule possible. Some of them were on regular runs back and forth while others moved over single operations. It is a whole pattern of life, little known to the settled people along the routes of the great trucks. I learned only enough about these men to be sure I would like to know much more.

If one has driven a car over many years, as I have, nearly all reactions have become automatic. One does not think about what to do. Nearly all the driving technique is deeply buried in a machinelike unconscious. This being so, a large area of the conscious mind is left free for thinking. And what do people think of when they drive? On short trips perhaps of arrival at a destination or memory of events at the place of departure. But there is left, particularly on very long trips, a large area for daydreaming or even, God help us, for thought. No one can know what another does in that area. I myself have planned houses I will never build, have made gardens I will never plant, have designed a method for pumping the soft silt and decayed shells from the bottom of my bay up to my point of land at Sag Harbor, of leeching out the salt, thus making a rich and productive soil. I don't know whether or not I will do this, but driving along I have planned it in detail even to the kind of pump, the leeching bins, the tests to determine disappearance of salinity. Driving, I have created turtle traps in my mind, have written long, detailed letters never to be put to paper, much less sent. When the radio was on, music has stimulated memory of times and places, complete with characters and stage sets, memories so exact that every word of dialogue is recreated. And I have projected future scenes, just as complete and convincing—scenes that will never take place. I've written short stories in my mind, chuckling at my own humor, saddened or stimulated by structure or content.

I can only suspect that the lonely man peoples his driving dreams with friends, that the loveless man surrounds himself with lovely loving women, and that children climb through the dreaming of the childless driver. And how about the areas of regrets? If only I had done so-and-so, or had not said such-and-such—my God, the damn thing might not have happened. Finding this potential in my own mind, I can suspect it in others, but I will never know, for no one ever tells. And this is why, on my journey which was designed for observation, I stayed as much as possible on secondary roads where there was much to see and hear and smell, and avoided the great wide traffic slashes which promote the self by fostering daydreams. I drove this wide, eventless way called U.S. 90, which bypassed Buffalo and Erie to Madison, Ohio, and then found the equally wide and fast U.S. 20 past Cleveland and Toledo, and so into Michigan.

On these roads out of the manufacturing centers there moved many mobile homes, pulled by specially designed trucks, and since these mobile homes comprise one of my generalities, I may as well get to them now. Early in my travels I had become aware of these new things under the sun, of their great numbers, and since they occur in increasing numbers all over the nation, observation of them and perhaps some speculation is in order. They are not trailers to be pulled by one's own car but shining cars long as pullmans. From the beginning of my travels I had noticed the sale lots where they were sold and traded, but then I began to be aware of the parks where they sit down in uneasy permanence. In Maine I took to stopping the night in these parks, talking to the managers and to the dwellers in this new kind of housing, for they gather in groups of like to like.

They are wonderfully built homes, aluminum skins, double-walled, with insulation, and often paneled with veneer of hardwood. Sometimes as much as forty feet long, they have two to five rooms, and are complete with air-conditioners, toilets, baths, and invariably television. The parks where they sit are sometimes landscaped and equipped with every facility. I talked with the park men, who were enthusiastic. A mobile home is drawn to the trailer park and installed on a ramp, a heavy rubber sewer pipe is bolted underneath, water and electric power connected, the television antenna raised, and the family is in residence. Several park managers agreed that last year one in four new housing units in the whole country was a mobile home. The park men charge a small ground rent plus fees for water and electricity. Telephones are connected in nearly all of them simply by plugging in a jack. Sometimes the park has a general store for supplies, but if not the supermarkets which dot the countryside are available. Parking difficulties in the towns have caused these markets to move to the open country where they are immune from town taxes. This is also true of the trailer parks. The fact that these homes can be moved does not mean that they do move. Sometimes their owners stay for years in one place, plant gardens, build little walls of cinder blocks, put out awnings and garden furniture. It is a whole way of life that was new to me. These homes are never cheap and often are quite expensive and lavish. I have seen some that cost $20,000 and contained all the thousand appliances we live by—dishwashers, automatic clothes washers and driers, refrigerators and deep freezes.

The owners were not only willing but glad and proud to show their homes to me. The rooms, while small, were well proportioned. Every conceivable unit was built in. Wide windows, some even called picture windows, destroyed any sense of being closed in; the bedrooms and beds were spacious and the storage space unbelievable. It seemed to me a revolution in living and on a rapid increase. Why did a family choose to live in such a home? Well, it was comfortable, compact, easy to keep clean, easy to heat.

In Maine: "I'm tired of living in a cold barn with the wind whistling through, tired of the torment of little taxes and payments for this and that. It's warm and cozy and in the summer the air-conditioner keeps us cool."

"What is the usual income bracket of the mobiles?"

"That is variable but a goodly number are in the ten-thousand- to twenty-thousand-dollar class."

"Has job uncertainty anything to do with the rapid increase of these units?"

"Well perhaps there may be some of that. Who knows what is in store tomorrow? Mechanics, plant engineers, architects, accountants, and even here and there a doctor or a dentist live in the mobile. If a plant or a factory closes down, you're not trapped with property you can't sell. Suppose the husband has a job and is buying a house and there's a layoff. The value goes out of his house. But if he has a mobile home he rents a trucking service and moves on and he hasn't lost anything. He may never have to do it, but the fact that he can is a comfort to him."

"How are they purchased?"

"On time, just like an automobile. It's like paying rent."

And then I discovered the greatest selling appeal of all—one that crawls through nearly all American life. Improvements are made on these mobile homes every year. If you are doing well you turn yours in on a new model just as you do with an automobile if you can possibly afford to. There's status to that. And the turn-in value is higher than that of automobiles because there's a ready market for used homes. And after a few years the once expensive home may have a poorer family. They are easy to maintain, need no paint since they are usually of aluminum, and are not tied to fluctuating land values.

"How about schools?"

The school buses pick the children up right at the park and bring them back. The family car takes the head of the house to work and the family to a drive-in movie at night. It's a healthy life out in the country air. The payments, even if high and festooned with interest, are no worse than renting an apartment and fighting the owner for heat. And where could you rent such a comfortable ground-floor apartment with a place for your car outside the door? Where else could the kids have a dog? Nearly every mobile home has a dog, as Charley discovered to his delight. Twice I was invited to dinner in a mobile home and several times watched a football game on television. A manager told me that one of the first considerations in his business was to find and buy a place where television reception is good. Since I did not require any facilities, sewer, water, or electricity, the price to me for stopping the night was one dollar.

The first impression forced on me was that permanence is neither achieved nor desired by mobile people. They do not buy for the generations, but only until a new model they can afford comes out. The mobile units are by no means limited to the park communities. Hundreds of them will be found sitting beside a farm house, and this was explained to me. There was a time when, on the occasion of a son's marriage and the addition of a wife and later of children to the farm, it was customary to add a wing or at least a lean-to on the home place. Now in many cases a mobile unit takes the place of additional building. A farmer from whom I bought eggs and home-smoked bacon told me of the advantages. Each family has a privacy it never had before. The old folks are not irritated by crying babies. The mother-in-law problem is abated because the new daughter has a privacy she never had and a place of her own in which to build the structure of a family. When they move away, and nearly all Americans move away, or want to, they do not leave unused and therefore useless rooms. Relations between the generations are greatly improved. The son is a guest when he visits the parents' house, and the parents are guests in the son's house.

Then there are the loners, and I have talked with them also. Driving along, you see high on a hill a single mobile home placed to command a great view. Others nestle under trees fringing a river or a lake. These loners have rented a tiny piece of land from the owner. They need only enough for the unit and the right of passage to get to it. Sometimes the loner digs a well and a cesspool, and plants a small garden, but others transport their water in fifty-gallon oil drums. Enormous ingenuity is apparent with some of the loners in placing the water supply higher than the unit and connecting it with plastic pipe so that a gravity flow is insured.

One of the dinners that I shared in a mobile home was cooked in an immaculate kitchen, walled in plastic tile, with stainless-steel sinks and ovens and stoves flush with the wall. The fuel is butane or some other bottled gas which can be picked up anywhere. We ate in a dining alcove paneled in mahogany veneer. I've never had a better or a more comfortable dinner. I had brought a bottle of whisky as my contribution, and afterward we sat in deep comfortable chairs cushioned in foam rubber. This family liked the way they lived and wouldn't think of going back to the old way. The husband worked as a garage mechanic about four miles away and made good pay. Two children walked to the highway every morning and were picked up by a yellow school bus.

Sipping a highball after dinner, hearing the rushing of water in the electric dishwasher in the kitchen, I brought up a question that had puzzled me. These were good, thoughtful, intelligent people. I said, "One of our most treasured feelings concerns roots, growing up rooted in some soil or some community." How did they feel about raising their children without roots? Was it good or bad? Would they miss it or not?

The father, a good-looking, fair-skinned man with dark eyes, answered me. "How many people today have what you are talking about? What roots are there in an apartment twelve floors up? What roots are in a housing development of hundreds and thousands of small dwellings almost exactly alike? My father came from Italy," he said. "He grew up in Tuscany in a house where his family had lived maybe a thousand years. That's roots for you, no running water, no toilet, and they cooked with charcoal or vine clippings. They had just two rooms, a kitchen and a bedroom where everybody slept, grandpa, father and all the kids, no place to read, no place to be alone, and never had had. Was that better? I bet if you gave my old man the choice he'd cut his roots and live like this." He waved his hands at the comfortable room. "Fact is, he cut his roots away and came to America. Then he lived in a tenement in New York—just one room, walk-up, cold water and no heat. That's where I was born and I lived in the streets as a kid until my old man got a job upstate in New York in the grape country. You see, he knew about vines, that's about all he knew. Now you take my wife. She's Irish descent. Her people had roots too."

"In a peat bog," the wife said. "And lived on potatoes." She gazed fondly through the door at her fine kitchen.

"Don't you miss some kind of permanence?"

"Who's got permanence? Factory closes down, you move on. Good times and things opening up, you move on where it's better. You got roots you sit and starve. You take the pioneers in the history books. They were movers. Take up land, sell it, move on. I read in a book how Lincoln's family came to Illinois on a raft. They had some barrels of whisky for a bank account. How many kids in America stay in the place where they were born, if they can get out?"

"You've thought about it a lot."

"Don't have to think about it. There it is. I've got a good trade. Long as there's automobiles I can get work, but suppose the place I work goes broke. I got to move where there's a job. I get to my job in three minutes. You want I should drive twenty miles because I got roots?"

Later they showed me magazines designed exclusively for mobile dwellers, stories and poems and hints for successful mobile living. How to stop a leak. How to choose a place for sun or coolness. And there were advertisements for gadgets, fascinating things, for cooking, cleaning, washing clothes, furniture and beds and cribs. Also there were full-page pictures of new models, each one grander and more shiny than the next.

"There's thousands of them," said the father, "and there's going to be millions."

"Joe's quite a dreamer," the wife said. "He's always figuring something out. Tell him your ideas, Joe."

"Maybe he wouldn't be interested."

"Sure I would."

"Well, it's not a dream like she said, it's for real, and I'm going to do it pretty soon now. Take a little capital, but it would pay off. I been looking around the used lots for the unit I want at the price I want to pay. Going to rip out the guts and set it up for a repair shop. I got enough tools nearly already, and I'll stock little things like windshield wipers and fan belts and cylinder rings and inner tubes, stuff like that. You take these courts are getting bigger and bigger. Some of the mobile people got two cars. I'll rent me a hundred feet of ground right near and I'll be in business. There's one thing you can say about cars, there's nearly always something wrong with them that's got to be fixed. And I'll have my house, this here one right beside my shop. That way I would have a bell and give twenty-four-hour service."

"Sounds like a good deal," I said. And it does.

"Best thing about it," Joe went on, "if business fell off, why, I'd just move on where it was good."

His wife said, "Joe's got it all worked out on paper where everything's going to go, every wrench and drill, even an electric welder. Joe's a wonderful welder."

I said, "I take back what I said, Joe. I guess you've got your roots in a grease pit."

"You could do worse. I even worked that out. And you know, when the kids grow up, we could even work our way south in the winter and north in the summer."

"Joe does good work," said his wife. "He's got his own steady customers where he works. Some men come fifty miles to get Joe to work on their cars because he does good work."

"I'm a real good mechanic," said Joe.

Driving the big highway near Toledo I had a conversation with Charley on the subject of roots. He listened but he didn't reply. In the pattern-thinking about roots I and most other people have left two things out of consideration. Could it be that Americans are a restless people, a mobile people, never satisfied with where they are as a matter of selection? The pioneers, the immigrants who peopled the continent, were the restless ones in Europe. The steady rooted ones stayed home and are still there. But every one of us, except the Negroes forced here as slaves, are descended from the restless ones, the wayward ones who were not content to stay at home. Wouldn't it be unusual if we had not inherited this tendency? And the fact is that we have. But that's the short view. What are roots and how long have we had them? If our species has existed for a couple of million years, what is its history? Our remote ancestors followed the game, moved with the food supply, and fled from evil weather, from ice and the changing seasons. Then after millennia beyond thinking they domesticated some animals so that they lived with their food supply. Then of necessity they followed the grass that fed their flocks in endless wanderings. Only when agriculture came into practice—and that's not very long ago in terms of the whole history—did a place achieve meaning and value and permanence. But land is a tangible, and tangibles have a way of getting into few hands. Thus it was that one man wanted ownership of land and at the same time wanted servitude because someone had to work it. Roots were in ownership of land, in tangible and immovable possessions. In this view we are a restless species with a very short history of roots, and those not widely distributed. Perhaps we have overrated roots as a psychic need. Maybe the greater the urge, the deeper and more ancient is the need, the will, the hunger to be somewhere else.

Charley had no answer to my premise. Also, he was a mess. I had promised myself to keep him combed and clipped and beautiful, and I hadn't done it. His fur was balled and dirty. Poodles do not shed any more than sheep do. At night, when I had planned this virtuous grooming, I was always too busy with something else. Also I discovered a dangerous allergy I didn't know he had. One night I had pulled up at a trucker's park where huge cattle trucks put up and cleaned their beds; around the park there was a mountain of manure and a fog of flies. Although Rocinante was screened the flies got in in their millions and hid in corners and would not be dislodged. For the first time I got out the bug bomb and sprayed heavily, and Charley broke into a sneezing attack so violent and prolonged that I had finally to carry him out in my arms. In the morning the cab was full of sleepy flies and I sprayed it and Charley had another attack. After that, whenever flying visitors invaded I had to close Charley out and air out the house or cab after the pests were dead. I never saw such a severe allergy.

Since I hadn't seen the Middle West for a long time many impressions crowded in on me as I drove through Ohio and Michigan and Illinois. The first was the enormous increase in population. Villages had become towns and towns had grown to cities. The roads squirmed with traffic; the cities were so dense with people that all attention had to be devoted to not hitting anyone or not being hit. The next impression was of an electric energy, a force, almost a fluid of energy so powerful as to be stunning in its impact. No matter what the direction, whether for good or for bad, the vitality was everywhere. I don't think for a second that the people I had seen and talked to in New England were either unfriendly or discourteous, but they spoke tersely and usually waited for the newcomer to open communication. Almost on crossing the Ohio line it seemed to me that people were more open and more outgoing. The waitress in a roadside stand said good morning before I had a chance to, discussed breakfast as though she liked the idea, spoke with enthusiasm about the weather, sometimes even offered some information about herself without my delving. Strangers talked freely to one another without caution. I had forgotten how rich and beautiful is the countryside—the deep topsoil, the wealth of great trees, the lake country of Michigan handsome as a well-made woman, and dressed and jeweled. It seemed to me that the earth was generous and outgoing here in the heartland, and perhaps the people took a cue from it.

One of my purposes was to listen, to hear speech, accent, speech rhythms, overtones and emphasis. For speech is so much more than words and sentences. I did listen everywhere. It seemed to me that regional speech is in the process of disappearing, not gone but going. Forty years of radio and twenty years of television must have this impact. Communications must destroy localness, by a slow, inevitable process. I can remember a time when I could almost pinpoint a man's place of origin by his speech. That is growing more difficult now and will in some foreseeable future become impossible. It is a rare house or building that is not rigged with spiky combers of the air. Radio and television speech becomes standardized, perhaps better English than we have ever used. Just as our bread, mixed and baked, packaged and sold without benefit of accident or human frailty, is uniformly good and uniformly tasteless, so will our speech become one speech.

I who love words and the endless possibility of words am saddened by this inevitability. For with local accent will disappear local tempo. The idioms, the figures of speech that make language rich and full of the poetry of place and time must go. And in their place will be a national speech, wrapped and packaged, standard and tasteless. Localness is not gone but it is going. In the many years since I have listened to the land the change is very great. Traveling west along the northern routes I did not hear a truly local speech until I reached Montana. That is one of the reasons I fell in love again with Montana. The West Coast went back to packaged English. The Southwest kept a grasp but a slipping grasp on localness. Of course the deep south holds on by main strength to its regional expressions, just as it holds and treasures some other anachronisms, but no region can hold out for long against the highway, the high-tension line, and the national television. What I am mourning is perhaps not worth saving, but I regret its loss nevertheless.

Even while I protest the assembly-line production of our food, our songs, our language, and eventually our souls, I know that it was a rare home that baked good bread in the old days. Mother's cooking was with rare exceptions poor, that good unpasteurized milk touched only by flies and bits of manure crawled with bacteria, the healthy old-time life was riddled with aches, sudden death from unknown causes, and that sweet local speech I mourn was the child of illiteracy and ignorance. It is the nature of a man as he grows older, a small bridge in time, to protest against change, particularly change for the better. But it is true that we have exchanged corpulence for starvation, and either one will kill us. The lines of change are down. We, or at least I, can have no conception of human life and human thought in a hundred years or fifty years. Perhaps my greatest wisdom is the knowledge that I do not know. The sad ones are those who waste their energy in trying to hold it back, for they can only feel bitterness in loss and no joy in gain.

As I passed through or near the great hives of production—Youngstown, Cleveland, Akron, Toledo, Pontiac, Flint, and later South Bend and Gary—my eyes and mind were battered by the fantastic hugeness and energy of production, a complication that resembles chaos and cannot be. So might one look down on an ant hill and see no method or direction or purpose in the darting hurrying inhabitants. What was so wonderful was that I could come again to a quiet country load, tree-bordered, with fenced fields and cows, could pull up Rocinante beside a lake of clear, clean water and see high overhead the arrows of southing ducks and geese. There Charley could with his delicate exploring nose read his own particular literature on bushes and tree trunks and leave his message there, perhaps as important in endless time as these pen scratches I put down on perishable paper. There in the quiet, with the wind flicking tree branches and distorting the water's mirror, I cooked improbable dinners in my disposable aluminum pans, made coffee so rich and sturdy it would float a nail, and, sitting on my own back doorsteps, could finally come to think about what I had seen and try to arrange some pattern of thought to accommodate the teeming crowds of my seeing and hearing.

I'll tell you what it was like. Go to the Uffizi in Florence, the Louvre in Paris, and you are so crushed with the numbers, once the might of greatness, that you go away distressed, with a feeling like constipation. And then when you are alone and remembering, the canvases sort themselves out; some are eliminated by your taste or your limitations, but others stand up clear and clean. Then you can go back to look at one thing untroubled by the shouts of the multitude. After confusion I can go into the Prado in Madrid and pass unseeing the thousand pictures shouting for my attention and I can visit a friend—a not large Greco, *San Pablo con un Libro*. St. Paul has just closed the book. His finger marks the last page read and on his face are the wonder and will to understand after the book is closed. Maybe understanding is possible only after. Years ago when I used to work in the woods it was said of lumber men that they did their logging in the whorehouse and their sex in the woods. So I have to find my way through the exploding production lines of the Middle West while sitting alone beside a lake in northern Michigan.

As I sat secure in the silence, a jeep scuffed to a stop on the road and good Charley left his work and roared. A young man in boots, corduroys, and a red and black checked mackinaw climbed out and strode near. He spoke in the harsh unfriendly tone a man uses when he doesn't much like what he has to do.

"Don't you know this land is posted? This is private property."

Normally his tone would have sparked a tinder in me. I would have flared an ugliness of anger and he would then have been able to evict me with pleasure and good conscience. We might even have edged into a quarrel with passion and violence. That would be only normal, except that the beauty and the quiet made me slow to respond with resentment, and in my hesitation I lost it. I said, "I knew it must be private. I was about to look for someone to ask permission or maybe pay to rest here."

"The owner don't want campers. They leave papers around and build fires."

"I don't blame him. I know the mess they make."

"See that sign on that tree? No trespassing, hunting, fishing, camping."

"Well," I said, "that sounds as if it means business. If it's your job to throw me off, you've got to throw me off. I'll go peacefully. But I've just made a pot of coffee. Do you think your boss would mind if I finished it? Would he mind if I offered you a cup? Then you could kick me off quicker."

The young man grinned. "What the hell," he said. "You don't build no fires and you don't throw out no trash."

"I'm doing worse than that. I'm trying to bribe you with a cup of coffee. It's worse than that, too. I'm suggesting a dollop of Old Grand-Dad in the coffee."

He laughed then. "What the hell!" he said. "Let me get my jeep off the road."

Well, the whole pattern was broken. He squatted crosslegged in the pine needles on the ground and sipped his coffee. Charley sniffed close and let himself be touched, and that's a rare thing for Charley. He does not permit strangers to touch him, just happens to be somewhere else. But this young man's fingers found the place behind the ears Charley delights to have rubbed, and he sighed contentedly and sat down.

"What you doing—going hunting? I see your guns in the truck."

"Just driving through. You know how you see a place and it's just right, and you're just tired enough, I guess you can't help stopping."

"Yeah," he said. "I know what you mean. You got a nice outfit."

"I like it and Charley likes it."

"Charley? Never heard of a dog named Charley. Hello, Charley."

"I wouldn't want to get you in trouble with your boss. Think I ought to drag ass now?"

"What the hell?" he said. "He ain't here. I'm in charge. You ain't doing no harm."

"I'm trespassing."

"Know something? Fella camped here, kind of a nut. So I came to kick him off. He said something funny. He says, 'Trespassing ain't a crime and ain't a misdemeanor.' He says it's a tort. Now what the hell does that mean? He was a kind of a nut."

"Search me," I said, "I'm not a nut. Let me warm up your coffee." I warmed it two ways.

"You make swell coffee," said my host.

"Before it gets too dark I've got to find a place to park. Know any place up the road where they'll let me stay the night?"

"If you pull over that way behind those pine trees nobody could see you from the road."

"But I'd be committing a tort."

"Yeah. I wish to Christ I knew what that meant."

He drove ahead of me in the jeep and helped me find a level place in the pine grove. And after dark he came into Rocinante and admired her facilities and we drank some whisky together and had a nice visit and told each other a few lies. I showed him some fancy jigs and poppers I'd bought at Abercrombie & Fitch, and gave him one, and I gave him some paperback thrillers I'd finished with, all loaded with sex and sadism, and also a copy of *Field & Stream*. In return he invited me to stay as long as I wished and said that he'd come by tomorrow and we'd do a little fishing, and I accepted for one day at least. It's nice to have friends, and besides I wanted a little time to think about the things I'd seen, the huge factories and plants and the scurry and production.

The guardian of the lake was a lonely man, the more so because he had a wife. He showed me her picture in a plastic shield in his wallet, a prettyish blonde girl trying her best to live up to the pictures in the magazines, a girl of products, home permanents, shampoos, rinses, skin conditioners. She hated being out in what she called the Sticks, longed for the great and gracious life in Toledo or South Bend. Her only company was found in the shiny pages of *Charm* and *Glamour*. Eventually she would sulk her way to success. Her husband would get a job in some great clanging organism of progress, and they would live happily ever after. All this came through in small, oblique spurts in his conversation. She knew exactly what she wanted and he didn't, but his want would ache in him all his life. After he drove away in his jeep I lived his life for him and it put a mist of despair on me. He wanted his pretty little wife and he wanted something else and he couldn't have both.

Charley had a dream so violent that he awakened me. His legs jerked in the motions of running and he made little yipping cries. Perhaps he dreamed he chased some gigantic rabbit and couldn't quite catch it. Or maybe in his dream something chased him. On the second supposition I put out my hand and awakened him, but the dream must have been strong. He muttered to himself and complained and drank half a bowl of water before he went back to sleep.

The guardian came back soon after sun-up. He brought a rod and I got out my own and rigged a spinning reel, and had to find my glasses to tie on the bright painted popper. The monofilament line is transparent, said to be invisible to fish, and is completely invisible to me without my glasses.

I said, "You know, I don't have a fishing license."

"What the hell," he said, "we probably won't catch anything anyway."

And he was right, we didn't.

We walked and cast and walked and did everything we knew to interest bass or pike. My friend kept saying, "They're right down there if we can just get the message through." But we never did. If they were down there, they still are. A remarkable amount of my fishing is like that, but I like it just the same. My wants are simple. I have no desire to latch onto a monster symbol of fate and prove my manhood in titanic piscine war. But sometimes I do like a couple of cooperative fish of frying size. At noon I refused an invitation to come to dinner and meet the wife. I was growing increasingly anxious to meet my own wife, so I hurried on.

There was a time not too long ago when a man put out to sea and ceased to exist for two or three years or forever. And when the covered wagons set out to cross the continent, friends and relations remaining at home might never hear from the wanderers again. Life went on, problems were settled, decisions were taken. Even I can remember when a telegram meant just one thing—a death in the family. In one short lifetime the telephone has changed all that. If in this wandering narrative I seem to have cut the cords of family joys and sorrows, of Junior's current delinquency and junior Junior's new tooth, of business triumph and agony, it is not so. Three times a week from some bar, supermarket, or tire-and-tool cluttered service station, I put calls through to New York and reestablished my identity in time and space. For three or four minutes I had a name, and the duties and joys and frustrations a man carries with him like a comet's tail. It was like dodging back and forth from one dimension to another, a silent explosion of breaking through a sound barrier, a curious experience, like a quick dip into a known but alien water.

It was established that my wife was to fly out to meet me in Chicago for a short break in my journey. In two hours, in theory at least, she would slice through a segment of the earth it had taken me weeks to clamber over. I became impatient, stuck to the huge toll road that strings the northern border of Indiana, bypassed Elkhart and South Bend and Gary. The nature of the road describes the nature of the travel. The straightness of the way, the swish of traffic, the unbroken speed are hypnotic, and while the miles peel off an imperceptible exhaustion sets in. Day and night are one. The setting sun is neither an invitation nor a command to stop, for the traffic rolls constantly.

Late in the night I pulled into a rest area, had a hamburger at the great lunch counter that never closes, and walked Charley on the close-clipped grass. I slept an hour but awakened long before daylight. I had brought city suits and shirts and shoes, but had forgotten to bring a suitcase to transport them from truck to hotel room. Indeed, I don't know where I could have stored a suitcase. In a garbage can under an arc light I found a clean corrugated paper carton and packed my city clothes. I wrapped my clean white shirts in road maps and tied the carton with fishing line.

Knowing my tendency to panic in the roar and crush of traffic, I started into Chicago long before daylight. I wanted to end up at the Ambassador East, where I had reservations, and, true to form, ended up lost. Finally, in a burst of invention, I hired an all-night taxi to lead me, and sure enough I had passed very near my hotel.

If the doorman and bellhops found my means of traveling unusual, they gave no sign. I handed out my suits on hangers, my shoes in the game pocket of a hunting coat, and my shirts in their neat wrapping of New England road maps. Rocinante was whisked away to a garage for storage. Charley had to go to a kennel to be stored, bathed, and Hollanderized. Even at his age he is a vain dog and loves to be beautified, but when he found he was to be left and in Chicago, his ordinary aplomb broke down and he cried out in rage and despair. I closed my ears and went away quickly to my hotel.

I think I am well and favorably known at the Ambassador East, but this need not apply when I arrive in wrinkled hunting clothes, unshaven and lightly crusted with the dirt of travel and bleary-eyed from driving most of the night. Certainly I had a reservation, but my room might not be vacated until noon. The hotel's position was explained to me carefully. I understood it and forgave the management. My own position was that I would like a bath and a bed, but since that was impossible I would simply pile up in a chair in the lobby and go to sleep until my room was ready.

I saw in the desk man's eyes his sense of uneasiness. Even I knew I would be no ornament to this elegant and expensive pleasure dome. He signaled an assistant manager, perhaps by telepathy, and all together we worked out a solution. A gentleman had just checked out to catch an early airplane. His room was not cleaned and prepared, but I was welcome to use it until mine was ready. Thus the problem was solved by intelligence and patience, and each got what he wanted—I had my chance at a hot bath and a sleep, and the hotel was spared the mischance of having me in the lobby.

The room had not been touched since its former occupant had left. I sank into a comfortable chair to pull off my boots and even got one of them off before I began to notice things and then more things and more. In a surprisingly short time I forgot the bath and the sleep and found myself deeply involved with Lonesome Harry.

An animal resting or passing by leaves crushed grass, footprints, and perhaps droppings, but a human occupying a room for one night prints his character, his biography, his recent history, and sometimes his future plans and hopes. I further believe that personality seeps into walls and is slowly released. This might well be an explanation of ghosts and such manifestations. Although my conclusions may be wrong, I seem to be sensitive to the spoor of the human. Also, I am not shy about admitting that I am an incorrigible Peeping Tom. I have never passed an unshaded window without looking in, have never closed my ears to a conversation that was none of my business. I can justify or even dignify this by protesting that in my trade I must know about people, but I suspect that I am simply curious.

As I sat in this unmade room, Lonesome Harry began to take shape and dimension. I could feel that recently departed guest in the bits and pieces of himself he had left behind. Of course Charley, even with his imperfect nose, would have known more. But Charley was in a kennel preparing to be clipped. Even so, Harry is as real to me as anyone I ever met, and more real than many. He is not unique, in fact is a member of a fairly large group. Therefore he becomes of interest in any investigation of America. Before I begin to patch him together, lest a number of men grow nervous, let me declare that his name is not Harry. He lives in Westport, Connecticut. This information comes from the laundry strips from several shirts. A man usually lives where he has his shirts laundered. I only suspect that he commutes to work in New York. His trip to Chicago was primarily a business trip with some traditional pleasures thrown in. I know his name because he signed it a number of times on hotel stationery, each signature with a slightly different slant. This seems to indicate that he is not entirely sure of himself in the business world, but there were other signs of that.

He had started a letter to his wife which also ended in the wastebasket. "Darling: Everything is going OK. Tried to call your aunt but no answer. I wish you were here with me. This is a lonesome town. You forgot to put in my cuff links. I bought a cheap pair at Marshall Field. I'm writing this while I wait for C.E. to call. Hope he brings the cont . . ."

It's just as well that Darling didn't drop in make Chicago less lonesome for Harry. His guest was not C.E. with a contract. She was a brunette and wore very pale lipstick—cigarette butts in the ash tray and the edge of a highball glass. They drank Jack Daniel's, a whole bottle—the empty bottle, six soda bottles, and a tub that had held ice cubes. She used a heavy perfume and did not stay the night—the second pillow used but not slept on, also no lipstick on discarded tissues. I like to think her name was Lucille—I don't know why. Maybe because it was and is. She was a nervous friend—smoked Harry's recessed, filtered cigarettes but stubbed each one out only one-third smoked and lighted another, and she didn't put them out, she crushed them, frayed the ends. Lucille wore one of those little smidgins of hats held on by inturned combs. One of the combs broke loose. That and a bobby pin beside the bed told me Lucille is a brunette. I don't know whether or not Lucille is professional, but at least she is practiced. There is a fine businesslike quality about her. She didn't leave too many things around, as an amateur might. Also she didn't get drunk. Her glass was empty but the vase of red roses—courtesy of the management—smelled of Jack Daniel's, and it didn't do them any good.

I wonder what Harry and Lucille talked about. I wonder whether she made him less lonesome. Somehow I doubt it. I think both of them were doing what was expected of them. Harry shouldn't have slugged his drinks. His stomach isn't up to it—Tums wrappers in the wastebasket. I guess his business is a sensitive one and hard on the stomach. Lonesome Harry must have finished the bottle after Lucille left. He had a hangover—two foil tubes of Bromo Seltzer in the bathroom.

Three things haunted me about Lonesome Harry. First, I don't think he had any fun; second, I think he was really lonesome, maybe in a chronic state; and third, he didn't do a single thing that couldn't be predicted—didn't break a glass or a mirror, committed no outrages, left no physical evidence of joy. I had been hobbling around with one boot off finding out about Harry. I even looked under the bed and in the closet. He hadn't even forgotten a tie. I felt sad about Harry.

S. J. PERELMAN

Ruth and Augustus Goetz*

Hollywood Knickerbocker Hotel
Hollywood, Calif.
December 4, 1939

Dear Kids,

You know all that shit about "we'd rather go by car any day" and "pfoo on airplanes and trains"? Well, disregard it.

Not that we had a bit of mechanical or tire trouble. Except for a whole day of driving snowstorms in the New Mexican mountains and half a morning of impenetrable fog thereafter in Arizona, the weather was good enough. But the food and the hotels and the endlessness of it—sometimes we thought we must go mad, and mad we went.

It took us exactly eight days, starting from Erwinna at ten o'clock Friday morning and arriving the following Friday afternoon at five. The car held up like a trouper, and without our conscious knowledge, the fact that it had a heater and

* Playwrights (*The Heiress*, etc.) and Bucks County neighbors (*Acres and Pains* is dedicated to them). Augustus Goetz died in 1958.

a de-icer for the windshield saved our lives in the snowstorms, because the snow kept freezing on the windshield as it fell.

Items encountered en route which might interest you are two. In Vinita, Oklahoma, we passed the Silver Dollar Cafe, the *spécialité de maison* of which was blared out in big neon letters "Nigger Chicken." The town happens to have a good share of negro residents, who must feel corking when they shuffle by the Silver Dollar. The other item was a lunch we had in Sayre, Okla. It was captioned "Virginia Ham Roll," which set our taste buds working like pistons. The ham roll consisted of greasy pie dough of the sort contained in five-cent pork pies. Imbedded rubber-like in this were strips of fried ham tasting slightly of kerosene. Over the pasty lay an inch of Dole's Hawaiian shredded pineapple. The vegetables were a stone-cold, glass-hard roast potato, some billiard-green string beans out of a can and floating in a water sauce, and two spoonfuls of tuna-fish salad using hemp instead of lettuce.

I don't know why I silhouette this particular meal when it was typical of all the food we had, but the hotels in three instances were even more horrendous. The first night, unable to make Wheeling, where we had stayed previously and knew there was a decent hotel, we stopped over at something called Greensburg, Penna. We got there after dark and barely managed to get up to our room, a filthy affair in the town's leading hotel called the Penn-Albert. Steam pipes ran through the room so we were unable to regulate the heat, and after dinner, we fell into bed. Immediately a roar of band music rose from the street. The town was having its annual Christmas shopping parade and turkey bingo. Thirty drum-majorettes were practicing under the windows, directed by a man's voice on a public address system. We closed the windows and were stifled, we opened them and were deafened. The hotel hung over the Reading station and every fast freight in the country passed through that night. The parade and shouting kept up till almost three the following morning, and you can imagine what we looked and tasted like the next morning.

At Tucumcari, New Mexico, we had a room in the Randle, a matchboard hotel with people clearing their throats all night and peeing into cuspidors. The worst horror was the Beale in Kingman, Arizona, which had a coating of fine gray fur over everything as thick as Gurke's coat.* Men walked up and down an alley contiguous to our room and three women in the next room came in about four and tried very hard to vomit up their drinks without much success.

---

* Gurke was the family schnauzer.

Here we are cached for the time being in the Hollywood Knickerbocker, where every prospect pleases and only price is vile. It is the kind of place that I imagine Mrs. Goetz and Mrs. West and other ladies with iron-gray permanents flock to; they're all sitting on a glassed-in porch downstairs listening to their veins cracking like ice in a Maine pond. Every so often a Cadillac shlurrs up to the door and a chauffeur lifts out somebody's mother and gives her the fireman's carry to a wicker chair. After she gets her breath, she starts bragging about how much money her son makes a year.

The kids and Lula got here in fine shape and are comfortably installed at Laura's brother's house, but he doesn't mind the noise because he's working at a studio, which is a great insulation against noise and worry. The Campbells* seem to be in similar good shape, Alan is delighted to be out here and is chirruping like a Kentucky cardinal, Dotty is a little less delighted and most of her improvisations on the four-letter words are already familiar to you. Otherwise the whole god damned place smells exactly like a laundry and the people have the fierce deranged stare of paretics. Coming back to the hotel from lunch in the only Hebe delicatessen in town with Laura, I just saw a lady of sixty strolling down the boulevard wearing a pair of shiny black silkateen pajamas with a lace collar and a brooch at the throat. She obviously wanted to tell me how much money her son was making, but I beat her to a stop light and hid behind a bougainvillea.

The temperature is about ninety-eight and everybody says we are in for another hot spell. The only thing Laura and I have accomplished thus far is to decide that this is *really* our last trip here, forever. If we can get the dough to make those changes in our house and repair that buckled bank balance, we hope to blow taps over our glorious career in this branch of the entertainment world. If our estimates are right and we have only one life to lead, it isn't going to be led here.

And here I am rattling away about poor little me and not a word about you. How is everything on Featherbed Lane in Keller's Church and Hicks Street in Brooklyn? Come on, give. Laura, of course, sends you her dearest locked inextricably with mine.

* Dorothy Parker (d. 1967) and Alan Campbell (d. 1963).

PETER EGAN

The Great GP Trek

"**O**kay, where are we going on this big bicycle trip?" my friend Bill Steckel asked me, exhaling the usual cloud of Gauloise smoke and signaling the waiter for two more *ballons de vin rouge*.

"Barcelona," I said, tossing a French car magazine on the table. "The race schedule says the Spanish Grand Prix is coming up in April, at Montjuich. By that time, the weather should be pretty good in the Pyrenees. We could get a couple of bikes and ride them down there. Take maybe two weeks. I figure it's about a thousand miles."

We were sitting indoors at a bistro in Paris, a place called La Chope, on Place de la Contrescarpe. The sidewalk tables were glassed in for winter, and just outside we could see *les clochards*, the famous winos of Paris, sleeping over the warm sewer grates with steam escaping around them.

At the bar a bunch of male Sorbonne students were arguing with muted savagery over some political problem, all of them dressed in tailored wool bell-bottoms, expensive shoes, shag hairdos, and short leather jackets. The Sorbonne, in 1971, produced the best-dressed revolutionaries in the world.

Bill Steckel and I were both bumming around Paris for the winter. I had recently gotten out of the Army, staying home just long enough to convert my $1100 of accumulated combat pay into a small wad of traveler's checks and an airline ticket to Europe. Bill was a business school graduate who'd managed a trucking company for two years and then decided to take his savings and travel.

We'd met at the Hotel Victoria, near the Panthéon. The Victoria was a Left Bank hangout for the five-dollar-a-day crowd, at a time when that was still a real-istic figure. I lived nearby at the Modern Hotel, which had been modern about the time of Napoleon's visit to Marengo. My room cost seven francs a day (about two dollars) and was shaped like a small slice of pie, defying rectangular furniture. The window looked out on an air shaft with a patch of sky at the top.

Bill was a big shambling guy who chain-smoked Gauloises and wore sport coats and bow ties at a time when the rest of the world's Youth Culture affected a kind of Basque shepherd/Marrakesh rug-dealer look. His Ivy League orthodoxy made him the only true eccentric in the hotel, and everyone was charmed by his easy good nature.

It was a great time to be in Paris. There were a lot of shiftless, good-time Americans around, keeping up the ancient bohemian tradition. During the day you could walk through the Louvre or the Jeu de Paume galleries unmolested by tour-ist crowds, or walk down the Seine to Shakespeare & Company, or look at the book stalls and drink coffee in the cafes.

At night a bunch of us would get on the Metro, ride to a distant restaurant such as Julien at the arches of St. Denis, and then drink our way home, bar-hopping from one corner bistro to another.

During one of these sybaritic evening hikes, I discovered that Bill had ridden a bicycle across the United States, from Seattle to New York, when he was eighteen. I'd never taken a long bicycle trip, but the idea was appealing. So we decided to bicycle somewhere in Europe at the first sign of spring. The Spanish Grand Prix beckoned.

Buying a bicycle in Paris was not easy. We'd look up the address of a bicycle shop in the phone book, go there, and find a narrow little store with a wall full of sprockets, alloy tubes, wire wheels, and racing hubs. The proprietor would ap-proach us with tape measures—wanting to check our inseams and sleeve lengths so he could *build* us a bike. For about $600. Thank you, no, *monsieur*, we have made a mistake.

Finally we found a big Peugeot factory showroom on the Champs Élysées, Bicycle City. We bought a couple of eight-speed touring models with lights, fenders, and luggage racks, for about eighty dollars each. Perfect. We rode them back to the hotel in rush hour, around the Arc de Triomphe, and lived. A good omen.

* * *

Early on a Monday morning in April, we said goobdbye to Paris and hit the cobble-stones, each of us with about forty pounds of worldly belongings on our luggage racks. Army surplus sleeping bags and shelter halves—courtesy of the flea market—were strapped to our handlebars. My old Nikon F was slung over the bedroll like a headlight. Our first night's objective was the youth hostel in Chartres, sixty miles from Paris.

On this ride, Bill stayed in lower gears, pedaling furiously, while I stretched it out in top gear. Neither of us had ridden a bicycle in five years, so Bill advised me to shift down and save my legs. "Too much work," I said.

We stopped for a look at Versailles and then approached Chartres, with the famous Cathedral towering in the distance like a ship on a sea of wheat fields. We reached the youth hostel at sunset. We had a typical youth hostel dinner of collectivist gruel, wrote a few postcards, and went to bed in the dormitory.

At midnight I awoke with my legs in spasm. Hundreds of small hand grenades were going off in my muscles. I couldn't straighten my legs, so I rolled out of my bunk, slammed to the floor, and crawled down the hallway to the shower room, hoping to run hot water on my legs. When I got there, I remembered two important things:

1. There is no hot water in French youth hostels.
2. Showers are operated by an overhead pull-chain. Unreachable, if you are a lowly quadruped.

So I crawled back to bed. Not having a gun to kill myself, I was still there in the morning.

We lost a day, as Bill taught me to walk again, then hit the road toward the Loire River valley. I shifted down and stayed there.

The second night, we pitched our tent against a tennis court fence in a park along the river, at Meung sur Loire. We woke up damp and sore, feeling generally like reprocessed dog meat (meung?), and vowed to stay in cheap hotels and youth hostels rather than camp again.

On the road, there were more lessons to be learned, the first being geographical.

France, it seems, is a tilted country, with the high end in the south. This large, tilted block of real estate is called the *massif central* and runs uphill all the way to the Pyrenees on the Spanish border. It gets steeper as you go south. And, in the spring, higher and colder, terminating in a border region that looks positively Canadian, with pine trees and snow. Nelson Eddy/Jeanette MacDonald country.

Another lesson was cultural.

The French people in small towns are warm and generous. Unless they drive cars. There is an invisible force field at the transom of every French car that turns perfectly nice people into murderous psychopaths. Presented with a natural victim like a bicycle on the road, French drivers like to honk, flash lights, swerve, and make extravagant Gallic gestures of lip and hand. At least they did then. So we took the most remote, untraveled roads we could find, south through Bourges, Montluçon, Clermont-Ferrand (not so remote), and St. Flour.

We also learned not to eat "lunch" on the road. Even at truck stops, the French *déjeuner* tends to be a five-course affair with wine. It leaves you feeling happy, numb, sleepy, fat, and nearly incapable of finding the men's room, let alone balancing a bicycle. Especially on a road filled with truck drivers who've just had the same lunch. We cut back to light, high-energy lunches of Suchard chocolate and the famous *beaujolais American*: Coca-Cola. Carbohydrate loading became a much-anticipated evening ceremony. Also meat, wine, cheese, dessert, and cognac loading. We loaded it all and still lost weight.

Speaking of health matters, I had to hand it to Bill; as we climbed higher into the mountains, breathing thinner and colder air, he never stopped smoking his Gauloises. I'd look over as we rounded an uphill low-gear hairpin and see him trailing small puffs of smoke, just like a train. He would occasionally pedal up beside me and suggest we stop for a cigarette break.

As the weather grew colder and the roads steeper, we began leaving our bicycles unlocked in front of hotels, in hopes someone would steal them. But every morning when we came out, they'd still be there. "What's wrong with these people?" Bill would ask. "Are they blind?"

Our worst day of the trip was a climb between St. Chéle and Millau, a tortuous uphill flog into a stiff mountain gale and sleet storm. We were in low gear, wearing our rain ponchos, when a truck sped by. The wind blast blew our ponchos up over our heads and stopped us dead in our tracks. Blinded, feet stuck in pedal traps, we fell over sideways, like toppled equestrian statues. Bill's cigarette was ruined in this crash, which called for a smoke break in the shelter of a nearby barn.

After about eighteen miles of progress for an afternoon's effort, we stopped for the night at the windswept little village of Millau. At the hotel desk, we trotted out our favorite question: "Are there many hills between here and———[fill in the name of the next town]?" In this case, Lodève.

"Mais, oui!" the concierge assured us, eyes growing large and frightened, like those of a superstitious innkeeper discussing werewolves in a Peter Lorre movie. She assured us it was impossible to get to the next town by bicycle and made uphill gestures of the arm, which I judged to be about eighty-five degrees in grade. Take the train, she told us. There's one tomorrow.

When we came out of the hotel in the morning, it was still raining and our bikes remained unstolen, despite our best efforts to park them at an appealing angle. Should we give up and take the train?

No. We decided to pedal one more day, then take the train if things didn't improve.

A few miles out of town we crested a beautiful gap in the mountains, a pass with cascading waterfalls next to the road. Ahead of us, the road ran downhill for as far as we could see along the rim of a massive, beautiful valley full of vineyards, spring flowers, and bright sunshine. Yet behind us it was still foggy and raining. A view into the South of France, like the gates of Heaven.

We coasted eighty miles downhill that day, through Lodève and Pézenas into ever warmer sunlight, never pedaling a stroke. After nine days of low-gear workout, we were gliding down like hawks on a thermal. All the way to the Mediterranean coast. When we got to Béziers, our brake pads were almost gone.

By following the coast, we skirted the worst of the Pyrenees and the ride down to Barcelona was easy. Both of us had lost fifteen pounds on the trip, and we were in great shape, able to pedal in high gear all day. After nighttime stops at Perpignan, Figueras, and Malgrat de Mar, we breezed into Barcelona on a sunny Wednesday afternoon, our thirteenth day of riding. We found a room at a cheap hotel just off the Ramblas, a wide, tree-lined pedestrian boulevard. Many women lived in the hotel, but they kept strange hours and seemed to come out only at night. Perhaps they were vampires.

Restaurants nearby served a strange but hearty combination of roast chicken, chicken soup, and Spain's interpretation of cheap champagne. Out on the Ramblas, elderly chaperones strolled with teenage girls while Spanish boys looked on, the braver ones politely introducing themselves to the chaperones and joining in the stroll. Just like traditional American courtship as we know it, only without cars, privacy, telephones, pizza, movies, loud music, and sex.

On Thursday, Bill—who was not a big racing fan—went to Gaudi's famous architectural wonder, the Church of the Holy Family, while I took a bus to watch Formula 1 practice at the Montjuich circuit, which is in a beautiful park up in the hills of Barcelona. The buses were packed, but when I got to the track, no one else got off.

They were all going to bullfights or the football championship-cup games. There was hardly anyone at the track. Just the teams and drivers, with a few random spectators wandering around, like an SCCA regional. The uniformed *Guardia Civil* allowed me to stroll right into the paddock with no ticket and no press pass.

Unreal.

But there I was, dodging a rental car as Jackie Stewart and his wife, Helen, drove up and parked next to the Tyrrell-Ford van. Stewart was in his rock star phase, at the peak of his powers, dressed in the famous Jackie Stewart hat and *Superfly* sunglasses, with plenty of hair to get the goat of crusty old FIA types. François Cevert showed up and shook hands with Stewart. Nearby, a young Jacky Ickx watched his Ferrari being unloaded. Mario Andretti suddenly appeared, standing right next to me, also watching the cars come down the ramps. Andretti had just won his first F1 race, at South Africa.

This was all impossible. I was sure someone would throw me out at any moment, but no one did. Not all day. Nor during the next two days of qualifying.

I wandered over to the Brabham trailer and looked at the new "'lobster-claw" car with its odd front ducting. A small crowd stood around the team motorhome, waiting for Graham Hill to come out. Eventually he did, emerging with a towel over one arm and a tray of small sandwiches held high. He passed sandwiches out to the mechanics without saying a word, holding his chin up like Jeeves the butler, then disappeared into the motorhome. Everyone laughed and applauded.

Just across the way, Rob Walker and John Surtees conferred with the Brooke Bond Oxo Surtees team's other driver, Rolf Stommelen. I stood next to them while they talked, like Woody Allen's *Zelig*. Ingratiating myself, chameleon-like into every historic tableau. Surtees, World Champion in cars and seven times on bikes. Should I say hello? No. It might break the spell and they'd throw me out. I decided that God had made me invisible, just this one day, as a special favor in compensation for my inability to play the trombone. Why wreck it?

It rained briefly late in the afternoon on Saturday, and everyone covered the cars with tarps. I walked past a car with its door open, and there was Pedro Rodriguez, watching the weather and waiting. He looked up and smiled. "Going out again?" I asked.

He shrugged. "I hope later the track will dry."

"Good luck," I said. He nodded graciously and autographed my race program, next to Andretti's signature. The paper was wet and the pen would barely write.

Rodriguez, who was going very fast in his Yardly BRM, would live to race in only three more Grands Prix. He was killed in a Group 7 race at the Norisring in Germany three months later.

Looking at the program now is a little sad. Besides Rodriguez, we would eventually lose Ronnie Peterson, François Cevert, Jo Siffert, Rolf Stommelen, and Graham Hill from the starting roster.

There is another revelation in the program too: I see in the list of drivers for the Formula 3 support race the names of James Hunt and Alan Jones. I hope I didn't elbow these guys out of the way to get a better look at Andretti's Ferrari, or ask one of them to hold my coat while I took a picture of Stewart.

Race day was terrific. Sunday, April 18, 1971.

After missing the start because there was only one ticket booth at the park gate, Bill and I found a good spot for watching the race. It was on a wall, looking down the uphill S-bend just past the Calle Méjico. Cars would come screaming in from the short bottom straight, then drift under hard power up through the curves, with much wheel-spin and tail-wagging.

Ickx's Ferrari led the first few laps, but Stewart's blue Tyrrell got by him and gradually pulled out a few seconds' lead. Late in the race, Ickx pushed harder and harder to catch Stewart, who drove one of the great races of his life to hold the lead and win. A first for the Tyrrell.

Looking down at the cars in the S-bend, I watched Stewart's tires just skim the Armco, first on one side and then the other, lap after lap, as he put the power down, howling and slithering up the hill. Each time, I would say to myself, "He can't get away with that again," but he always did. For nearly two hours. It was one of the most masterful displays of control, bravery, and concentration I've ever seen. Ickx, too, was tremendously fast, but I think his 12-cylinder Ferrari had a little more power than Stewart's V-8. Stewart was simply inspired that day. And on many other days, as it turned out.

Chris Amon finished third, after a great drive in his Matra-Simca, and Pedro Rodriguez was fourth. A fine day of racing—classic battles in a beautiful setting—and a wonderful first GP. I didn't know it then, but I would never again have so much freedom to wander around a GP circuit or its paddock. Not even years later as a working journalist, with full press credentials. Spain was a dreamlike aberration.

After that weekend, Bill and I sold our bikes to a Barcelona bicycle shop for forty dollars and took a night train to Montreux, Switzerland, on our way back to Paris. We were supposed to meet some friends there, but they didn't show. So Bill and I checked into the youth hostel and climbed a nearby mountain.

We struggled all day to climb the peak and got to the top only to discover there was a parking lot full of tour buses on the summit and a paved highway down the backside. We decided not to plant the American flag, or notify *National Geographic*.

Another train took us back to Paris where summer tourist crowds had already descended on the city, turning waiters and bartenders surly for the season. Homing instinct and poverty hit us simultaneously, so we packed up and flew back to the United States. In New York, Bill lent me forty dollars so I could buy a Greyhound ticket to Madison, Wisconsin.

Two days later, after nearly three years of living out of rucksacks, backpacks, panniers, and duffel bags, I was home. Barb and I were married later that summer, and I went back to school.

When I think back on this trip, the most remarkable part is that I almost didn't take it. With $1100 of Army separation pay burning a hole in my pocket, I came very close to using the money as down payment on a car—a brand-new MGB.

Now, twenty-one years later, you can still buy an early seventies MGB: we have a nice one in our garage, and I see others for sale nearly every day in the paper. Cars we can always find, and they are easy to restore. Good times with young friends in Paris, however, and bicycle rides to the 1971 Spanish Grand Prix have become much harder to arrange.

JACK KEROUAC

On the Road

The car belonged to a tall, thin fag who was on his way home to Kansas and wore dark glasses and drove with extreme care; the car was what Dean called a "fag Plymouth"; it had no pickup and no real power. "Effeminate car!" whispered Dean in my ear. There were two other passengers, a couple, typical halfway tourist who wanted to stop and sleep everywhere. The first stop would have to be Sacramento, which wasn't even the faintest beginning of the trip to Denver. Dean and I sat alone in the back seat and left it up to them and talked. "Now, man, that alto man last night had IT—he held it once he found it; I've never seen a guy who could hold so long." I wanted to know what "IT" meant. "Ah well"—Dean laughed—"now you're asking me impon-de-rables—ahem! Here's a guy and everybody's there, right? Up to him to put down what's on everybody's mind. He starts the first chorus, then lines up his ideas, people, yeah, yeah, but get it, and then he rises to his fate and has to blow equal to it. All of a sudden somewhere in the middle of the chorus he *gets it*—everybody looks up and knows; they listen; he picks it up and carries. Time stops. He's filling empty space with the substance of our lives, confessions of his bellybottom strain, remembrance of ideas, rehashes of old blowing. He has to blow across bridges and come back and do it

250

with such infinite feeling soul-exploratory for the tune of the moment that everybody knows it's not the tune that counts but IT—" Dean could go no further; he was sweating telling about it.

Then I began talking; I never talked so much in all my life. I told Dean that when I was a kid and rode in cars I used to imagine I held a big scythe in my hand and cut down all the trees and posts and even sliced every hill that zoomed past the window. "Yes! Yes!" yelled Dean. "I used to do it too only different scythe—tell you why. Driving across the West with the long stretches my scythe had to be immeasurably longer and it had to curve over distant mountains, slicing off their tops, and reach another level to get at further mountains and at the same time clip off every post along the road, regular throbbing poles. For this reason—O man, I have to tell you, NOW, I have IT—I have to tell you the time my father and I and a pisspoor bum from Larimer Street took a trip to Nebraska in the middle of the depression to sell flyswatters. And how we made them, we bought pieces of ordinary regular old screen and pieces of wire that we twisted double and little pieces of blue and red cloth to sew around the edges and all of it for a matter of cents in a five-and-ten and made thousands of flyswatters and got in the old bum's jalopy and went clear around Nebraska to every farmhouse and sold them for a nickel apiece—mostly for charity the nickels were given us, two bums and a boy, apple pies in the sky, and my old man in those days was always singing 'Hallelujah, I'm a bum, bum again.' And man, now listen to this, after two whole weeks of incredible hardship and bouncing around and hustling in the heat to sell these awful makeshift flyswatters they started to argue about the division of the proceeds and had a big fight on the side of the road and then made up and bought wine and began drinking wine and didn't stop for five days and five nights while I huddled and cried in the background, and when they were finished every last cent was spent and we were right back where we started from, Larimer Street. And my old man was arrested and I had to plead at court to the judge to let him go cause he was my pa and I had no mother. Sal, I made great mature speeches at the age of eight in front of interested lawyers . . ." We were hot; we were going east; we were excited.

"Let me tell you more," I said, "and only as a parenthesis within what you're saying and to conclude my last thought. As a child lying back in my father's car in the back seat I also had a vision of myself on a white horse riding alongside over every possible obstacle that presented itself: this included dodging posts, hurling around houses, sometimes jumping over when I looked too late, running over hills, across sudden squares with traffic that I had to dodge through incredibly—"

"Yes! Yes! Yes!" breathed Dean ecstatically. "Only difference with me was, I myself ran. I had no horse. You were a Eastern kid and dreamed of horses; of course we won't assume such things as we both know they are really dross and literary ideas, but merely that I in my perhaps wilder schizophrenia actually *ran* on foot along the car and at incredible speeds sometimes ninety, making it over every bush and fence and farmhouse and sometimes taking quick dashes to the hills and back without losing a moment's ground . . ."

We were telling these things and both sweating. We had completely forgotten the people up front who had begun to wonder what was going on in the back seat. At one point the driver said, "For God's sakes, you're rocking the boat back there." Actually we were; the car was swaying as Dean and I both swayed to the rhythm and the IT of our final excited joy in talking and living to the blank tranced end of all innumerable riotous angelic particulars that had been lurking in our souls all our lives.

"Oh, man! man! man!" moaned Dean. "And it's not even the beginning of it—and now here we are at last going east together, we've never gone east together, Sal, think of it, we'll dig Denver together and see what everybody's doing although that matters little to us, the point being that we know what IT is and we know TIME and we know that everything is really FINE." Then he whispered, clutching my sleeve, sweating, "Now you just dig them in front. They have worries, they're counting the miles, they're thinking about where to sleep tonight, how much money for gas, the weather, how they'll get there—and all the time they'll get there anyway, you see. But they need to worry and betray time with urgencies false and otherwise, purely anxious and whiny, their souls really won't be at peace unless they can latch on to an established and proven worry and having once found it they assume facial expressions to fit and go with it, which is, you see, unhappiness, and all the time it all flies by them and they know it and that *too* worries them no end. Listen! Listen! 'Well now,'" he mimicked, "'I don't know—maybe we shouldn't get gas in that station. I read recently in *National Petroffious Petroleum News* that this kind of gas has a great deal of O-Octane *gook* in it and someone once told me it even had semi-official high-frequency *cock* in it, and I don't know, well I just don't feel like it anyway . . .' Man, you dig all this." He was poking me furiously in the ribs to understand. I tried my wildest best. Bing, bang, it was all Yes! Yes! Yes! in the back seat and the people up front were mopping their brows with fright and wishing they'd never picked us up at the travel bureau. It was only the beginning, too.

In Sacramento the fag slyly bought a room in a hotel and invited Dean and me to come up for a drink, while the couple went to sleep at relatives', and in the hotel room Dean tried everything in the book to get money from the fag. It was insane. The fag began by saying he was very glad we had come along because he liked young men like us, and would we believe it, but he really didn't like girls and had recently concluded an affair with a man in Frisco in which he had taken the male role and the man the female role. Dean plied him with businesslike questions and nodded eagerly. The fag said he would like nothing better than to know what Dean thought about all this. Warning him first that he had once been a hustler in his youth, Dean asked him how much money he had. I was in the bathroom. The fag became extremely sullen and I think suspicious of Dean's final motives, turned over no money, and made vague promises for Denver. He kept counting his money and checking on his wallet. Dean threw up his hands and gave up. "You see, man, it's better not to bother. Offer them what they secretly want and they of course immediately become panic-stricken." But he had sufficiently conquered the owner of the Plymouth to take over the wheel without remonstrance, and now we really traveled.

We left Sacramento at dawn and were crossing the Nevada desert by noon, after a hurling passage of the Sierras that made the fag and the tourists cling to each other in the back seat. We were in front, we took over. Dean was happy again. All he needed was a wheel in his hand and four on the road. He talked about how bad a driver Old Bull Lee was and to demonstrate—"Whenever a huge big truck like that one coming loomed into sight it would take Bull infinite time to spot it, 'cause he couldn't *see*, man, he can't *see*." He rubbed his eyes furiously to show. "And I'd say, 'Whoop, look out, Bull, a truck,' and he'd say, 'Eh? what's that you say, Dean?' 'Truck! truck!' and at the *very* last *moment* he would go right up to the truck like this—" And Dean hurled the Plymouth head-on at the truck roaring our way, wobbled and hovered in front of it a moment, the truckdriver's face growing gray before our eyes, the people in the back seat subsiding in gasps of horror, and swung away at the last moment. "Like that, you see, exactly like that, how bad he was." I wasn't scared at all; I knew Dean. The people in the back seat were speechless. In fact they were afraid to complain: God knew what Dean would do, they thought, if they should ever complain. He balled right across the desert in this manner, demonstrating various ways of how not to drive, how his father used to drive jalopies, how great drivers made curves, how bad drivers hove over too far in the beginning and had to scramble at the curve's end, and so on. It was a hot, sunny afternoon. Reno, Battle Mountain, Elko, all the towns along the Nevada road shot by one after another, and at dusk we were in the Salt Lake flats with the lights of Salt Lake City infinitesimally glimmering almost a hundred miles across the mirage of the flats, twice showing, above and below the curve of the earth, one clear, one dim. I told

Dean that the thing that bound us all together in this world was invisible, and to prove it pointed to long lines of telephone poles that curved off out of sight over the bend of a hundred miles of salt. His floppy bandage, all dirty now, shuddered in the air, his face was a light. "Oh yes, man, dear God, yes, yes!" Suddenly he stopped the car and collapsed. I turned and saw him huddled in the corner of the seat, sleeping. His face was down on his good hand, and the bandaged hand automatically and dutifully remained in the air.

The people in the back seat sighed with relief. I heard them whispering mutiny. "We can't let him drive any more, he's absolutely crazy, they must have let him out of an asylum or something."

I rose to Dean's defense and leaned back to talk to them. "He's not crazy, he'll be all right, and don't worry about his driving, he's the best in the world."

"I just can't stand it," said the girl in a suppressed, hysterical whisper. I sat back and enjoyed nightfall on the desert and waited for poorchild Angel Dean to wake up again. We were on a hill overlooking Salt Lake City's neat patterns of light and he opened his eyes to the place in this spectral world where he was born, unnamed and bedraggled, years ago.

"Sal, Sal, look, this is where I was born, think of it! People change, they eat meals year after year and change with every meal! *EE!* Look!" He was so excited it made me cry. Where would it all lead? The tourists insisted on driving the car the rest of the way to Denver. Okay, we didn't care. We sat in the back and talked. But they got too tired in the morning and Dean took the wheel in the eastern Colorado desert at Craig. We had spent almost the entire night crawling cautiously over Strawberry Pass in Utah and lost a lot of time. They went to sleep. Dean headed pellmell for the mighty wall of Berthoud Pass that stood a hundred miles ahead on the roof of the world, a tremendous Gibraltarian door shrouded in clouds. He took Berthoud Pass like a June bug—same as at Tehachapi, cutting off the motor and floating it, passing everybody and never halting the rhythmic advance that the mountains themselves intended, till we overlooked the great hot plain of Denver again—and Dean was home.

It was with a great deal of silly relief that these people let us off the car at the corner of Twenty-seventh and Federal. Our battered suitcases were piled on the sidewalk again; we had longer ways to go. But no matter, the road is life.

ACKNOWLEDGMENTS

I would like to gratefully acknowledge the invaluable assistance of Edward P. Alterman and Stephanie A. Miles in compiling and preparing the material for this anthology. This project was P. J. O'Rourke's idea, and for that he should get free beer for life.

ACKNOWLEDGMENTS

"Juan Manuel Fangio" by Denise McCluggage first appeared in *Autoweek*, June 1985. Copyright © 1985 Denise McCluggage. Reprinted by permission of the author.

"The Man Who Could Do Everything" by Ken Purdy. Reprinted by permission of the author and the author's agents, Scott Meredith Literary Agency, L.P., 845 Third Avenue, New York, New York 10022.

"A Letter" by John Weitz from *Automobile Magazine*, Vol. 10, No. 10. Copyright © 1996 John Weitz. Reprinted by permission of author.

"Heck, Mes Amis, It's Only Ol' Cale" by Bob Ottum. The following article is reprinted courtesy of *Sports Illustrated* from the July 13, 1981, issue. Copyright © 1981, Time Inc. "Heck Mes Amis, It's Only Ol' Cale," Bob Ottum. All rights reserved.

"Tragic Superhero of American Racing" by Griffith Borgeson first appeared in *Of Men and Cars*, 1960, as "The Stutz That Wasn't." Copyright © 1960 Griffith Borgeson. Reprinted by permission of author.

"Stand on It!" by Bill Neely and Bob Ottum. Copyright © 1973 Bill Neely and Bob Ottum. Reprinted by permission of authors.

"Out of Control!" by Dan Gerber. Copyright © 1974 Dan Gerber. Reprinted by permission of author.

"Followers" by Jim Harrison. Copyright © 1982 Jim Harrison. First appeared in *Selected and New Poems*. Reprinted by permission of author.

"History of the Studebaker Corporation" by Bruce McCall first appeared in *Automobile Magazine*, Vol. 1, No. 4. Copyright © 1986 Bruce McCall. Reprinted by permission of author.

"The Bugatti" by Ken Purdy. Reprinted by permission of the author and the author's agents, Scott Meredith Literary Agency, L.P., 845 Third Avenue, New York, New York 10022.

"Car v. Bike" by L. J. K. Setright. First appeared in *The Car Magazine Literary Supplement*, July 1969. Copyright © 1969 L. J. K. Setright, *Car Magazine*. Reprinted by permission of the author and *Car Magazine*.

"Down the Hatch" by Ronald Barker from *The Motorist's Weekend Book*, edited by Michael Frostick and Anthony Harding. Copyright © 1960 Ronald Barker. Reprinted by permission of the author.

ACKNOWLEDGMENTS

"One Fake Ferrari" by Jean Lindamood. First appeared in *Automobile Magazine*, Vol. 1, No. 7. Copyright © 1986 Jean Lindamood. Reprinted by permission from author.

"Rex Harrison Memorable in 'Amateur Driver' Role" by Noel Harrison. First appeared in *Autoweek*, December 1991. Copyright © 1991 Noel Harrison. Reprinted with permission of the author.

"Wilf the Wheelman" by Nick Brittan. First appeared in *Car Magazine*, February 1967. Copyright © 1967 *Car Magazine*. Reprinted by permission of *Car Magazine*.

"Back Door Beauty . . . and Finally a Bit of Serious Drag Racing on the Strip" by Hunter S. Thompson. From *Fear and Loathing in Las Vegas* by Hunter S. Thompson. Copyright © 1971 by Hunter S. Thompson. Reprinted by permission of Random House Inc.

"Streaked!" by Ian Fraser. First appeared in *Car Magazine*, February 1967. Copyright © 1967 *Car Magazine*. Reprinted by permission of *Car Magazine*.

"Log of the Earthtoy Drifthumper" by Jim Harrison. First appeared in *Automobile Magazine*, Vol. 1, No. 4. Copyright © 1986 Jim Harrison. Reprinted by permission of author.

"Slow Down and Die" by Dave Barry. From *Dave Barry's Greatest Hits* by Dave Barry. Copyright © 1988 by Dave Barry. Reprinted by permission of Crown Publishers, Inc.

"On the Horns of a Dilambda" by Ronald Barker. First appeared in *Car Magazine*, April 1969. Copyright © 1969 Ronald Barker, *Car Magazine*. Reprinted by permission of the author and *Car Magazine*.

"On the Road" by Calvin Trillin—From *Uncivil Liberties*, published by Ticknor & Fields. Copyright © 1979, 1982 by Calvin Trillin. Originally appeared in *The Nation*.

"Night Driving" by Joyce Carol Oates. Copyright © 1989 Joyce Carol Oates. Reprinted with permission of author.

"Not from the Back Seat" by Lydia Simmons from *Michigan Quarterly Review*, Vol. XIX, No. 4/XX, No. 1 (Fall 1980/Winter 1981). Reprinted by permission of Michigan Quarterly Review.

ACKNOWLEDGMENTS

"Hiro Yamagata's Holy Ghost XX Century Automobiles" by Allen Ginsberg. Copyright © 1994 Allen Ginsberg. First appeared in *Hiro Yamagata: Earthly Paradise*. Reprinted by permission of author.

"Car Prestige" by Ernest Hemingway. Reprinted with permission of Scribner, a Division of Simon & Schuster, Inc., from *Ernest Hemingway: Dateline Toronto*, edited by William White. Copyright © 1985 by Mary Hemingway, John Hemingway, Patrick Hemingway, and Gregory Hemingway.

"My Brave New Face" by Jamie Kitman. First appeared in *Automobile Magazine*, Vol. 7, No. 8. Copyright © 1992 Jamie Kitman. Reprinted by permission of author.

"Border Patrol" by P. J. O'Rourke. First appeared in *Automobile Magazine*, Vol. 2, No. 1. Copyright © 1987 P. J. O'Rourke. Reprinted by permission of author.

"Travels with Charley" by John Steinbeck. From *Travels with Charley* by John Steinbeck. Copyright © 1961, 1962 by The Curtis Publishing Co., © 1962 by John Steinbeck, renewed 1990 by Elaine Steinbeck, Tom Steinbeck, and John Steinbeck IV. Used by permission of Viking Penguin, a division of Penguin Books USA, Inc.

"Ruth and Augustus Goetz" by S. J. Perelman. From *Don't Tread on Me: The Selected Letters of S. J. Perelman* by S. J. Perelman, edited by Prudence Crowther. Copyright © 1987 by Abby Perelman and Adam Perelman. Preface and introduction © 1987 by Prudence Crowther. Used by permission of Viking Penguin, a division of Penguin Books USA, Inc.

"The Great GP Trek" by Peter Egan. First appeared in *Road & Track*, May 1992. Copyright © 1992 Peter Egan. Reprinted by permission of the author.

"On the Road" by Jack Kerouac. From *On the Road* by Jack Kerouac. Copyright © 1955, 1957 by Jack Kerouac; renewed © 1983 by Stella Kerouac, renewed © 1985 by Stella Kerouac and Jan Kerouac. Used by permission of Viking Penguin, a division of Penguin Books USA, Inc.